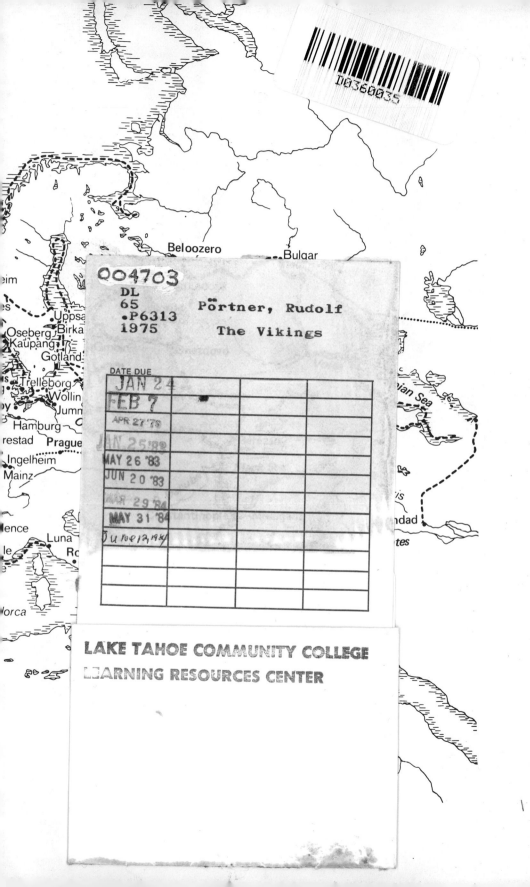

The Vikings

Rudolf Poertner

The Vikings

Rise and Fall of the Norse Sea Kings

Translated and Adapted by

Sophie Wilkins

St. James Press
London

St. Martin's Press
New York

Contents

Part Five
Trade

Part Six
The Mirror of Myth

Part Seven
Finale

Appendix

Foreword

The Christian monks made devils out of them—the chroniclers in their monasteries manufactured ravening wolves out of the Norse clans and peoples who burst out of their historical anonymity about 800 and then for three centuries filled the countries and seas of Europe with their noise, their temperament, their explosive vitality. By means of such propaganda the scribes avenged themselves on these emissaries from hell for showing so little respect for their own affluent peace. The slogans and images they coined were passed on a thousandfold and remained current—until one day fashion decreed that they be turned into their opposite.

The ill-advised prophets of Nordic supremacy transformed the monsters into heroes, decorated them with the medals and insignia of Germanic purity, and then sent them galloping off on Odin's eight-legged horse into an imaginary historical opera. The sober gray northern atmosphere was transformed into a mythological fog, where they could develop their conception of race, the ethics of a master race, the self-deification of a people, couched in a bombastic pseudoscientific language (greatly at odds, incidentally, with the hard, bony monosyllables of the Norse sagas).

This could be why the Vikings again have a bad public image in our day—why there is a certain underground tendency to see in them the original "blond beasts" after which the Nazis sought to pattern their own ideal, already programmed, progeny. In historical novels and books for children the Vikings continue to flourish as ruthless adventurers and intrepid discoverers. Hollywood has built whole Viking fleets and in consequence, to make them pay, has had to turn out one oceanic Wild West film after the other, in which Nordic antiquity has long since degenerated into journalistic trash and opulent spectacle.

Independently, historians, archaeologists, and philologists have recently studied the world of the Vikings in their own ways and accumulated new insights and new knowledge.

What have they learned? The Viking world was far more differentiated than it has ever been represented. The old stereotypes won't do. A life of richness and fullness has been revealed to us—a life which was never suspected behind the illuminated facade of traditional histories. It is a world of enormous historical substance. It came and went as an episode of European history—an inextricably integrated and integrating component of that history.

The Vikings themselves were no-nonsense peasants who lived like their forefathers off the sparse produce of their hard cold soil—and yet they devised the most imaginative mythological scenario of the post-classical era; their poetry, composed according to extremely strict rules, was full of hidden allusions and incredibly complicated turns and devices. They were constantly feuding with each other and at war with the rest of the world, but always obeyed their ancient moral code, the ultimate guardian of which was the clan.

They built the best and swiftest ships of their time, oceangoing clippers that could nevertheless be parked on a beach, and in these ships they crossed oceans and inland seas like riders crossing deserts and steppes. They stripped the European coastlands, relieved whole populations of the continent of untold riches, and penetrated deep inland unscathed. They attacked cities and monasteries, fortresses and farms, set them on fire, pillaged them and took along everything that looked usable: gold and jewels, altar cloths and swords, liturgical vessels and pretty girls. But they were also efficient colonizers. They discovered the Atlantic islands, colonized Iceland and Greenland, and set foot on American soil 500 years before Columbus.

They carried on long wars with France and the Anglo-Saxon kingdoms, they founded states in the Mediterranean, created the kingdom of Kiev in Russia, served as guards and generals to the Byzantine emperors, and were omnipresent between the Volga and Newfoundland, Iceland and Sicily, Birka and Constantinople. But they were also itinerant merchants of great daring, at home in all the markets of Europe, hard-headed businessmen trading easily in Arabic, Frankish, and Anglo-Saxon currencies. Their craftsmen made tools and utensils unsurpassed in their unyielding functionalism. Their goldsmiths and woodcarvers created works whose designs are still a fertile source of ideas for contemporary arts and crafts in northwestern Europe.

In a word, they were effective within an immense radius of activity. Their vitality released many forces. The "heroic" was only a part of their fiercely fruitful life.

They were a little of everything: peasants, explorers, colonizers; the most audacious seafarers and the most feared fighters of their time. Pirates and traders. Heroes, merchants, and villains. Industrious craftsmen and intelligent organizers. Killers and artists. Maniacal savages and cool accountants. Though crassly individualistic and contemptuous of state power, they were obedient sons of their clans.

This book seeks to do justice to the many aspects of their life and talents. It wants to extinguish the bogeyman image created by the Christian monks as well as the Siegfried interlude of the race fanatics—to get away from the fogs of Nordic mythology, from the windy adventurers of historical-trivia literature, from the muscular superstars of the big Hollywood colorscreens. Instead, it seeks to set down a sober account of everything we know today of the complicated, contradictory, exciting world of the Vikings.

In making this attempt at an inventory, I have tried to be as precise and dispassionate as possible, in order to tell it as it was. New questions and new insights always keep changing our traditional body of knowledge, making it appear in a new light. Every generation must "earn" its history afresh by rewriting it. This too I have tried to do here. The description of social, spiritual, and scientific structures is more important than battles and affairs of state. Not the great heroes of the high point in Norse history, but the anonymous common people are the true heroes of this book. To track down this common man behind the eruptive forces, the wars, the rattling of arms of Viking times has been the purpose of this fresh discovery of Norseland.

Rudolf Poertner

Bonn, June 1971

Part One

Signal Fires

Raiders on Lindisfarne

June 8, 793
Vikings, Norsemen, Varangians
Where the World Ends . . .
Dudo's Hypothesis: Polygamy?
Springboards to Expansion

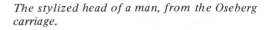

The stylized head of a man, from the Oseberg carriage.

June 8, 793

June 8, 793 is a date written in blood and fire in the Anglo-Saxon Chronicle. The day began peacefully enough on the Holy Island of Lindisfarne, near the east coast of Northumbria, with the monks making the best of the fine early summer weather, bringing in an unusually rich hay harvest.

Toward noon, ships with huge square sails were sighted on the horizon, speeding shoreward. Their approach was soon watched eagerly by the monks, who were far too settled in their peaceable, trustful ways to scent any trouble or danger.

The island abbey of Lindisfarne was founded in 635 A.D. by Celtic monks from Iona, a rocky island off the west coast of Scotland. From their base at Lindisfarne these monks did missionary work throughout eastern England under the gentle guidance of St. Aidan. After him it was St. Cuthbert, a shepherd who rose to be prior, who grafted onto the harsh disciplines of the Irish and Scottish anchorites his Benedictine concern for active wisdom and charity. Within fifty years of its founding, Lindisfarne was a noted center of monastic learning and arts in Northumbria, especially renowned for the beautifully illuminated manuscripts turned out in its scriptorium. The best known of these, and one of the finest works created in the early Middle Ages, is the Lindisfarne Bible, dated c. 700 A.D. Throughout the eighth century the fame of Lindisfarne spread to the Continent, approaching that of such august monasteries as Lorsch and Echternach, Fulda and Reichenau.

But on that shining June morning of 793 when tall sails swooped into the shallows of the island shore, all hell broke loose upon Lindisfarne. Men streamed from the vessels with bloodcurdling yells, swinging axes and swords, hurling themselves upon the defenseless, trusting monks. They threw them to the ground and ''killed them, bound and captured some, put many to flight, stripped off their clothes, and exposed them to ignominious mockery. Many were drowned in the sea.'' No one was spared, not servants, not even the women. The invaders stripped the place of everything movable, beginning with the church treasure; they defiled places of worship, overturned altars, destroyed the library, plundered cellar and storerooms, slaughtered cattle and sheep in the pasture, set all buildings on fire. When the roaring victors boarded their dragon-headed vessels again, only smoking ruins and corpses were left on the bloodstained beach of the deserted island.

Contemporary accounts, such as the Anglo-Saxon Chronicle, may inject a bit of melodrama into this story, including rumors of weird omens heralding the fearful visitation, of tempests and tornadoes uprooting the trees, of winged dragons with flaming nostrils flying over the lonely island, and a rain of blood dripping from the roof of St. Peter's in York during Lent that year. But apart from such embroidery, the actual events seem to have been rendered accurately. A bas-relief in stone from the period shows on one side two men kneeling beneath a dominant cross, with sun, moon, and the Hand of God above, symbols of faith and the Christian way of life. The reverse shows a horde of warriors, athletic men in tight leggings and doublet-like tunics, lifting swords and battle axes over their heads.

The attack on Lindisfarne, like a flare signaling the beginning of the Viking era, was only the first Viking raid to be recorded. Many more came thick and fast in the succeeding years, according to the chronicles:

794 Vikings raid the monasteries of Jarrow and Wearmouth on the east coast of England.
795 St. Columba's monastery on Iona and settlements on the Lambey Island in Northern Ireland are plundered.
797 Kintyre in Scotland, and the Isle of Man are burnt and plundered.
799 Islands off the coast of Frisia and Aquitaine are terrorized.
800 Murdering and looting, Vikings take over the Faroe Islands.
802 Attacks are renewed on the monastic settlements of Iona.
806

All the raids followed the same pattern. Dragon ships appeared out of the blue and their well-trained fighting men were swarming all over before any defense could be organized. They murdered whoever crossed their path, raped and abducted young women, filled their ships with booty; then, in a few hours, they were gone. There was nothing anybody could do about this kind of piracy.

Vikings, Norsemen, Varangians

Who were these red-blond invaders from the North whose terrible reputation began troubling Europe about 800—just when the papal coronation of Charlemagne as Emperor of Rome promised peace through federation of Europe's principalities—and who continued to threaten her coasts for another two and a half centuries? Where did they come from? What drove them on?

They were called Vikings, a name that may be derived from the Latin *vicus*: a place, market place, village, settlement, camp—as in Sles*vic* or Schles*wig*, originally Sliaswic, the town on the Schlei River. In which case the name would mean "men of the camp," "the settlers," or the like. Among the many other possible derivations are *vik* meaning bay, *vig* meaning battle, *vige* meaning to withdraw or escape. The linguist Fritz Askeberg has suggested the masculine *viking*, meaning a sea warrior on a long voyage from home. Even in its feminine form *viking* can be interpreted to mean "departing," "excursion," "absence."

But they were also called *normanni* or Norsemen; *ascomanni* or men of the ash trees; *rus*, in Slavic, after Swedish *ruotsi*, oarsmen; *madjus*, meaning "heathen monsters," by the Arabs; *Varangians*, in Russia.

A wide choice of names and derivations. Where they came from is far more certain: the North of Europe: Denmark, Sweden, Norway. That vast Scandinavian peninsula with its precipitous mountain ranges, deep fjords, intricately indented coastline, making a massive land bridge from the Baltic to the Atlantic, was their native soil.

Where the World Ends . . .

To the peoples of Western Europe, Scandinavia was a world they had barely heard of: immeasurable, undisclosed, indeed inaccessible, matted with immense virgin forests like a gigantic unkempt bearskin. Only its long fretted coastline with its many bays, and a few sheltered valleys of the interior enjoying a favorable climate, held clearings where settlers made a hard living by fishing, tilling the soil, and keeping livestock.

It was a world virtually unknown, its existence barely noted by contemporaries elsewhere; the few, scanty records of this forbidding northern world that have come down to us seem to have been written in dread and loathing. A map of Viking settlements in Scandinavia must be pieced together from the findings of the archaeologists, so few are the names of rivers, mountain ranges, and other geographical landmarks that have come down to us from the earliest chronicles. We are fairly certain, however, that the three northern peoples had already settled into their present habitat. There were Danes on Jutland and the islands of the western Baltic, as well as throughout Skane, the mildest, most fertile southern part of Sweden. The Svea tribe clustered around Lake Mälar and Old Uppsala. West and east Gotland, parts of the Värmland forests, and some areas of southern Norway were inhabited by Goths. But the long indented coastline on the Atlantic, reaching far up into the polar regions, belonged entirely to the Norwegians, who came in contact with Lapps and Finns only in the tundras and steppes of its northernmost parts.

Settlements were concentrated in only a few areas. In Jutland, for example, they kept to the north of the Eider River, which separated the Danes from the German Saxons to the southwest, and from the Slavic Abodrits and Wends to the southeast. As late as the eleventh century, when Adam of Bremen was the first to attempt a factual description of the uninviting North, Jutland was held to be largely a barren wasteland. He wrote:

> Cultivated fields are few. The land is quite unsuitable for human habitation. Only where the fjords interlace are there settlements of any size, such as Slesvic, also called Haithabu [Hedeby].

He has more encouraging things to say of Zealand, of some other fertile, productive islands, and he names two surviving towns, Odense and Roskilde, the first Danish capital. Archaeologists have confirmed his accounts in essentials, so we may assume that at least eastern Fyn and western Zealand were thickly populated about 800 A.D., and produced the rich harvests mentioned by Adam, who goes on to say:

> Once the island of the Danes lies behind you, a new world opens up in Sweden and Norway; these are two extensive, virtually unknown territories of the North, of which Norway can hardly be crossed on foot in a month, nor Sweden in two.

In Sweden, he knows something of Gotland, the town of Skara, northern Värmland and Helsingland and, southward, the Baltic sea coast. "In the east it extends as far as the Ripheic Mountains"—i.e., the Lappland massif—"where immense, desolate spaces, snow, and hordes of human monsters make further progress impossible." Behind Birka, the trading island near present-day Stockholm, lay the rich, fertile, habitable Lake Mälar region. Gotland, too, had prospered enough to support even a merchant class.

To Adam, Norway was the end of the world:

> Its coast forms the shore of the raging ocean, and also reaches the Ripheic mountains, where the world comes to a weary end. Norway is the most barren of all countries because of its rugged mountains, its extreme cold, suitable only for raising live stock. . . . the herds are pastured in deserted places, and the people live on such husbandry, the milk of the animals serving to feed them, the wool to clothe them.

The only sizable settlement he names is Trondheim, the center of Viking Norway.

At the time of the Lindisfarne raid, the numerous Scandinavian tribes lived side by side, more or less separately, loosely organized. Power was generally vested in family and clan, though Sweden already had an enthroned king. Denmark, too, had a firmly established ruler for a brief period around 800 A.D. This may have been partly why the smallest of the three northern countries was the first to launch a large Viking naval expedition.

Dudo's Hypothesis: Polygamy?

The reasons for the Vikings' sudden eruption from anonymity have been grounds for much speculation by historians, though no completely satisfying answers have been found to this day. Long before Lindisfarne, the southward migrations toward Spain, Rome, and Constantinople of the Goths, Vandals, Burgundians, Herulians, and other northern Teutonic tribes had left behind vast deserted regions which it took from the fourth to the eighth century to fill up again. Except for scanty reports of small undertakings along the Frisian and Gallic coasts, the Shetland Islands, and Ireland, there is nothing in the chronicles of the time that even confirms the existence of the northern seagoing tribes. Then at the end of the eighth century this incredible outbreak, this 250-year-long liberation of Viking energy, this powerful eruption.

The ecclesiastics who kept book on their times had an answer for this sudden change. The Vikings were God's scourge, His judgment upon a sinful mankind. It took another two centuries before someone tried to understand the Vikings as a phenomenon in their own right, leaving God out of it. Dean Dudo of St. Quentin saw in polygamy the root cause of Viking expansion. By this time enough Danes had settled in Normandy (which was named for them as the "northmen") that their ways could be observed and studied. Their preference for more than one wife at a time, unlike the good Christians who had to content themselves with one, if any, had attracted some attention. Adam of Bremen had noticed too that the Swedes "know no bounds . . . and are sinful like the Slavs, Parthians, and Moors" with regard to women. Dudo hypothesized that the too rapid growth of population caused by polygamy drove the Vikings to forage for other men's goods and lands.

But polygamy, simply for material reasons, must have been the habit of the rich and notable only, and this would not have led to a generalized overpopulation like that suggested by Dudo. However, inheritance laws may have aggravated the situation of the rich, specifically the law of primogeniture by which all landed property must go to the eldest son. The powerful landed families found themselves with too many young empty-handed malcontents to be provided for in the style to which they felt entitled by birth. Dudo reports, in this regard, that "according to ancient custom" a certain number of such younger sons were chosen by lot and driven out with orders to go and conquer new homes for themselves "in which henceforth they could live peaceably."

Dudo's statement reflects an awareness of constant internal squabbles, of the Vikings' endless fighting among themselves. These Norse fishermen, hunters, and seafarers were given not only to lusty wenching but to heavy drink; the combination could and did lead from friendly practical jokes to bloody fights, thence to blood feuds And clan wars, sometimes literally overnight. Those of the loser's sons who were left alive were well advised to seek their fortunes elsewhere. After the election of a king there would also be losers who might find a pirate expedition an excellent way to compensate, even possibly to come back rich enough to win the next election.

Scholars like the Danish historian Johannes Brøndsted, who find such reasons insufficient or, as he says, "too arbitrary," seek the cause of the Viking migrations in a possible deterioration of their home climate. Such a deterioration, said to have begun long before Carolingian times, undermined the traditional economy, dependent as it was on extensive animal husbandry. The Norwegians changed over to agriculture and finding new areas of settlement, but the barrenness of the land ended by driving them out to sea. As Adam puts it:

> Banished from their homeland by poverty they now wander round the world and bring home as booty what other countries produce in plenty.

Even the relatively southerly and fertile lands of the Danes and the Swedes, being correspondingly more thickly settled, in time suffered from exhaustion of the soil, as some archaeological evidence indicates; so whether they were poor in land, or their land was poor in yield, it was land hunger too that drove them to seek their fortunes abroad.

Springboards to Expansion

None of this would have been enough to set in motion such a worldwide expansion if it weren't accompanied by the Vikings' natural readiness to risk death and danger, and their passion for and knowledge of the sea—a passion that struck their contemporaries as true madness. The destinations to which they sailed followed from the nature and position of their countries. Their voyages, which ended by

Europe during the Viking Age.

embracing the whole of Europe as if in the many-suckered grip of an octopus, moved along geographically prescribed lines:

Danes headed southward to the rich coasts and riverlands of Carolingian Europe, west to southern England and Ireland, south again to Spain, and throughout the Mediterranean.

Swedes crossed the Baltic and from their footholds along its eastern coastline gradually penetrated the immensities of Russia in a southeasterly direction all the way to Constantinople.

The Norwegians' southwesterly route brought them to Scotland, Ireland, and the smaller Atlantic island groups; westward they found Iceland, Greenland, Labrador, and Newfoundland in the Western Hemisphere.

To avoid oversimplification it must be said that the Danes also threatened the Wendish coast and the Prussians along the Baltic Sea; the Swedes exacted tribute on the Mediterranean; and the Norwegians participated in the invasions of France and England. But this doesn't alter the overall picture. The three main targets of the Viking expansion—the coastlands of Western Europe, the rivers and forests of Eastern Europe, and the great islands and northwestern coasts of the North Atlantic—lie within the natural line of sight of the three Scandinavian countries.

The first recorded Viking expeditions were, like the Lindisfarne adventure, mere petty raids for private gain, on the initiative of minor chieftains and their ferocious gangs. But by the beginning of the ninth century, under Godfred the Dane, they had tasted enough of success to prepare for enterprises of some magnitude.

Part Two

Searchers, Finders, Takers

TRAN SIVIT ET VENIT A

HAROLD H

HIC EXEVNT: CABAILL DEN AVIBV

A Hundred Years
of War with France

David and Goliath
Terror from the Rhone to the Pyrenees
Fleet after Fleet of Dragon Ships
The Rhine in Flames
The Siege of Paris and the Battle on the Dyle
Duke Rollo Baptized
Women of France Conquer their Conquerors

Pictures from the Bayeux tapestry showing the building and departure of the Norman invasion fleet to England.

David and Goliath

King Godfred the Dane caused great displeasure among Frankish historians. They pictured him as an arrogant braggart who had the impudence to intrude upon Charlemagne's realm. What bothered them most was his boastful declaration, shortly before his death, that he was about to march on Aachen and burn the Emperor's palace to the ground.

This was in the year 810, when the Frankish Empire was the greatest power in Europe and its ruler, Charlemagne, the most imperial head of state and military leader Europe had known since Julius Caesar.

The great Christian Emperor had little cause to worry about the heathen Danes in the first decade of his reign. He even had his own corps of Norse chieftains living and carousing in good fellowship with his own Frankish nobles at the imperial Court of Aachen, or Aix-la-Chapelle. Diplomatic relations with the little Viking kingdom of Denmark, well consolidated as it was by the turn of the century, were correct, if not cordial. A Danish delegation, led by a certain Halfdan, is even known to have attended the parliament at Lippspringe in 782. In 807 another chieftain, also named Halfdan, brought a great retinue to Charlemagne's court, to offer himself as vassal to the Holy Roman Emperor.

Even the increasingly frequent Viking raids around the turn of the century against the Frisian and Gallic coasts did not seem to seriously hinder relations between Franks and Danes. Charlemagne went about strengthening his defenses, restoring an old watchtower at Boulogne, setting up regular watchfires at night, building ships, and taking personal tours of inspection to see his orders carried out. Even proud landholders had to serve on ships of the Frankish coast guard, and it was probably this force which helped divert the Viking captains' attention from Frisia and Aquitaine to England and Scotland for the next few years.

Real trouble between the Frankish kingdom and Denmark did not arise until after Charlemagne, in 804, had forcibly evicted the rebellious North Albigensian Saxons from their lands and given them to his allies, the Slavic Abodrits. Suddenly Franks and Danes, who had lived at a respectful distance from each other, separated by Transelbian Saxons, were close neighbors and had to keep a mistrustful eye on one another. Charlemagne, by this time fighting Arabs in the Mediterranean, learned once more that a conqueror's work is never done as long as every new boundary line becomes a frontier breeding new enemies.

In fact King Godfred seems to have feared becoming a sacrifice to Charlemagne's lust for power. He obviously believed attack was the best defense. He had already countered the establishment of a Frankish camp at Hollingstedt near Harburg in 804 by an impressive display of his fleet. Now, four years later, he penetrated into Abodrit country, took the Slav trading center of Reric, evacuating its merchants to Slesvig, and began the construction of the Danework (*Danevirke*), that formidable, still largely extant fortification that unambiguously marked the southern boundary of his little realm.

A year after this demonstration of his might Godfred entered into negotiations with Charlemagne. Little is known about these talks. But by this time Charlemagne must have realized the intransigence and potential danger of his enemy. At any rate he established in 810 at Itzehoe the first Frankish base east of the Elbe to serve as a bridgehead offensive for a campaign against Denmark.

Godfred anticipated his attack, however, by landing in Frisia with two hundred ships, thus securing a strong strategic position. His forces settled in the country, he collected a hundred pounds of silver toward the cost of his campaign, and was preparing to march against Aachen, as announced—a plan that left a tangible shock upon the Carolingian court biographer Einhard.

Before the undertaking got underway, however, Godfred was assassinated. The danger was temporarily lifted. A year later Godfred's brother Hemming made peace with the great western Emperor of Christendom, who was probably happy to have gotten off so cheaply.

Modern historians have drawn two conclusions from this first altercation between Franks and Danes. First, that Godfred was not the idle braggart so contemptuously dismissed by the monk chroniclers of the time, but a cunning, energetic and able ruler, a David confronting the Carolingian Goliath with bravado. Second, that this Goliath was vulnerable, since his interminable un-defended coastline along the Channel and the Atlantic was at the mercy of any attack from the sea.

Terror from the Rhone to the Pyrenees

Godfred's attack was thus aborted by rivals at his own court who preferred peace with Charlemagne. Indeed there was peace for the next few years, since Charlemagne was old and weary, and Denmark was paralyzed by internal dissension over who should occupy the now vacant throne.

When Charlemagne died in 814, however, Denmark's inner turmoil was intensified by the return of Godfred's sons from Sweden, where they had taken refuge when their father was murdered, to challenge the two kings Heriold and Reginbert, maintained by Frankish power in Denmark. The struggle dragged on for many years, in a sort of chronic guerrilla warfare staged by the Frank-supported partisans from neighboring Abodrit country, with minimum success. Finally in 826 Heriold approached Charlemagne's successor, Louis the Pious, for protections and reinforcements, in exchange for which he let himself be baptized at Mainz, with his wife and son, nephew, and a large retinue. As a Christian vassal of the Holy Roman Emperor, the former puppet king of Denmark was now made Count of Rustringen, a royal fief between the Jade and Weser rivers, territory which is today part of northern Germany; from here Heriold was to be in charge of Christianizing the North. It was at this time and under Heriold's sponsorship that the renowned Ansgar of Corvey set out on his first great missionary voyage northward.

This effort to create something in the nature of a Christian-Danish kingdom-in-exile did not pacify the Danish attacks—quite the contrary. Perhaps even encouraged by this Frankish interference in Danish internal affairs, Viking raids increased in number and vigor, drawn by the easy accessibility of areas rich in booty such as the mouths of the Seine and Loire rivers, the islands of Ré and Noirmoutier with their wealthy monasteries and their large stores of salt—a luxury in medieval times. They came to Flanders for its cattle, sailed all around the coast of Brittany, collected enough loot to fill their ships for the homeward voyage—perhaps to Denmark, perhaps already as far as Ireland, where the first Viking colonies had taken root.

And they kept coming back, the more relentlessly as Louis's power crumbled. In 833, Louis the Pious capitulated to his victorious sons at the Battle of Colmar. The ensuing civil war rocked the powerful kingdom to its foundations and started off a decade of almost uninterrupted Viking attacks, which netted the raiders money, weapons, wine, cloth, spices—all sorts of consumer and luxury goods to whet their growing appetite for more.

The chronicles of these years bear witness to the relentlessness of the Viking attacks, lootings, killings, conflagrations:

834　Danes lay waste to Frisia, then march via Utrecht to Dorestad where they loot, kill those inhabitants they don't take prisoner, and destroy parts of the town by fire.

835　Vikings again destroy Dorestad and the monastery of Noirmoutier which is then dissolved.

836　They burn down Antwerp and Witta-on-the-Maas and extort tribute from the Frisians after hitting Dorestad once more.

837　On June 17 they surprise and kill a great number of the coast guard at Walcheren, rob the inhabitants, kill the Christian Dane Hemming, carry off many women, and again lay rich Dorestad under tribute.

838 A great storm destroying the entire Danish pirate fleet proves more effective than the weak Emperor's reinforced coast guard.

839 Another attack on Walcheren, and a rumored attack on Cologne (according to Adam of Bremen).

840 The Annals of Fulda refer to the Frankish market town of Dorestad as fief of the Vikings—Dorestad was paying regular protection money to the pirates. (From this point on Frisia ceased to suffer Viking attacks, being virtually their property, possibly till the end of the century.)

The steady hammering by the Viking terror gave rise to a sense of helplessness and consequently a depressing belief that the end of the world was at hand, a mood which gradually spread over the whole of the Frankish kingdom. As early as 834 one chronicler wrote that the kingdom was impotent, the people increasingly wretched day by day. Signs of doom were noted everywhere: fires in the shape of dragons, immense hurricanes and flames over the sea, comets, streams of light in the sky, stars trailing fire—clearly the Day of Judgment was at hand, and the bloodthirsty heathens from the north were the instruments of God's wrath. Bishop Prudentius of Troyes was only one of many who exhorted all the faithful to repent and mend their ways, lest fearful visitations to come make an end of their world altogether, with fire and sword.

The rough Norsemen had no such qualms or terrors, but went on lustily making the most of their victims' weaknesses in leadership and morale, for their own pleasure and profit.

Fleet after Fleet of Dragon Ships

Louis the Pious died in 840 on an island in the Rhine, near his beloved Ingelheim. Three years later, at Verdun, his sons partitioned his realm—a new situation, even for the Vikings. The coast between the Eider and the Weser now belonged to Louis the German; that between the Weser and the Scheldt to the Emperor Lothar; and that between the Scheldt and the Pyrenees to Charles the Bald. If the agreement was designed to enable three to rule in the place of one, at peace with one another, it was a signal failure. Not only were the three brothers constantly at war with one another, but each was always available to his brothers' enemies as an ally; together they wasted the empire's best fighting men and leaders in their relentless struggle for their own interests. The monk Regino of Prüm sadly comments on the Battle of Fontenoy, which in 841 led to the partition of the realm, that here ''the Frankish

Viking from Sigtuna, about one inch high in the original, carved in elkhorn.

fighting forces were so decimated that they were no longer able to protect the existing boundary lines, let alone expand them.'' Twenty years later another chronicler, the monk Ermentarius, wrote that ''the brothers' warring with one another was making their enemies beyond the borders stronger than ever: the coasts were left unguarded, foreign wars neglected while civil war raged within the country, and more ships kept coming bringing Norsemen without end.''

The three kings also had to contend with all the actively self-seeking rebels among their own vassals, often influential potentates in their own right, who were eager to come to terms with the invading Vikings to help undermine the power of the Crown. The Vikings, for their part, found such alliances expedient, particularly in Brittany and Aquitaine.

In 841, only a year after the death of Louis the Pious, the Danes came freely sailing up the mouth of the Seine and burnt down Rouen. Thereupon the Emperor Lothar made over all of Walcheren to King Heriold and his brother Rorik, to make the two Danish princes his allies against his own brothers, Louis and Charles. A year later Viking freebooters ravaged Quentovic, the third great trading center on the Frankish coast after Dorestad and Rouen. In June 843, a fleet of ''only 67 sails'' moved unhindered against Nantes; the Vikings massacred the inhabitants, whom they surprised in the midst of their traditional Midsummer Day festivities. The pilots in this case, as well as for the raids upon the banks of the Garonne in 844, were probably provided by the local Frankish aristocracy. In 845 Hamburg and Paris too went up in flames.

Six hundred Viking ships are supposed to have landed at Hamburg that year. The whole settlement was razed, including Bishop Ansgar's mission center. Early in March, a hundred and twenty dragon ships sailed up the mouth of the Seine, led by King Ragnar—the Ragnar Lodbrok of the Viking Saga—and took Rouen, then Carolivenna, twenty miles from St. Denis, then Paris, demolishing all three in Viking fashion. The Frankish forces, though outnumbering the invaders and better armed, were so demoralized they dared not counterattack. After long negotiations, Charles the Bald bought off the Vikings with 7,000 pounds of silver, an immense treasure with which they withdrew from the ravaged capital, to receive a triumphal welcome from King Horik of Denmark at their homecoming. Eventually a large part of this hoard came back to France, when in the fall of 845 King Horik diverted a few wagonloads of it to Louis the German in reparation for the sack of Hamburg. After all, East Franconia, militarily the strongest of the three kingdoms, was next door neighbor to Denmark; Horik's timely diplomatic concession averted retaliation by Hamburg, and in fact bought eighty years of peace between Elbe and Eider.

But the coasts and river mouths of West Franconia continued to be exposed to

Viking attacks. Saintes, Périgueux, Limoges, and Tours were burnt and plundered more than once. Bordeaux was put under siege in 847 and taken in 848. The day of the hit-and-run raid was long since over. From the middle of the century onward, Brittany and Aquitaine were under Danish rule; Danes, with Norwegian reinforcements, were spread out along the coasts, with the island of Noirmoutier, at the mouth of the Loire, serving them as a permanent base for their raiding expeditions. They held other islands and strongpoints as well, fortified by palisades and equipped with barns and winter quarters.

Chaos and uncertainty kept spreading deeper into the terrified, desperate country. There are constant references in the chronicles to relics of the saints being moved hither and yon by the refugees, out of the heathen invaders' reach; finally they seemed to be permanently on the move. An increasing part of the population, too, was sucked into the maelstrom of refugees, and as always when war brings extremes of deprivation and fear to men in large numbers, the entire moral and social structure of the country collapsed.

By 853, the Parliament of Servais was forced to concede to the dispossessed the right to settle where they would, while threatening to penalize heavily any landowner who would try to enslave the refugees. Highwaymen made the roads unsafe; robbers and thieves attacked isolated farms and decimated the cattle.

Many of the homeless peasants banded together in quasi-military formations and tried parleying with the Vikings on their own hook, sometimes even with success. But the Franconian nobles soon began to fear the native peasant militia, and saw in them a further incentive to side with the foreign oppressors. In league with the Vikings, they fought not only their own king but the peasant bands as well, thus plunging whole regions into disorder and demoralization. This went on for another fifty years before the Viking tide reached its crest.

The Rhine in Flames

Three events determined the course of those final decades of the ninth century: the seven-year war that began in 860 over possession of Oiselle (present-day Jeufosse), an island in the Seine; the "great army" expedition of 879-92; and the invasion of northern Franconia which began in 900 and ended in 912 with the founding of the Dukedom of Normandy.

In the long struggle over Oiselle the French learned for the first time to use Vikings against Vikings as a "secret" weapon of high effectiveness. Charles the Bald paid a chieftain named Weland 5,000 pounds of silver plus produce to smoke out his compatriots on the island. The device did not work too well this first time, since Weland also accepted 6,000 pounds of silver from the other side in return for stopping his siege short of victory. Nevertheless, this early double agent seems to have started a trend; more and more the Franks came to hire their erstwhile enemies for ready cash to defend them against invaders of their own kind. They were the best mercenaries to be had for the job.

However, there was no stemming the onrush of the Viking "great army" for long, even by cash or trickery. Beaten back by Alfred the Great in England, they turned again to the continent. On April 12, 879, the great fleet of dragon ships landed at the mouth of the Scheldt, and within a few days Ghent was going up in smoke. From there a series of foraging and plundering expeditions took them across Flanders and Frisia into Lorraine and as far as Provence.

By the time Louis t' German died in his palace at Frankfurt in January 882, the central kingdom of Lorraine had disappeared from the map. Ancient Roman towns like Maastricht, Liège, Jülich, Neuss, Cologne, and Bonn, with their far-famed churches and monasteries, their markets and trading centers, were laid waste. The Imperial Palace at Aachen was burnt to the ground, and the Vikings' horses were stabled in the Imperial Chapel. By the time the Norsemen had finished razing Trier's Roman landmarks, on Easter Monday, April 10, they must have felt satisfied with their collection, for they returned to their ships at Elsloo to fill them with the loot.

They were still taking huge tribute in the bishopric of Rheims when a vast army composed of Franks, Alemanni, Bavarians, Thuringians, Saxons, Frisians, and Langobards advanced on Elsloo under the leadership, of Charles the Fat and encircled the Viking troops stationed there. But instead of attacking, as his immense army was reputedly longing to do, the inert and timid king merely sent emissaries to bribe the trapped Vikings into leaving voluntarily. His offer was 2,080 (some say 2,412) pounds of gold and silver; if their king Godfrey would be converted to Christianity, he could have Christian Frisia for his own.

Godfrey wasted little time in accepting baptism along with several wagonloads of treasure as a baptismal gift from Charles the Fat, by now sole king of the Franks. Godfrey settled with his troops in the Rhine delta, of which he was henceforth the rightful lord and master. From here he continued to make war against France. So did his brother Sigfred, who withdrew from Elsloo only to entrench himself on the lower Scheldt River—this after he had sworn never to set foot on French soil again.

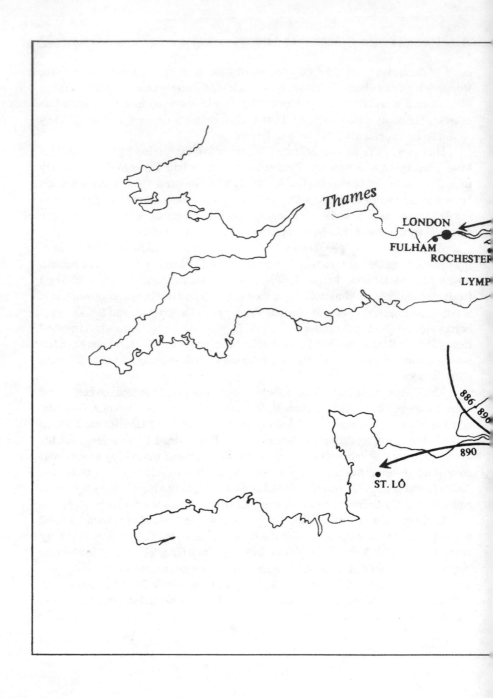

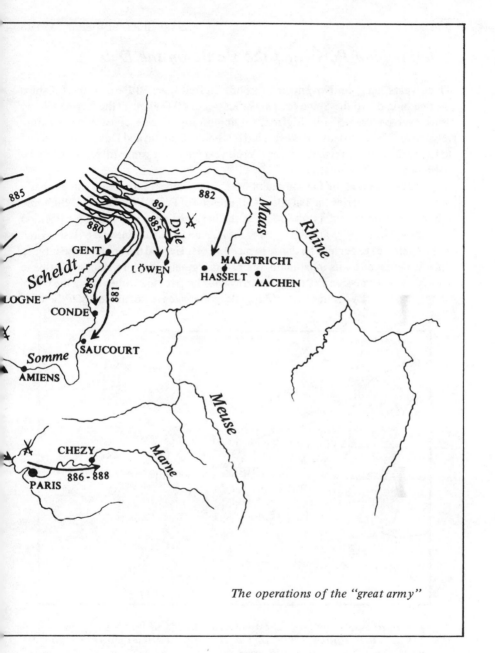

The operations of the "great army"

The Siege of Paris and the Battle on the Dyle

Three years later, on November 24, 885, Sigfred reached Paris with 700 ships
—stretching down the Seine for two miles—and 40,000 men, the largest Viking
army ever on French soil. Sigfred, relying on his shock tactics, expected little
resistance. The Parisians, however, led by Bishop Geuzlin and Duke Odo, refused
to be intimidated and risked a siege. A full year later they were still resisting all the
onslaughts of "the great army."

In July, 886, at the Parliament of Metz, the princes of the realm categorically
demanded that Charles the Fat come to the rescue of Paris. With much ill-humored
reluctance, Charles led a relief force to the besieged city, and took up a position
just below Montmartre and the walls of Paris. And yet again, instead of lashing out
at the enemy as expected, he chose to buy him off. He sold the honor of the city, so
bravely defended by its inhabitants against such great odds, for a shameful bribe in
money, and permission to "the great army" to camp for the winter along the banks
of the Rhone. By giving the Viking despoilers leave to move their field of

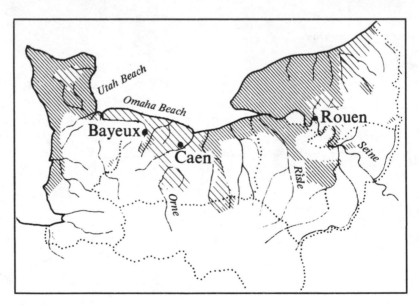

*The territory of the great D-Day invasion of World War II was firmly in
Viking hands around 900 A.D. The cross-hatched areas indicate regions
where Norse place names still predominate.*

operations to Burgundy, the sluggish king was getting some of his own back on the warlords of Burgundy, with whom his relations were none too good.

The humbled kingdom drew a deep breath of relief, therefore, when after Charles's inglorious death in 887, a Franconian king at long last drove out the Norsemen by force of arms instead of paying tribute. In 891, at Louvain, on the Dyle River—in the Duchy of Brabant, today divided between Belgium and the Netherlands—Arnulf of Carinthia encircled a strong contingent of Vikings, and in a swift attack "chased hundreds of thousands into the river so that the river bed, filled with the dead, appeared dry" as the Fulda annalist has it.

Although "the great army" did not retreat to England until the following year, beaten not so much by the might of French arms as by epidemics and the great drought of 892, the Austrian's victory on the Dyle, coming after the famed resistance of Paris, had a profound psychological effect on the natives. The myth of Viking invincibility had evaporated.

Besides, the population had learned a great deal about self-defense and fighting back, in so many years of daily skirmishes. Rivers were now guarded with fortified bridges, chains, and other obstacles; bands of men on horseback had effectively fought off Norsemen who were on the move; the townspeople had learned to sell their lives dearly behind their quickly rebuilt walls and fortifications; country seats surrounded themselves with wide moats and high palisades. The lowlands of the Rhine, Scheldt, Meuse, Seine and Loire still have the remains of thousands of these moats and earthworks to show.

By the end of the ninth century victory came far less easily to the Vikings than it had in the beginning. However, the continental forces were still disorganized, the coastline of France still as exposed to attacks as ever. A compromise was called for, and it was achieved in 911, resulting in the foundation of the Duchy of Normandy.

Duke Rollo Baptized

Not all of the "great army" had returned to England in 892. Particularly in the area of the lower Seine there were numerous enclaves where the invaders had remained, part pirates, part settlers. They terrorized the peasants into supplying them with meat and produce, exacting more and more tribute, while at the same time starting to cultivate the land and raise cattle themselves. Rouen lay at the center of the region they controlled, and here the Viking prince Rollo (also called Hrolf or Rolf) had established himself at the turn of the century.

Probably of Danish extraction, Rollo had come by way of England to Western

France and gained fame there as a warrior and brigand. But after suffering a severe rebuff at Chartres in 911, he seems to have done some serious rethinking about his strategic position—as did the Frankish royal counselors. Rollo agreed to parleying with the French.

It was a clever decision. The time had come to consolidate his position. The opposing powers found themselves in a certain balance. The Normans encountered fierce resistance whenever they tried to penetrate beyond their own territory, but their territory itself was not under attack.

In the late fall of 911 at St. Clair, Charles the Simple, surrounded by a host of clerics schooled in diplomacy, met with Rollo and his Viking chieftains. Since it was only a matter of legalizing the status quo they soon reached an agreement. Rollo was now to be Duke of the province to be known as Normandy, held by him as a royal fief, and was given the hand of Princess Gisela, Charles's natural daughter, in marriage. He, for his part, agreed to regard Charles as his liege lord, and to be converted to Christianity. The baptism of the handsome Duke in 912 is considered to mark the end of the Viking attacks on Western Europe. Rollo encouraged his own men and other immigrants to settle, defended his territory against his Viking cousins, and kept faith with the king, who in turn respected him and his independence.

Under Rollo's successors, immigration from England, Denmark, and Norway went on, as Normandy expanded steadily westward from the Seine. Place names like Osmundiville, Regnelot, Torberville, and Ulveville still echo the names of immigrants Asmund, Ragnar, Torbjörn, and Ulf. Also of Norse origin are names of settlements ending in -gard, -land, -tofte, and -torp.

Colonization by the Northmen changed the social structure as well. The best of the arable lands and pastures had formerly belonged to a few large landholders; the Vikings brought in many free, small landholders, peasants independent and secure enough to rebel against and defeat the attempts of the new upper class, by the end of the tenth century, to reinstitute the old feudal system of serfdom. The immigrants kept to their own way of life for a long time, including marriage customs somewhat at variance with Christianity.

Women of France Conquer Their Conquerors

When the sources regretfully mention marriage *more danico* or Danish style, they simply mean polygamy. Many settlers kept a number of wives, in proportion to their property and wealth—native women, for the most part, to judge by documents on Normandy that give, between 911 and 1066, three hundred

Scandinavian names for men, but only six for women. Hence the Romance language of the women became the colloquial language, while the Teutonic speech of the men came to be used chiefly on official occasions and in male-dominated occupations. The fishermen of the Cotentin Peninsula, for example, have to this day many words of Norse origin in their vocabulary. So one could say that the French women reconquered their conquerors by way of their language and cultural heritage.

Nevertheless, Normandy long retained its special character as a foreign body in the land. The noisy vitality of its inhabitants, descendants of adventurous seafarers, was often noted with amazement and apprehensiveness by the monks who kept up the chronicles to the end of the Middle Ages, as if the ancient fear of the Vikings were still haunting them.

But apart from a few minor incidents, the "barbarians from the North" were quiescent for nearly a hundred and fifty years. Then renewed unrest drove them to conquer England and create, in Sicily, that warlike kingdom of mercenaries which later formed, for fifty years, the core of the great Hohenstaufen Empire.

Pincers Around Europe

Denmark North of the Thames

England, too, felt the fist of the Vikings throughout the ninth century. When the attacks began, Britain was still splintered into many small suzerainties feuding with each other. But the southern part of the country was united in 819 by King Egbert of Wessex and managed to fight off the large invasions of the next decade. So the Vikings turned to central England, East Anglia and Northumbria, where by mid-century they had well established militant settlements. From these bases they launched pillaging expeditions, exacting tribute and terrorizing the country with increasing ferocity as the Anglo-Saxon peasants staunchly fought back—in one reported instance, the peasants flayed some captured Danes and nailed their trophies up on the church door.

The first large-scale Viking invasion is reported in the chronicles of 835. After this date the raids became a yearly plague. To give a brief review of the most important dates only:

838 East Anglia and Kent are invaded by Danish robber bands.

839 350 dragon ships come up the Thames to plunder Canterbury and London.

850 In Kent, the invaders winter in England for the first time.

866 Three "great heathen armies" land in East Anglia, led by the brothers Ivar the Boneless, Ubbi, and Halfdan, sons of Ragnar Lodbrok, all heroes of the Nordic sagas. They conquer York an settle down behind its ancient Roman walls.

867 All of Northumbria falls to the united Danish-Norwegian forces.

870 They penetrate Wessex, but come up against stubborn resistance by King Ethelred and his brother Alfred.

871 Defeated at Reading, they remain powerful enough to settle in London, take tribute from King Alfred, and further colonize Northumbria, northeast England, and East Anglia, so that all the territory northeast of the Thames is in Scandinavian hands.

Nevertheless the year 871 was a turning point. It was the year King Alfred came to the throne of Wessex: an unlikely, ailing man, who in the course of the next three decades managed to oust the invaders from southern England. He was the first to organize a methodical resistance against the Norsemen. He formed a regular army, including even the small landholders, and carefully trained it for action by extensive maneuvers. Above all, he built a fleet of his own, with whose powerful squadrons the Viking dragon ships would soon have to contend. Thus he was the first to meet the enemy on hitherto uncontested ground—the sea they had come to consider all their own—where he would try to stop them before they could land, and failing that, at least harass them before they could escape with their booty. Such was the beginning of the Royal British Navy.

For seven years Alfred paid tribute to the enemy to gain time for his preparations. Then he struck: in 878, at Edington in Wessex, King Alfred so trounced the hordes of invaders that the great majority of their survivors preferred to go seek their fortune on the continent instead, and succeeded; it was they who made up the "great army" that terrorized France from 879 until 892. A smaller number remained northeast of the Thames, which they continued to colonize up to Northumbria. Their territory became known as the Danelaw, where Danish laws and customs prevailed for centuries to come.

It took Alfred eight years more to win back London. He also made a treaty with the Danish King Guthrum, stabilizing their common frontiers for a few years of peace until, in 892, remnants of the "great army" returned from France, and fighting broke out anew. But Alfred's defense plan proved itself once more, as did his guerrilla tactics designed to wear down the enemy. After his son Edward destroyed the anchored ships of a great Danish expeditionary force in 899, the Viking terror became a thing of the past, as it did ten years later in France.

Surviving Viking crew members made for the Seine, including, probably, Rollo, the future Duke of Normandy, on what probably was his first journey to the continent. The majority of the Danes, however, returned to their lands north of the Thames, territory they were to transform into fertile farmland in the centuries to come. There they lived side by side with the original inhabitants, forgetting warfare and its upheavals together, even though they kept a certain social distance.

Turgeis, A Norwegian, Founds Dublin

The barren, sparsely populated groups of islands in the North Atlantic and the Irish Sea had been plundered, settled, and colonized by Vikings long before the attacks on England, as had large parts of Scotland and Ireland. The first to fall—perhaps even before Lindisfarne—were the twenty-three Shetland Islands off the north coast of Scotland, which offered subsistence to fishermen and sheepherders. They made good naval bases for further conquests by the mobile dragon ships. The Norwegians were early masters of the "island hopping" which Americans and Japanese learned to practice in the Pacific in World War II. To the north, the bleak Faroe Islands between Scotland and Iceland, which had hitherto served only as

Picture of a ship on a Gotland picture stone.

places of penance for Scottish and Irish hermits, did not escape the Vikings' grasp. The surviving hermits returned to their monasteries in England. The Vikings stayed on, though they might break the monotony of their Spartan existence by sailing for Norway in the summer, to plunder their own native villages, according to the thirteenth-century Icelandic historian Snorri Sturluson.

Southward from the Shetlands, the Northmen took, one after the other, the Orkneys, the Hebrides, and other islands off the west coast of Scotland. Northern immigrants also settled on the Scottish coast, which explains why the extreme northwestern point of Scotland is called *Suther*land. Later, the Isle of Man in the Irish Sea became a Norwegian colony, trading station, and base for provisioning the pirate ships.

Finally, Ireland itself, land of cranks and geniuses, refuge of individualists, the last European stronghold of the Celts, ruled by numberless little chieftains nursing their endless feuds, rich in monasteries whose monks had disseminated Irish art and religious fervor far and wide throughout the continent. When the hardy, rapacious killers from the North descended on Ireland, the blood they spilled, the land they ravaged, were memorialized in an outcry of Homeric grandeur. One anonymous chronicler wrote:

> They laid waste the island from end to end. They looted the homes of chieftains, the churches and holy places; they destroyed shrines, holy relics, beautiful places of worship which they stripped of all their splendid ornaments. For these rabid, savage, merciless heathen felt no reverence nor respect nor forbearance for the holy places; no church or holy of holies was safe from them, for they fear neither God nor man. It were easier to number the sands by the sea, the grass of the fields, the stars in the sky, than to relate all that the Irish people . . . , man or woman, youth or maid, layman or cleric, freeman or serf, suffered at their hands of humiliation, violence, and oppression.

The facts bear him out. By 830 the Norwegians held the coasts of the Emerald Isle and part of the interior in the south. In 839 their Sea King Turgeis brought a strong fleet to northern Ireland, proclaimed himself King of All Strangers in Erin, founded Dublin, destroyed many shrines and chapels, and presented himself as a heathen priest at Christian places of pilgrimage. Provoked beyond endurance by such affronts to their religious sensibilities, the Irish, who finally caught up with the evildoer in 844, drowned him in Loch Nair.

Unexpected help arrived toward the middle of the century from Danish bands that had occupied the southern part of the island. Irishmen and Danes joined forces to drive the Norwegians northward, a struggle in which both sides outdid themselves in brutality and treachery, each seeking to exterminate the other. It was of course the population of the countryside that suffered the most, as the Irish Chronicle eloquently relates.

The Norwegians, however, were soon back again. Under Olaf the Pale they reconquered Dublin and drove the Danes off the island. Before long they were fighting among themselves, and after King Halfdan came from northern England to join battle with the others, sheer chaos reigned until Ireland, bled white by incessant warfare, won a brief peace of exhaustion around 900. Twenty years later the Norwegians took firm hold again, and Ireland remained a Viking colony for almost all of the Tenth century, especially under the three kings descended from Ivar—Sigtrygg, Gudrod, and Olaf Kvaran. On the Island of Sages and Saints there was "a Norwegian king in every district, a chieftain in every clan, a steward in every village, a warrior in every homestead" according to the Irish Chronicle.

They destroyed an ancient culture and reduced the entire population to a primitive struggle for bare survival during which "no bard nor philosopher nor musician followed his calling." Not until the year 1000 did the Irish find a leader in King Brian, who roused the anger and feline toughness of the natives and drove out the invaders, so that fifty years later "beautiful, bejeweled damsels could again travel unmolested through the land." By this time England, however, had all but become a Danish colony.

An Anglo-Saxon St. Bartholomew's Massacre

The century had gotten off to a good start under King Alfred's son Edward, who carried on his father's successful strategy of slowly pushing into Viking territory, quietly building strongholds and permanent garrisons to consolidate his gains, and risking minimal provocation. Since the Danes in England were being harassed by Norwegians from Ireland and Scotland, Edward's son Athelstan gradually won back the disputed territories, so that by 940 the Kings of Wessex extended their rule to Mercia, Northumbria, York, and many parts of the Danelaw. (This did not prevent the Norwegians from proclaiming Eric Bloodaxe King of Northumbria and York ten years later.)

Athelstan's sons, Edmund and Edgar, managed to keep the invaders at bay, while tolerating Viking settlements within the conquered parts of the Danelaw, even granting them a certain independence. An edict of Edgar's in 970 states: "In return for the loyalty they have always shown me, I have permitted and shall continue to permit the Danes to have such good laws as they shall deem fit."

The two brothers reigned as England's legitimate sovereigns, and won the respect of the Vikings; Danish and Celtic princes rowed the royal galley at Edgar's coronation in 973. From that day on he bore the resounding title King of England and Sovereign of the Sea and Island Kings. But by the end of the century the Danes were harassing the coasts of England again, collecting tribute money, the so-called Danegeld: they sailed from port to port threatening death and Destruction unless the population could raise sufficient ransom. In 994, London was forced to find 16,000 pounds of silver overnight before a joint Danish-Norwegian armada, one of the most powerful Viking fleets on record, agreed to move on without damaging the city.

This fresh outbreak of Danish blackmailing expeditions coincided with the reign of Edgar's weakling son, Ethelred the Unready. A timid man provoked beyond endurance, he permitted himself one shocking burst of violence: on November 13, 1002, he ordered *all* the Danes within his realm put to death. Unluckily for him, Gunnhild, sister of the Danish King Sven Forkbeard, lost her life in this massacre. Immediate Danish reprisals struck Oxford and Cambridge, among other places. Ten years later Forkbeard, still unappeased, brought a huge fleet of dragon ships to the mouth of the Thames. However, London was defended by the Viking Torkil, mercenary to the Anglo-Saxon kings. Forkbeard marched on, without waiting for London to surrender, conquered Wessex, and drove Ethelred into an ignominious flight to his Norman cousins across the Channel. Three years later, after Sven Forkbeard's death, all England was incorporated into King Canute's realm, making the North Sea a Danish inland sea.

The Rise and Fall of King Canute

Denmark was the first of the northern countries to be consolidated, under King Godfred, but it did not outlast its founder for long. Even while Danish pirate kings terrorized all western Europe, there was no ruler of note back home.

Norway, on the other hand, evolved in the ninth century from a cluster of tribal kingdoms toward the formation of a central government. The stars of this drama of Norwegian unification were Queen Asa, her son Halfdan the Black, and that King Harald who would not cut his flaming locks until the last holdout among the rebels had been dealt with: Harald Fairhair, as he was called.

Harald had eleven wives, with whom he produced a veritable army of offspring. One of his sons, Eric Bloodaxe, bled himself white in the struggle for England while another, Haakon the Good, made the best of his father's success in subduing rebellion, and gave Norway a long-lasting peace. For the first time in memory, many Norwegians died peacefully of old age, not only during his reign but also that of his successor, Haakon the Second, ''The Great Jarl'' (Earl) who also kept the peace in his own realm instead of carrying war to others. But in his old age the Great Jarl's relentless pursuit of the country's daughters led to peasant uprisings and his own ignominious end—he was beaten to death in a pigsty.

His successor was the renowned Olaf Tryggvason, ''the most glorious hero of Norwegian Viking times.''

In the meantime, Denmark had become reunited under three rulers: Gorm the Old, who reunified the islands off Jutland before his death in 950; his son Harald Bluetooth, who moved the boundaries of his realm northward as far as southern Norway, though he was forced by the German Emperor Otto the Great to give up Hedeby and submit to baptism; and Harald Bluetooth's son, Sven Forkbeard, one of Denmark's greatest rulers, who prepared the way for Danish hegemony under Canute the Great.

It was under Sven Forkbeard, in the year 1000, that the Danes won their decisive victory against the Norwegians, in the sea battle of Svold where Olaf Tryggvason, sailing into battle in the *Long Serpent*, the most beautiful and strongest of Viking ships, lost his life and his fleet. The next turning point came in 1016, when Ethelred's son Edmund was defeated by Canute at the battle of Ashingdon in Essex. Edmund later ceded all of England except Wessex to the Danes, who got Wessex as well when Edmund died a few months afterward. In 1030, when Canute won a crushing victory at Stiklarstadir over Norwegian King Olaf the Pious (St. Olaf), ''a good and exceedingly mild man'' who had converted his subjects to Christianity, he took over the rest of Norway. Viking history reached its culmination in Canute's kingdom. Only five years later, however, Olaf's son, Magnus the Good, was back on his father's throne, and by 1042 the Danes had lost England again.

1066: Normans Invade England

In 1042 Ethelred's son Edward reassumed the throne of England, which Canute's successors were too weak to hold. Edward had spent thirty of his forty years in Normandy, in the company of Norman knights and princes of the Church, whose life style he had adopted.

Edward (''the Confessor'') spoke French, cultivated French manners, and was given to an excessive romantic piety, all of which did not consort well with the rough-and-ready ways of the Anglo-Saxon court. He also surrounded himself with Norman friends and advisers, upon whom he bestowed generous grants of land and lucrative offices, paving the way for the Norman conquest well before the appearance of William the Conqueror.

But the Anglo-Saxon princes, led by his brother-in-law Harold, knew how to defend themselves. While Edward the Confessor concentrated on his pious studies and exercises and on his pet project, building Westminster Abbey, Harold of Wessex, a worldly man experienced in warfare, gradually took over the government. When Edward died in 1066, childless, and was duly buried in Westminster Abbey, the Anglo-Saxon princes naturally elected Harold, scion of the powerful Wessex royal house, King of England.

But at this point another claimant to the throne of England came forward: William, Duke of Normandy, called the Bastard because of his illegitimate birth as

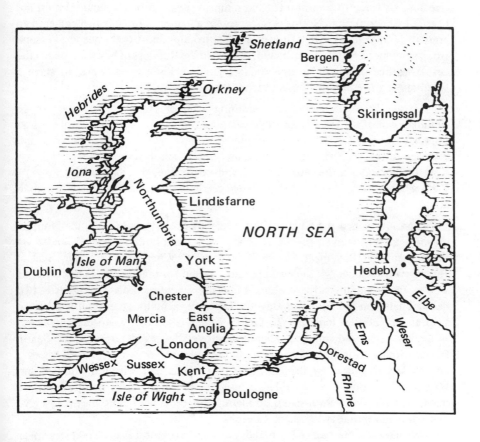

The British Isles.

offspring of Robert I (sometimes identified with the hero of medieval legend, Robert the Devil) and a laundress. William argued that Edward the Confessor had actually bequeathed him the crown of Wessex in 1052, in gratitude for hospitality enjoyed in Normandy. Furthermore, William had conferred knighthood on Harold of Wessex during a stay at Rouen, thus making the Anglo-Saxon William's vassal—and a vassal could not, in the feudal order of the day, be his liege lord's superior!

With promises he subsequently never kept, William obtained from the Pope a dispensation for his war against Harold. Also on his side were all the knights of Normandy, the finest fighting men in Europe, whom he managed to bribe, threaten, or force to join him for the planned invasion of England. He did not restrict his recruiting to Normans only, and in a matter of months had gathered an army of 65,000 men, with a fleet of 400 battle ships and 1,000 transport vessels. He even induced Harald Haardraade, or Harald the Ruthless of Norway, one of the heroic figures of Norse history and a legend in his own lifetime, to stage a simultaneous invasion of England from the northwest.

Harald Haardraade, before becoming king of Norway, had risen to be Commandant of the Guards for the Byzantine Emperor at Constantinople. As an Imperial General for Greece he is reputed to have won countless victories and captured fortresses between Jerusalem and Sicily, among others. Yet in 1066, as King of Norway, he lost his life at Stamford Bridge, outside the city walls of York, where young Harold of Wessex succeeded in beating back the Norwegian army.

Harold reached the Channel too late, however, to hold back the Norman invaders at sea or even on the beaches. William's huge army had landed on September 28, 1066, near Pevensey in Sussex. When the two armies met at Hastings on October 14, the ensuing battle lasted for nine hours. (The battle, as well as the preparations for William's invasion, were recorded for posterity two decades later on the so-called Bayeux Tapestry, actually an embroidered linen strip about 230 feet long and 20 inches wide.) The host of Norman invaders, brilliantly organized and led, all but destroyed the even larger Anglo-Saxon forces. Young King Harold was brought down by an arrow that pierced his eye, and hacked to pieces by the Normans into whose hands he fell, blinded and bleeding. The monks responsible for his interment needed the help of his royal mistress, Lady Edith Swansneck, to identify his remains, before they could give him Christian burial at Waltham Church.

William, the Bastard of Normandy, known henceforth as the Conqueror, was crowned King of England at Winchester on Christmas Day, 1066. The son of Vikings, it was he who gave medieval England its political, cultural, and social character and thus influenced the island's entire subsequent history. There were no further invasions after 1066; the island has kept itself intact for over nine hundred years.

England was not alone in falling to the "restless, landless sons of Normandy." In the second half of the eleventh century they created a number of states and city-states on the Mediterranean whose influence was long felt in the history of Europe.

Dark Red Seabirds on the Mediterranean

Legend has it that even Charlemagne, on a visit once to the South of France, saw Norse dragon ships appear and disappear along the coastline. Around 840 an Arab reported sighting a fleet of Viking ships "like a swarm of dark red seabirds." Such ships in 827 invaded the northern Spanish kingdom of Asturias, probably coming from Noirmoutier. Another major attack came in 844, when a Viking fleet of 54 longboats descended on the coast of Cordoba, besieged Lisbon for thirteen days, threatened Cadiz, burnt the suburbs of Seville, and laid waste the orange groves by the Guadalquivir (at that time known as Wadi el-Kebir), before taking their booty back to their strongholds on the west coast of France.

Fifteen years later a Viking fleet of 62 ships set out from Brittany for the Mediterranean on one of the most daring expeditions in the history of naval warfare—it was to last three years. The pirate crews—led by the Sea King Hasting, with Björn Ironside, the son of Ragnar Lodbrok—ravaged Algeciras, bloodied Morocco, plundered Mallorca, occupied the Rhone delta and sailed upriver as far as Valence, sacked Pisa, Ficsole, and the no-longer-extant Luna (which they mistook for Rome), and terrorized all the waters between Spain, Italy, and North Africa, burning down cities and villages, loading their ships with loot and prisoners. On the way back they ran into a heavy storm on the Bay of Biscay in which they lost all but seventeen ships. The survivors landed at Pamplona and picked up—or should one say "lifted"?—30,000 dinari from the governor there, before finally getting back to Nantes in 862, laden with rich Moorish saddles and harness, dazzling Arab robes, ornaments and jewelry, and bringing home many dark-skinned slaves.

For a long time thereafter the Mediterranean countries were left in peace by the Norse marauders, and the next Viking assaults, when they did come a hundred years later, concentrated on Asturias and Lisbon only. The sea between Gibraltar

and Syria still belonged to "the competition"—the Saracens, second only to the
Vikings in piratical fierceness. Not until the eleventh and twelfth centuries were
the Arabs gradually driven back by Franco-Norman mercenaries, out of southern
Italy And Sicily, back to North Africa.

About the time King Canute was making war on England, in the second
decade of the eleventh century, Viking mercenaries in the pay of the Byzantine
Emperor were defending his territories in Apulia and Calabria against the Sicilian
Saracens and the many Italian city-states and dukedoms trying to expand southward while fighting each other. By the end of the third decade of the century the
Normans had prevailed, and founded an independent dukedom at Aversa. They
threw out the Greeks, divided the land among themselves, and formed the first of
the powerful Viking satellite states on the Mediterranean.

Their leader was the legendary Duke Robert Guiscard, one of twelve sons of
Count Tancred of Hauteville. In 1059 he received all of southern Italy for his fief
from Pope Nicholas II. In 1084 he freed Pope Gregory VII, then under siege by
Emperor Henry IV (in his own interest, the Pope being his patron), eliminated the
last of the Greek strongholds in the south, and began the conquest of Sicily, which
was completed by his brother Roger in 1091, six years after Robert Guiscard died
of the plague.

It was Roger's son who united the various Norman states in southern Italy into
the "Kingdom of the Two Sicilies" which, under his able rule, became a great
power, indeed the most flourishing state, economically and culturally, in the
Europe of that day. Under Roger II, Saracens, Greeks, Jews, Italians and Normans
made Palermo one of the great cities of southern Europe, a center of continental
power, dominating the entire Mediterranean region at the dawn of the twelfth
century.

Varangians in Russia

As early as the seventh century, Vikings had found yet another route southward,
from Sweden via Lake Ladoga, the great Russian rivers and the Black Sea to
Constantinople, which they called *Miklagard*, the Great City. Archaeological
finds on Helgö and Gotland indicate that trade went on between Sweden and the
lands around the Caspian Sea and the Indian Ocean centuries before the so-called
Viking Age. And there is evidence of a systematic colonization of the Baltic coast
during the eighth century. From their many small fixed trading points along the
eastern shores of the Baltic, the Vikings could move across the Gulf of Finland to
the southern shores of Lake Ladoga. Their settlement at Old Ladoga, as it is called

today, was convenient for reloading goods from seagoing dragon ships to the smaller boats used inland. Undaunted by the vast reaches of virgin forest or by hostile Slav .tribes, they moved slowly from Ladoga along the Russian rivers deeper into the mainland. By the mid-ninth century they had crossed the Volkhov to the source of the Volga and from there to Bulgar, the great trading post at the confluence of Volga and Kama—terminal point of the great Silk Route from the Far East and portal to the lands of the Caliphs.

More important historically is the fact that, by way of the Volkhov and the Dnieper, they reached Kiev about 864, and made it an outpost for their territorial expansion. In the tenth century it became the center of a powerful kingdom stretching across the whole of western Russia from the Baltic Sea to the Black Sea. Here King Vladimir I (St. Vladimir) was baptized in 987, and opened the country to the missionaries from Constantinople—and therewith to the rites of the Eastern Church, a matter of far-reaching consequence. The Vikings were known as the *Rus* in this part of the world, and the name gradually was applied to their subjects as well. Kiev became known as "the Mother of Russian cities"; the Vikings' eastern domain became the cradle of Christian Russia.

Rurik and the Nestor Chronicle

Most of early Viking history in Russia is obscure, undocumented, and still under dispute for many reasons, including ideological differences. The present Soviet government does not care to regard Swedish conquerors as the founders of the first great Russian city, and is inclined to question the sources of such theories. Claims that the Swedish Vikings not only ruled but opened up all of western Russia are based essentially on the Nestor Chronicle, written around 1100 in Kiev's Pechersky Monastery, though the oldest copy still in existence dates from the fourteenth century. It tells of Slavic tribes unable to establish law and order among themselves and therefore inviting three foreign princes to rule over them. The chosen three were brothers. They came, with their kinsfolk and all the Rus, to settle in three places: the oldest brother, Rurik, in Novgorod; the second, Sineus, at Beloozero; and the third, Truvor, in Izborsk. This tale is bound to seem suspect even to non-Slavic historians. Several readings have been exploited in various ways, but neither linguistic nor archaeological researches have as yet come up with much firm evidence one way or another.

However, it may be said with some certainty that the Rus-Varangian peoples from Sweden established themselves as rulers in the Dnieper region in the course of the ninth century, and extended their territory beyond Kiev to include all of the

The Eric stone in the Viking collection of the Slesvig-Holstein Museum. The text runs: "Thorulf, vassal of Svein, erected this stone for his companion Eric, who met his death when warriors besieged Hedeby, he was a helmsman, a well-born warrior."

The small Sigtrygg stone, in the Viking collection of the Slesvig-Holstein Museum. The text runs: "Asfrid, the daughter of Odinkar, made this memorial for King Sigtrygg, her and Knuba's son. Gorm engraved the runes."

Ukraine as far as the Black Sea. But though they were mentioned as foreigners in the chronicles as late as the eleventh century, the Swedes in western Russia assimilated with the natives as rapidly as their Danish counterparts in Normandy. Since they were mostly traders interested in the turnover of goods, rather than pirates and brigands killing for booty, their pattern of conquest is more peaceable than that of the Vikings in the West, even though skirmishes, feuds, and encounters with hostile natives were not uncommon.

Byzantium's Foreign Legion

There were also regular campaigns against the mighty Byzantine Empire, such as Grand Duke Helgi (Oleg) led in 865. He laid Constantinople under siege in the following year and won a trade agreement permitting the Varangian traders to pitch their booths outside the city walls. In 907, according to the Nestor Chronicle, the Varangians put wheels on their ships and sailed them on land against the Holy City under a favorable wind, so effectively that they won important concessions once more. In 913-14 the Varangians invaded from the Black Sea with five hundred ships, crossing the narrow Volga-Don land bridge (the site of the present Volgograd, formerly Stalingrad) to the Caspian Sea, for an attack on Iraq and Azerbaidzhan. In 941 Rurik's son Igor brought a strong fleet to Constantinople; this time his ships were destroyed by "Greek fire"—a kind of Molotov cocktail made of naphtha, pitch, and sulphur, sent to the target by means of arrows, spears, or copper tubes. Prince Igor returned to the attack in 944, this time with a huge cavalry contingent, and succeeded, like his predecessor Helgi, in winning a lucrative trade agreement with guarantees of valuable privileges to the Varangian traders. The document, reproduced in the Nestor Chronicle, is also of linguistic interest in that, like the earlier one of 907, it contains on the Russian side names of almost exclusively Nordic origin.

The Byzantine Emperor, by about 970, apparently had learned to swallow the same bitter pill as Charlemagne and the Franconian princes had: if you can't lick 'em, hire 'em. He began employing these ferocious daredevils for good money to fight his enemies. Varangians—the name may mean "the hoarse-voiced" or "allies"—formed the Imperial Guards, became important functionaries at court, and became the nucleus of the Eastern Empire's armies. Many of these crack troops—"beanpoles" to the Greeks—lost their lives defending the Byzantine Empire, particularly in battles against Arabs and Bulgars. Their Commander-in-Chief was the Adjutant General to the Emperor, in whose absence he held the keys to the gates of the city.

One such commander was Harald Haardraade—"Harold Hardnose" could be an English equivalent—Imperial Tax Collector at Kiev, Chief of the Swedish Guards at the Court of Constantinople, a victorious Imperial General many times over. As King of Norway, Harald lost his life in 1066, an ally of William the Conqueror. An exemplary Viking hero, he personifies the Scandinavian peoples' immense vitality and their bravery in war—including a readiness to risk their lives at all times, even when fighting for pay. With such flaming energies they managed to put their brand on four continents, one of which, Europe, they kept on her knees for centuries. By the time Robert Guiscard's Normans and the Eastern Empire's Varangians clashed on the Adriatic in the struggle for Durazzo (Durrës), they were omnipresent from the Atlantic to the Volga, from the Arctic to the Mediterranean. They had also, by this time, pushed across the Atlantic to the Western Hemisphere, five hundred years before Columbus.

Voyagers to Vinland

Butter Dripping from Every Grass Blade

First stop on the way to the New World was Iceland, and the first man to bring word of it back home was a Viking named Gardar Svavarson, a Swedish farmer from Zealand, married to a Norwegian woman whose parents had settled in the Hebrides. To collect his wife's dowry, Gardar set out for a voyage of several weeks' duration, but just off the Orkneys he was overtaken by a storm that drove him far off his course. He was forced to land on the coast of a large, deserted island, where he spent the winter.

When he returned the following summer, he told his story of the vast unknown island in the North Atlantic, which he named Gardarsholm, after himself. That was in the year 861. Some time later another gale blew the Norwegian shipowner Naddod to Gardarsholm. He climbed a mountain for a bird's-eye view, saw rocky plains, bare precipices, and snowy mountain peaks, and named the uninhabited, uninviting country Snowland. His report must have roused the Norwegians' curiosity. Another Norwegian, Floke Vilgerdason, coming from the Faroes, found its southern shore rich in fish and bird life and settled in for the winter, but lacking winter feed for his cattle, which perished, he too sailed back home, quite disgruntled. His name for the island, Iceland, was the one that stuck.

But one of his men, a peasant named Thorolf, saw the island with different eyes and effectively publicized his own report, full of enthusiastic descriptions of Iceland's fertile green valleys "so rich that butter dripped from every grass blade." His stories earned him his nickname, Thorolf Butter (Smör), and the credit for having set in motion a wave of migrants westward from Norway to the place he praised so highly, according to the thirteenth-century Icelandic *Landnamabok* or Land Register.

The first Norwegian settlers on Iceland were political emigrés, casualties of the forcible unification of Norway, which threatened their hereditary rights and burdened them with taxes. King Harald Fairhair, the empire builder from whom they fled, enjoys a bad press in Iceland to this day.

After a three-week voyage in open boats, the emigrants were rewarded by landing on an island far more in accord with Thorolf Smör's mouthwatering descriptions than Floke's or Naddod's bleak reports. Behind a chain of islands swarming with birds they found lush green meadows and streams teeming with fish. Birch woods provided them with material for making charcoal, bog iron ore supplied metals, driftwood came floating in on the tide, and sea lions and whales were plentiful along the coast. All in all, it was inviting enough to draw more

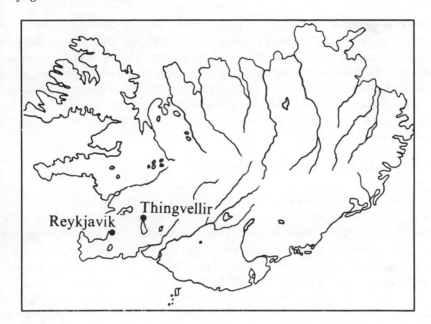

Iceland: the island on the Arctic Circle, 500 miles from the European mainland, 200 miles from Greenland. Iceland was discovered by Sctoch-Irish monks, and settled and colonized by Norwegian peasants after 860 A.D.

immigrants every year, not only from Norway but also Celts from the British Isles.

Iceland turned out, in fact, not to be entirely uninhabited. The Scandinavian immigrants had been preceded by Celtic penitents; hermits, full of zeal and naively astounded to find that here, hundreds of miles north of Scotland, they could see well enough at midnight during the summer months to pick the lice out of their clothing "just as if it were broad daylight," to quote the Irish monk Dicuil the Geometer.

These Christian holy men did not stay long once the detested heathen had arrived. They abandoned their wretched huts, boarded their tiny boats made of willow wood and hides, and rowed themselves back home. They left behind bells, croziers and other appurtenances of their calling, including many books illuminated in a curious, fantastic style that inspired many imitators.

The wave of immigration that began in 874 brought about 30,000 inhabitants to the island before starting to recede about 930. They lived in accordance with their traditions as a community of free farmers, proud of their independence, though in fact they were ruled by a few powerful families. This situation was not affected by the official founding of a state in 930, "the only wholly free republic in the world at that time" ruled by a parliament, the Althing, which met every summer on a lava-covered plain at Thingvellir. Here it made decisions, such as the one to Christianize the island, in 1000, devised new laws, and administered justice in accordance with the old laws, which were not committed to writing until 1148. The fact that this government had no executive branch eventually led to the opening up of Greenland.

"Greenland" and Eric the Red

In about 960 the Norwegian Thorvald Asvaldsson, having killed one of his neighbors in his homeland, emigrated to Iceland. He was permitted to settle in the north, in Drangaland, where the poor, stony soil provided less than subsistence for his ever-increasing family. At Thorvald's death his son Eric, nicknamed the Red, took over the homestead, married a girl of good family, and did his best to keep his family alive. But he was a hothead like his father, quick to take offense, and a few years after his marriage he too committed manslaughter—two sons of a neighbor lay dead. Outlawed for three years by the Althing, Eric Thorvaldsson, aged thirty, left Iceland in 982, sailing westward into exile, looking for "the country which Gunnbjorn Ulf-Krakason saw when he was adrift on the sea to the west of Iceland." Gunnbjorn's sighting went back to the year 900, and had inspired no westward rush of exploration, since he had seen nothing more than fog, ice floes, and snow-capped cliffs.

After several days' voyage westward Eric, too, saw only steep cliffs lashed by waves, completely inaccessible. Not until he drifted south with the ice, sailed around Cape Farewell, and then turned northward again did he come to more habitable land. Greenland's southwest coast, warmed by the Gulf Stream which encouraged some vegetation, looked relatively hospitable. Sailing from bay to bay, fishing, hunting, and catching birds, Eric thoroughly explored that rugged, indented coast for possibilities of settlement. Deep inside the fjords he found green valleys, sheltered by high mountains from the world of perpetual ice and snow. Here the climate was more favorable to life, streams were full of fish, and coastal waters were populated, like those in Iceland, with sleek seals and great whales.

Eric spent three long winters on that coast, and logged thousands of sea miles before he came home to tell his fellow Icelanders of the riches awaiting them. He was inspired to call the vast island in the Arctic Ocean Greenland, on the grounds that "many would want to go there if it had so promising a name." That name, in

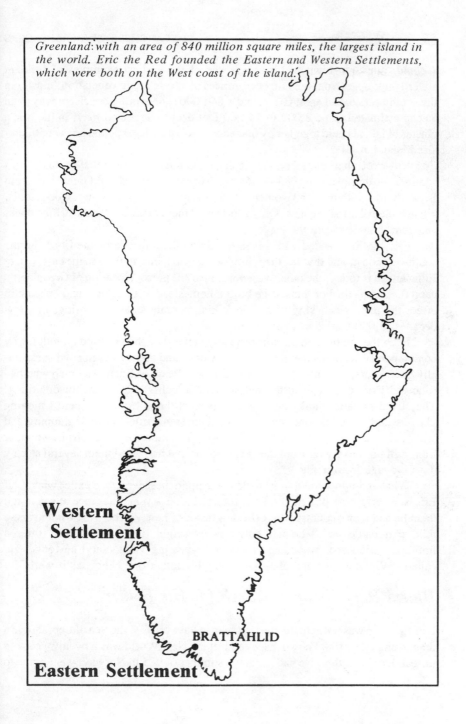

Greenland: with an area of 840 million square miles, the largest island in the world. Eric the Red founded the Eastern and Western Settlements, which were both on the West coast of the island.

Western Settlement

BRATTAHLID

Eastern Settlement

Iceland, must go down in history as one of the earliest examples of brilliant advertising: apart from the rare occurrences of sparse arctic vegetation, mostly in the southwest coastal area, Greenland's 840,000 square miles consist mostly of an icecap estimated to be 8,000 to 14,000 feet deep! Greenland may, in fact, be a cluster of islands held together by that enormous arctic icecap, and not a continent-sized island at all.

However that may be, the Icelandic *Landnamabok* tells us that "this summer"—this was in 985—"twenty-five ships sailed to Greenland from Breidafjord" with men and women, old and young, horses and cows, wood, tools, kitchen utensils, fishing nets. Only fourteen of them made it. "Some drifted back, and some sank beneath the waves."

Eric the Red landed with seven hundred others in one of the fjords on the southwest coast, and divided them into two groups, one settling to the east, where Julianehaab is today, the other westward, near the present location of Greenland's capital, Godthaab. For himself he built a homestead at Ericfjord, and became in effect the uncrowned king of a little Viking peasant state numbering, in a few decades, 3,000 Christian souls in all.

Even though the climate was probably better then than it is today, judging by contemporary accounts mentioning birch woods and apples that ripened in especially good years, Greenland was not a farmer's dream of Eden. The men who had followed Eric to Greenland did not succeed in cultivating grain, for one thing. They lived in dank, murky huts, under constant threat from the island's moving glaciers and pack ice, and survived off their lean cattle and their trapping and fishing. It was a life at the edge of starvation, without bread or sun, fruit, wood, or iron, a life of misery far from the expectations that had lured them several stormy days' voyage from home.

What an impression it must have made upon these wretched exiles when Leif Ericsson, offspring of Eric the Red, returned after a year's absence at sea to tell them he had seen a country where the dew tasted of honey, where the winter was so mild that cattle could be left outdoors overnight, boundless forests offered limitless varieties of wood, and even grape-bearing vines could be found. He called it Vinland, or Land of Wine, going his father one better, as it were.

Bjarni Herjolfsson's Search for His Father

Leif Ericsson was not actually the first man to have crossed the Sea of Labrador in a dragon ship. The first known discoverer of the New World was a twenty-year-old in search of his father. He had spent the summer of 985 in Norway, went home to

Iceland in the fall, and found his family's farm deserted; his parents had joined Eric the Red's expedition to Greenland. So Bjarni, the son of Herjolf, set sail for Greenland with a crew none of whom had ever navigated the Greenland sea. They made good progress for three days, looking only for the land that lay westward and would loom up out of the sea, crowned with icecapped mountains, when Iceland disappeared behind them. But then, according to *The Greenlanders' Saga*, a family chronicle begun about 1200, the favorable wind dropped, northerly gales blew up and drove them nobody knew where in the thick mist. It was many days before the sun broke through again and they could take stock of their position.

"So they sailed on for a whole day and a night. Then they sighted land and wondered what country this might be. And Bjarni did not think that this could be Greenland" so they sailed along the coast, "and saw that there were no high mountains here, only forest and gentle hills." They sailed on northward for two days before they sighted land again, but it was flat and covered with endless forest, so it could not be Greenland, which was reputed to have great glaciers. After three more days at sea under a steady southwesterly breeze they at long last saw a high and mountainous country with gigantic glaciers loom up out of the sea. But Bjarni shook his head once more and did not drop sail; it soon turned out to be only a small island.

On they sailed with the same wind, as fast as "ship and rigging could stand." Four days later they sighted land for the fourth time, and this time Bjarni was satisfied that it fitted the description of Greenland he had in mind, and looked for a place to land. They reached a spit of land with some boats beached on it. "And on this spit of land lived Bjarni's father . . . and Bjarni stayed with him as long as his father lived, and went on living there after his father's death." So content was Bjarni to have reached his goal that he hardly spoke of his long erratic voyage. It wasn't until fifteen years later, while he was in Norway, that he was questioned as to why he had never gone on land anywhere during his long voyage. Perhaps it dawned on him then that he had sighted the coast of a new world. On his return to Greenland he gave vivid and detailed descriptions of his odyssey.

Eric the Red and his sons heard about Bjarni's discoveries, and since they were in command on Greenland, it fell to the eldest, Leif, to find out if there was anything in them. He bought Bjarni's own, proven vessel, equipped it, manned it with a crew of thirty-five, and sailed westward on the course Bjarni had taken fifteen years before. It was in the year 1000. Nearly 500 years before Columbus.

Leif the Lucky

The voyage went as planned. The *Greenlanders' Saga* records that "the first land they sighted was the land Bjarni had seen last." But they found it to be a wasteland of rocks and glaciers and named it Helluland, meaning Land of Flat Stones, and returned to their ship.

They easily found the second place described by Bjarni, and liked it far better, with its white sand beaches behind which stretched interminable dark green forest. They named it Markland, meaning Woodland, and sailed on for two more days before a stiff northeaster, until they sighted land again. This time they went ashore on a small outlying island, where they knelt to pluck the rich dewy grass and tasted it. They had never tasted anything so sweet. It made such an impression that Leif Ericsson spoke of it again and again after his return.

After sailing through the narrows between the island and a cliff that jutted out northward into the sea, they dropped anchor and waded ashore close to a river that came from a lake further inland. It seemed a perfect place to spend the winter. "Both the sea and the river were swarming with salmon bigger than any they had ever seen. The land was so rich in vegetation that it seemed capable of feeding the cattle even in winter, there being no frost, and the grass only slightly withered by the cold. Nor did day and night differ so much in length as they did in Greenland or Iceland."

When they had finished building their winter quarters, Leif—a tall, powerful man and an astute leader in every way—divided his men into two groups, one to remain at the camp, the other to go out and explore the country. One evening, to Leif's distress, one member of the expedition failed to return: Tyrkyr the German, who had lived with Eric the Red's clan for many years and was regarded as a father and mentor by Leif. A search party of fifteen set out to look for him. But they had not gone far before they ran into him, coming toward them in an extraordinary state of excitement. The little man with his flat, freckled face was quite beside himself—rolling his eyes, grimacing, and babbling in German, until finally they managed to remind him that he must speak their language. When they finally understood what he was saying, they found it hard to believe. Tyrkyr insisted he had found vines bearing grapes. When Leif expressed doubt, Tyrkyr indignantly reminded him that he, the German, had grown up in a country full of vineyards and certainly knew what he was talking about.

When Leif's party put out to sea for their return voyage, with a cargo of timber and grapes, they were blessed with a favorable wind all the way home. After his return, he was known as Leif the Lucky, according to *The Greenlanders'*

Saga, which also notes that the next Vinland expedition was led by Leif's brother Thorvald. Thorvald wintered in the sycamore house built by Leif's men and set about exploring the country methodically, finding the white beaches, fertile river valleys, and dense forests reported by Leif.

Thorvald's men found no sign of previous settlement, until one day they stumbled upon a deserted barn. After the second winter they encountered people for the first time—nine natives in three boats made of hide stretched over a framework of willow wands. They killed eight of them, but the ninth got away and roused his tribe; a whole squadron of canoes appeared and showered the Greenlanders' river bank encampment with a hailstorm of arrows. Thorvald was mortally wounded. They buried him on a land spit, setting a cross at the head and foot of his gravemound. Then they loaded their ship with grapes and timber and sailed homeward after an absence of almost three years.

The next Vinland expedition, undertaken by Thorstein, another of Leif's brothers, and a crew including a few graybeards who had participated in earlier voyages, was blown off course by unfavorable weather and kept adrift at sea for weeks before it returned to Brattahlid, its mission unaccomplished.

That would have been around the year 1006.

Thorfinn Karlsefni, Merchant Seafarer

The dream of that land of rich meadows, wine, wheat, and giant salmon remained to haunt the icebound colonists of Greenland—something to talk about, inevitably, during those endless winter nights and whenever men gathered together over their beer. There it was, only ten days by sea, as good as uninhabited, with its sweet grasses and woods that stayed green even in winter.

One night Eric the Red talked about it with two visiting ship owners, Thorfinn Karlsefni, a well-to-do merchant who had contributed much barley to make that year's traditional Christmas beer flow copiously, and Bjarni Grimolfsson, also a merchant ship owner. Both men had come to Greenland in pursuit of trade, and found themselves trapped by the early onset of winter. That same winter Karlsefni married Eric's daughter-in-law Gudrid. During the festivities the beer flowed, the sagas were recited, and much talk of the overseas paradise stirred men's adventurous hearts.

Early the next summer at Brattahlid three stout dragon ships were made ready for the voyage. The third of the three ships belonged to the Eric clan—Eric wanted to make sure his interests were well represented on this colonizing expedition. His ship was led by one Thorhall the Hunter, with Freydis, an illegitimate daughter of

Eric's, and her husband Thorvard, as members of his party. The three ships held 140 men, domestic animals, tents, axes, weapons, supplies, all sorts of merchandise, and an unknown number of women—enough to make it a serious undertaking to settle and breed in the new land overseas.

The three ships at first followed the coastline north, until they reached the polar stream which, with the help of a steady north wind, carried them south past Helluland and Markland. Two days later the green wooded coastland rose up ahead, out of the dull gray sea. They landed on a small island so full of birds "that a man could hardly set foot on land without stepping on an egg." They spent the winter on a bay they called Straumfjord; but it was a hard winter, with little game or fish; even those eggs were not edible. In the spring, Thorhall left with nine men—they ended up as serfs in Ireland, where Thorhall died.

Thorfinn and Bjarni sailed further south and found a river delta rich in wild wheat, vines in the woods and on the hills, and fish in every brook. "They dug pits where the tide reached its highest point, and at ebbtide found halibut stranded in these pits. The woods were full of all kinds of game." They had reached their promised land at last.

But early one morning nine canoes appeared on the lake, filled with "ugly little men with unkempt hair and staring eyes in their broad faces." The strange men came on land but stayed at a respectful distance, staring at the Norse settlers in amazement before they disappeared again. They did not come back until the following spring, after a carefree winter the cattle had indeed spent outdoors, "looking after themselves." Suddenly one day the skin boats filled the lake in front of their settlement, so many that the lake looked "black as coal." According to *Eric the Red's Saga*, there was an interval of mutual suspiciousness, then the natives began to bring pelts ashore, trading them for red cloth from the settlers. Unluckily, Thorfinn's red ox chose this moment to come bellowing out of the woods, so frightening the natives that they leaped into their canoes and paddled away.

Three weeks later they were back, this time in a clearly hostile mood. They attacked the Viking settlers with terrifying howls and hurled whining missiles that added to the infernal noise, pressing so hard from every side that the settlers were driven into a rocky gorge. Here, with the help of their women, led by the fearless Freydis, the colonists managed to defend themselves. The battle convinced Thorfinn Karlsefni that the natives would never allow the settlers to live in their southern outpost peaceably, and they all withdrew back to Straumfjord, where they spent the following three years.

Trouble arose, after three hard winters, over the women. "The unmarried men interfered with the married women and there was much strife and unrest.'' Under the circumstances, enthusiasm for further exploration waned, and Karlsefni decided to break off the whole undertaking and return to Greenland. Bjarni's ship was driven off course and eventually reached Ireland. Karlsefni made it back to Brattahlid, but with little profit to show for his voyage. His booty consisted only of two native boys—called Skraelings, a term meaning cowards, because they preferred to fight with bow and arrow rather than man-to-man according to Viking custom—they had captured at the last moment on the coast of Markland. He eventually retired to Iceland with his wife Gudrid and his son Snorri, born in Vinland—the first white native American known to history. Later, Karlsefni had many more children; his was a family with fortune on its side, according to the Greenlanders' Saga.

Salmon, Wine, Wild Wheat

A fifth voyage to Vinland, led according to the sagas by Eric's daughter Freydis, with two Icelandic brothers named Helgi and Finnbogi to help her, brought two ships to Leif's original settlement. Troubled with dissensions among the participants from the beginning, it culminated in a bloodbath—Freydis butchering the two brothers and all the women with her axe! Freydis had clearly inherited the family tendency to impatience that began with Eric the Red's father; in any case, she returned to Greenland the following spring. Hers is the sort of story that arouses skepticism, not only with regard to itself but to all the sagas. Fridtjof Nansen, the great Norwegian polar explorer, is one such doubter; he dismissed all of the Eric and Karlsefni sagas as pure fantasy, daydreams recorded as fact.

But recent studies prove that the sagas contain a hard core of truth; there are too many details showing an exact knowledge of nautical and geographical conditions to be entirely imaginary. Bjarni's highly factual account of the voyage in search of his father, in particular, cannot be dismissed as a daydream. His authentic ship's logbook contains data so precise and verifiable that a voyage could be charted by these alone. A Norwegian who checked them out minutely, A. W. Brogger, believed that Bjarni reached the American east coast at South Labrador, about six hundred miles from Greenland. He then passed by the dangerous Labrador coast, and the third country he saw, with its steep precipices and glaciers, must have been the extreme southern tip of Baffin Island, whence a southeasterly course took him to Greenland.

Leif Ericsson's voyage is harder to reconstruct, what with all the mariner's yarns embroidered on and around it, and so the exact position of his Vinland remained ambiguous for a long time. It could have been anywhere between Newfoundland and Florida. After due consideration of all these possibilities, however, the general consensus narrowed the choice down to the area between New York and Boston—in other words, the states of Connecticut and Massachusetts, largely because of three constantly recurring details in the sagas: the salmon, the vines, and the wild-growing wheat.

Salmon, a typical cold-water fish, is not found south of 41° latitude—that is, no further south than New York. Wild vines do not grow north of 46°, and wild wheat grows up to 48°, but their average occurrence would be at about 42° latitude. The Vikings' Vinland would accordingly be situated between 41-42° latitude, within reach of Boston, which quite rightly has set up a monument to Leif Ericsson—especially since the plant secretion known as "honey dew" he discovered and made so much of is not uncommon in these latitudes. And the Indians of the American east coast did in fact use missiles emitting the kind of yowling or whining sound reported in the sagas.

All in all, then, the written sources alone provide enough internal evidence that the Vikings of Greenland indeed reached the New World a number of times, established settlements there, and mastered the problems of navigation involved in sailing there and coming back.

Helge Ingstad Finds Vinland

Archaeological evidence of the Vikings' trip to the New World has been harder to pin down. A runic inscription on a stone found in the Norwegian district of Ringerike makes definite reference to one of the Vinland voyages. On the other hand the "Kensington Stone" found in Minnesota, which was once regarded as definitive proof of the Viking adventure in the New World, has long since been unmasked as a forgery.

This stone, dug up in 1898 by a Minnesota farmer and wholly surrounded by the roots of a seventy-year-old tree, was certainly not of recent vintage. When the runes were deciphered, it turned out to be dated 1362. It tells of an expedition by eight Swedes and twenty-two Norwegians from Vinland westward into the North American continent. The farmer, Olaf Ohman, his Scandinavian neighbors, and a number of scientists devoted much attention to this stone, and one scientist in particular, Hjalmar R. Holand, virtually devoted his life to proving it authentic. Unfortunately runologists have found so much wrong with the inscription that they've determined it cannot pass muster. The language, for example, is not Old Norse, but a mix of Swedish, Norwegian, and English; the runes are not

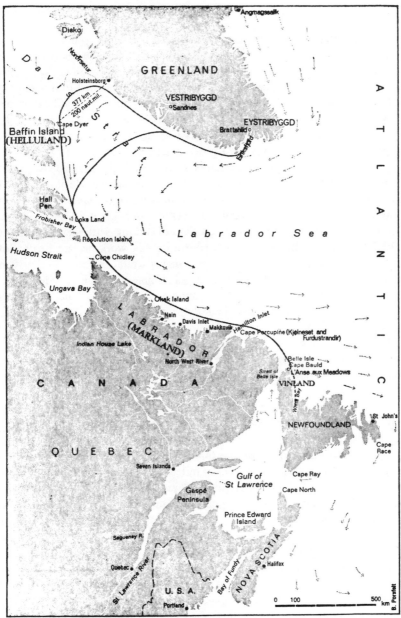

*Probable Viking routes between Greenland and North America. Repro-
duced from Helge Ingstad's* Westward to Vinland.

characteristic of the fourteenth century; the date is written in Arabic sequence—if genuine, a unique phenomenon among all runic signs, since the early stones tend to be dated by the early rulers, and later ones use Roman numerals or spell out the date in words. The mysterious forgery has not been explained to this day.

It wasn't until the 1960's that archaeology came to history's aid with a major and indisputable contribution to solving the riddle of Vinland. A Norwegian, Helge Ingstad, waged a campaign for nearly a decade to track down the legendary Vinland of his ancestors with the help of modern science and technology.

Like so many of the great discoverers in the field, Helge Ingstad was not even a professional archaeologist. As Governor of Spitzbergen he made headlines in the thirties by annexing a wide coastal strip of northeastern Greenland to Norway. He got his first experience in archaeology working with his wife, Anne Stine, a professional archaeologist, on the excavation of Viking settlements in southern Greenland. That was in 1953. In the course of this work he came to his own conclusions about the location of Vinland: that it would be more northerly than hitherto supposed, not so irrevocably tied to a climate favorable to wild grapes as we understand it today, and most likely situated in Newfoundland. He gave his reasons in his book, *Land Under the Pole Star.*

Then Ingstad went to work, methodically preparing to prove his theory. He already knew all the relevant literature: Adam of Bremen's history of the Church, *The Greenlanders' Saga,* the Icelandic *Annals.* He studied old maps, probed the navigational data in the sagas, memorized the topography of Newfoundland. Then, in a chartered cutter, he thoroughly explored the American northeastern coastline with its many rugged islands, studied the flora and fauna, talked with Eskimos and Indians, asked everyone he met about possible remains of ancient buildings. In a plane borrowed from the Canadian government, he took long flights for a bird's-eye view of the topography, in between explorations by sea and by land. He had traveled thousands of miles by boat, by plane, and on foot, and found nothing to save him from discouragement, when one day a man answering Ingstad's routine, by then almost automatic questions scratched his head and remembered something—he'd once heard tell of ''house-sites'' at a place on the north coast of Newfoundland, and could even name a man up there who knew more about it. ''I felt as if I had hooked a large salmon,'' writes Helge Ingstad; it was indeed a lucky tip, but he had earned it.

The site to excavate, eventually, turned out to be a bay on the peninsula L'Anse aux Meadows, not far from Cape Bauld, nine degrees south of the Eastern Settlement on Greenland. There, where the Labrador drift meets the tributaries of the St. Lawrence, he found green meadows, a fresh-water stream, arable land, gently sloping shores, game in the forests, ample driftwood and fish in the sea—precisely as described in the original Norse tales and documents. Ingstad was immediately impressed with the similarity of this terrain to that of the Norse settlements in Greenland. But best of all, he noticed some "indistinct, overgrown elevations in the ground, practically level with the grass and the heather. There was no doubt about it, these must be sites of houses, and very old ones." And completely untouched, so far.

Ingstad's excavations went on for years. But success was assured after only two summers. From the beginning the signs that this was Leif's original settlement site were propitious. More and more people came to participate in the dig. By 1962 there were archaeologists, geologists, pollen analysts, specialists of all kinds, from Sweden, Norway, Canada, from Iceland and Newfoundland working together. Nor was there any lack of visitors, despite the near-arctic climate. Aircraft came in swarms; a bishop turned up with a whole retinue of blackrobed clergymen, a high government official with his staff; finally, the Governor of Newfoundland dropped by.

The results were eventually summed up in Ingstad's book about the first discovery of America, *Westward to Vinland*:

Eight larger or smaller house-sites have been excavated, one of them a smithy; also four boat-sheds, and three large outdoor pits, of which two must have been cooking pits, and in the third of which charcoal must have been produced, probably for the use of the smith in his work. . . . The housesites display characteristics very similar to the way of building known from the Norse area during the Viking Age. At L'Anse aux Meadows we find house plans of the 'long-house' type, as in Greenland and . . . Iceland . . . the hearths [also] parallel [those] to be found in Greenland and Iceland, as for example the long fire and the ember pits.

Among the objects found we might mention: a few stone tools, some very rusty nails, fragments of iron, a small piece of smelted copper, a stone lamp like those known from medieval Iceland, a whetstone for needles, a fragment of bone needle of the Norse type. In addition, we have the most important find, the soapstone spindle-whorl of unquestionable Norse type.

He concludes:

Twelve carbon datings (C-14) from the different sites . . . date back to a time somewhat before or after A.D. 1000, the latest date indicated by the

C-14 method is A.D. 1080 + − 70 (i.e., the time of Leif Eirikson's voyage and those of his successors) . . . An evaluation of the archaeological material can hardly lead to any other conclusion than that the sites at L'Anse aux Meadows must be Norse and pre-Columbian.

That this was indeed none other than Leif Ericsson's original settlement could not be proved with finality, of course. The scant but remarkably accurate data in *The Greenlanders' Saga*, however, make it probable. The voyage from Greenland to L'Anse aux Meadows, which appears to be so uncommonly difficult because of the innumerable fjords, bays, and islands in this part of the world, is basically quite simple.

Once the voyagers had crossed the Davis Strait, there was only one thing for them to keep in mind on the southward journey: namely, not to lose sight of the land to the west. They had first to sail along the coast of southern Baffin Island and then steer due south along the extensive coast of Labrador until the northern part of Newfoundland appeared straight ahead. Great Sacred Island would then be an unmistakable landmark, and L'Anse aux Meadows lay just behind that island.

It was as simple as that. By enlarging only a little upon the terse statement in the saga, Leif Eiriksson could sit in his large hall in Greenland and give others sailing directions which could not be misunderstood.

Does this mean that the original American colony of the Viking settlers from Greenland has been found, beyond the shadow of a doubt? Not quite. In spite of all the recognition justly accorded to Ingstad's explorations, despite the spinning wheel and the C-14 datings, the remains at L'Anse aux Meadows are not considered to have been incontrovertibly dated, though they certainly look like an Iron Age find of Nordic character.

But no one seriously questions that Helge Ingstad has discovered the actual route. It is certain that there are traces of Viking settlements at the northern tip of Newfoundland, and that the area around Cape Bauld formed at least a part of mythical Vinland. The name Vinland, incidentally, is interpreted by Ingstad as Land of Meadows, rather than Land of Wine. (Old Norse *vin* - meadow; *vín* - wine.) It was meadowland such as this, land on which cattle could graze far into the winter, that the Norsemen longed for; by comparison with such a necessity, wild grapes would be merely a welcome luxury.

Part Three

Viking Society

The Ethics of the Fist

Brighthaired and Tall as Date Palms
Valkyries on Sunday
Keelbirds, Battlestormfish, Wound-Bees
Swordsmanship
The Death of a Poet
Vengeance as Duty
The Good Life, Viking Style
The Wisdom of Odin

The large picture stone of Lärbo on
Gotland. The bas-relief stone is over 8 feet
high. A dramatic battle scene is taking
place in the semicircular upper section.

Brighthaired and Tall as Date Palms

Rollo, the first Duke of Normandy, is reputed to have been so tall and heavy that they could not find a horse strong enough to bear his weight. The tall good looks and noble bearing of the Vikings are noted in the Fulda chronicle. The Arab Ibn Fadlan felt like a dwarf in the presence of the Varangian traders he met on his travels: "Never before did I see men with more perfect bodies," he wrote, "tall as date palms, with coppery fair hair."

Archaeological and anthropological findings have rather dashed these impressions. Their skeleton measurements fix the average height of the ancient Danes at 1.70 meters, and that of the Swedes at 1.72 meters—5' 10" at most, and hardly as tall as date palms. But statistical averages based on reconstructions of time-worn remains do not necessarily belie contemporary witness. The Norsemen were in any case probably at least a hand's breadth taller than their Central European contemporaries and a head taller than the Arabs.

Viking strength, endurance, toughness, their insensitivity to cold, wet, and all weathers, including the enervating heat around the Mediterranean which sapped the pugnacity of even their Teutonic ancestors, were constantly noted. Again, present-day research tends to dampen this vision of supermen. The damp mists and icy winds of northern latitudes produced their quota of rheumatic and other afflictions; crooked hips and backs were not uncommon, according to the analysis of skeletons found in Norway and Jutland. But these are the bones of those who stayed at home, or came home to die, not those of the roaring young men who went out to ravage the world and dazzled their victims and allies alike while doing so.

We know hardly anything about their facial features. A broad, strong-featured woman's face on a Swedish bronze buckle and a narrow warrior's head with a prognacious jaw, carved in bone, highlight by their rarity the epoch's lack of interest in realistic portraiture; nor were the chroniclers and poets interested in describing individual physiognomy. Written sources indicate that the early Vikings prided themselves on long hair and shaggy beards; best of all were blond and chestnut curls. The Normans on the other hand seem to have preferred crew cuts and shaven faces as fighting men; only civilians such as shipbuilders might wear bushy hair and moustaches. Headgear did not come into use until the twelfth century.

Valkyries on Sunday

Dress received considerably more attention, judging by such relics as the Oseberg and Bayeux tapestries, the Gotland runic stones, the valkyries of Öland and Uppland, and the so-called Golden Dwarf of Eketorp. Men most often wore a linen or woollen tunic to mid-thigh or knee, form-fitting so the waist was emphasized with or without a belt, and cut to show off a mighty biceps and torso. If the ends of the tunic were pushed under the belt, the thighs were also exposed, particularly if the men wore *broche* or *bruche* (cognate to our *breeches*), a kind of shorts. The Bayeux tapestry shows Norman woodcutters, boatbuilders, sailors, cooks and farmers so dressed while at work. Normally long leggings were worn with the tunic, close fitting at first but expanding, with time and prosperity, into wide, baggy trousers in all colors. Gentlemen wore smart cloaks fastened with decorated clasps under the chin or on the shoulder; green garters with loose ends indicated high rank. Even William the Bastard dressed like a peacock.

At home, the rich liked their tunics and trousers trimmed with precious furs, notably beaver and sable. Varangian merchants described by Arabs wore their cloaks over one shoulder, giving an effect of senatorial dignity. The uncovered arm was tattooed or painted "from the tip of the nail up to their necks" with ornaments, trees, and figurative designs.

They also had a passion for spiral bracelets, gold rings, and diadem-like headbands. The tombs of Birka yielded remarkably fine embroideries of gold wire, gold and silver lace, and splendid gold brocades. The warrior of Mammen in mid-Jutland was wrapped in a cloak with appliquéd embroideries; his armbands were padded silk worked in gold wire, and so was his elaborate headband.

Women wore, over a long pleated linen shirt (wool was worn next to the skin only for penance), a gown made in two parts and suspended on two clasps in front, and over this a sleeveless cape, varying in length. On the Oseberg tapestry the "buxom, prosaic, and clearly middle-aged matrons" seem to sail along in their wide-flowing robes like Valkyries on Sunday. But there are also young girls on one of the Oseberg chariots in miniskirts and boots, looking casual and sexy.

Ibn Fadlan's fascinating travel reports go into great detail about the Viking love of jewelry and ornaments of all kinds:

"Every one of these women wears on her breasts a metal box, with a ring and a knife attached, of iron, silver, copper, or gold, depending on her husband's wealth. They also wear neck rings of gold or silver. For every 10,000 dirhems [a dirhem was an Arabic silver coin weighing three grams] a man owns, his wife gets a neck ring to wear."

Ornament from the Swedish island Öland.

Rings and chains, clasps and pins, gold-embroidered necklaces, and pearl-studded bibs such as found in the Birka tombs also enhanced appearances and did their share for a husband's or father's credit rating. Natural beauty was prized, too, of course, and much is made of the women's dazzling white arms and their abundant long golden hair, on which great care was lavished. Both sexes appear to have used eye make-up, incidentally, according to the Arab Ibrahim Al-Tartushi, who visited Hedeby in 950 or thereabouts.

Viking dress emphasized vanity, snobbishness, conceit and vulgar effects: naked arms and muscles, gaudy breeches, scarlet silk robes. In short, the naive ostentation and dandyism of the newly rich.

Keelbirds, Battlestormfish, Wound-Bees

Their language, too, tended to be showy, windy, crudely overblown—like an unintended parody of what was best in the language of the bards. They excelled at veiled and gnomic references, bombast, circumlocution, alliterative excesses, overweight metaphors. Gold being a "dragon's hoard," a woman wearing gold was necessarily a "goddess of the dragon's hoard." Toes became "foot-twigs," a fallen comrade-in-arms an "Odin's oak," poetry "Odin's mead." When it came to referring to their ships, their fancifulness knew no bounds, from keelbird to foam-leaper, fjord-elk to swan-of-the-seagod. The sword was a battlestormfish, a bloody branch, a millstone-biter; the arrow a wound-bee.

At the other extreme, they loved short, pithy epithets, especially nicknames with a certain strange folk charm. The *Rigsthula*, a mythological poem, names its characters Stiffbeard and Sheafbeard, Brakenose and Codbiter, Fatbelly, Wolfsbrat. Kings were not exempt from such satiric labels; quite the contrary, to judge by Harald Harefoot, Harald Bluetooth, Ingjold Evilbrooder, Eyvind Braggart, Eric Bloodaxe, Sigurd Snakeeye, Olaf Lapking, and Lady Aud the Deep-Eyed. (Edith Swansneck's name, however, should serve as a reminder that this sort of naming was rather widespread medieval practice.) Their language runs the full gamut from emotional athletics to cool, malicious realism.

Swordsmanship

A man's strength was his highest virtue. Weakness meant shame, failure, dishonor; indeed, it was a crime punishable by death. And a Viking feared many things more than death; death, in fact, was not supposed to be feared at all. To become strong, to remain strong, to prove his strength at all times was a man's aim in life.

His strength was—as one Viking actually said in so many words—his one article of faith.

Since weak, sickly children were exposed to the elements, the cult of physical prowess began at birth. A child was raised to be tough. Physical exercise in stone throwing, running, jumping, riding, climbing, swimming, were basic disciplines in which a child had to prove himself; he learned to handle weapons in the nursery. The Icelandic sagas are abrim with respect for physical achievement. Harald Bluetooth was an admired snowshoe runner. Gunnar of the *Njals Saga* leapt across man-high obstacles in full armor, and across streams over six yards wide. Olaf Tryggvason, the superman of Nordic history, was reported to have run across the oars of his ship while his men were rowing with them, and to have shot a wooden ball from a boy's head with bow and arrow. He could juggle three swords while standing on his ship's railing, hurl two spears while catching one coming at him in full flight, and outswim a fish and outrun the fastest horse.

Mythical or not, such stories testify to the high esteem in which the Norsemen held sports and the arts of war. A Viking boy's playthings were axes, spears, and swords. He learned early that a freeman never went unarmed, at work or play. Dueling with swords was passionately practiced; blood had to be spilt. Life was cheap, including one's own. Death in battle was glorified. Death and killing was the all-pervasive theme of saga and life, from early childhood. The sagas provide numerous examples. A five-year-old, excluded from a children's game because he had not yet learned to spill blood, and unable to sleep that night with humiliation, got quietly out of bed, took his father's spear and thrust it into a horse's flank. When the horse was dead he lay down on his bed-bench and fell contentedly asleep. A seven-year-old, beaten in wrestling by a boy four years his senior, fetched an axe and split his playmate's skull with it. A twelve-year-old, unfairly reprimanded by his father, killed his father's valued steward, whereupon, the story goes, "Neither father nor son ever spoke of it, not in peace nor in anger, and so the winter passed." A young man riding home with an exceptionally fine new sword of glinting steel, double-edged, supple and light, reveled in the feel of it, slicing away at bushes and treetops on his way. As he neared home, one of his father's serfs came toward him. Without a second's reflection, and with one blow, he severed the man's head from his body—then galloped home to give the family a joyful report on his expertise with the fine new sword.

The Death of a Poet

"Thou shalt not kill" was no part of the Viking code, but there were certain rules of the game, formal requirements to be observed, at least among equals. Combatants were expected to risk their own necks. A decent robber confronted his victim out in the open, unlike a despicable thief. Killing from ambush or under cover of darkness was dishonorable, and penalized in some cases by outlawing and exiling the convicted perpetrator.

The hero of the *Egils Saga*, for example, captured by a farmer, escapes with the captor's silver. It then occurs to him that to make off with the silver in this underhand way is to be no better than a sneak thief. So he sets fire to the house, bringing the man and his family out into the open, face to face with him; then one by one he stabs them to death. Having won his booty "honestly," i.e. at some risk to himself, he can now go home with a clear conscience.

The same code required the utmost in self-control, a stoical equanimity in the face of danger, pain, even death. To convey extreme anguish, a story teller may let his silent hero's shirt of mail split apart, but a brave man has no tears under any circumstances, does not groan when wounded, does not move a muscle when hit. The poet Thormod, pierced by an arrow "near the heart," drags himself into a barn where the wounded are being cared for by a wise woman. There he asks for a pair of tongs and with his own hands extracts the arrow from his body, remarking half in jest, as the blood flows: "What a well-nourished heart, for which I must thank our king." With these words he dies upright against the side of the barn. An exemplary Viking death.

The way to live is exemplified by a figure from the Nordic sagas called the Bright Jarl, a kind of Siegfried character born of a god and a mortal woman who "held high his shield, carved his own bows, hunted to hounds, sat well in the saddle, wielded his sword, hurled his lance, swam in the water, read the runes, understood the language of birds, fought for land, gave of his gold, guarded the law, married, and begot many sons." Writing and especially reckoning were not included in the accomplishments of a man of high status and honor.

Honor, reputation, the esteem in which a Viking was held by his peers and his community—everything in life turned on that.

Vengeance as Duty

Where life and death were cheap, honor was sacred, infinitely vulnerable, to be defended at all times, at any cost. The slightest insult, even unintended, could have the effect of a mortal injury. A harsh word, a slap, a laugh at the wrong moment could set the machinery of vengeance in motion. The sons of Njal killed a man for making a denigrating remark about their father's beardlessness. The beauty Hallgerd, to avenge a beating by her husband Gunnar, refused him a few strands of her long hair for a new bowstring with which to fight off his enemies who were gaining on him, and calmly watched him die. The Icelander Thorleif was hit with a cook's ladle by his countryman Arnbjord aboard ship. Years later, when he sought a girl in marriage, her brother required him first to heal "the porridge marks" he had suffered in that quarrel. Irrespective of the disproportion between the injury and the expected retaliation, Thorleif bowed to this judgment. Many men died in a long-lasting clan feud as a result.

Vengeance was a moral imperative. A man who hesitated to avenge an insult exposed himself to general contempt and was often brought to book by his own family. Women, including mothers, were as relentless as men in this respect. No honor without vengeance, no life without honor. Countless feuds were bound to result; over five hundred of them are recorded by the Icelandic sagas alone. For the sake of vengeance long and dangerous voyages were undertaken as far as Greenland and Constantinople; lives and fortunes were sacrificed. Successful revenge received public acclaim for decades, especially if it came long after the heat of the moment had passed. The greater the foresight and cunning with which revenge was planned, the more it was celebrated.

The single-minded ferocity with which vengeance was pursued gradually came to be modified in thickly settled areas like Jutland. It became possible to appease the demands of honor by making material reparation, as determined by the Thing in juridical session. A scale of tariffs must have developed which set a price on insults suffered, balancing the numbers of dead on each side, fixing the value of serfs against that of free men, and establishing the difference that was to be made good in horses and sheep. In the words of the *Eyrbyggja Saga*, "The wounds of men were made good and amends made for any excess on one side or the other. And they parted reconciled." But the civilizing effect of community life was a long time taking hold. Of the five hundred feuds mentioned in the Icelandic sagas, only about thirty were settled peaceably by the Althing.

The Good Life, Viking Style

When a case was settled, the satisfied parties sat down to a sumptuous feast at which honey mead was drunk in copious drafts. Such banquets, like those following agreement on a commercial deal, a betrothal, and the like, usually went on until the participants were completely drunk; for drinking, too, was a ritual act and had its own mystique. A banquet, like a sacrificial feast, was a foretaste of the endless feasting and drinking in Valhalla—it encompassed heaven and earth in its magic. The men tried to get themselves into this godlike state of total drunkenness at least two or three times a year, goading each other on to drink more and more, faster and faster. Boastfulness, self-aggrandizement, highly imaginative and in-flated "true" stories would lead to disagreements, disputes, and quarrels, until in the end the mead-soaked hall was strewn not only with the bodies of guests who had passed out peacefully but with the dead and wounded.

> Many men meet in the mead-hall,
> Friends feasting, then fighting,
> Raving and rudely ranting,
> Till guest deals death to guest.

While elation still ran high, men would be moved to outdo each other and make all sorts of foolhardy promises to perform feats of extreme daring. Such a vow was made by placing hands on the yule boar dedicated to the god Frey, and draining the sacred cup. A vow was sacrosanct and occasioned bitter regrets when the man was sobered up, since there was no escaping the promises made. The sagas imply, however, that men would eat and drink themselves into a state of insensibility not for the sake of the orgy itself, but for its mystic values, as confirmation of their manhood, their strength, their closeness to their gods, of what they called their salvation—not in the Christian sense of the word, of course, but closer to the German *Heil* so well remembered as the universal greeting instituted under Hitler. The word *Heil*, a cognate of both our *heal* and *whole*, hence *holy*, means essentially health, wholeness, in the sense of being saved from all the ills flesh is heir to; it includes triumphant success, ultimately a kind of earthly apotheosis. And it is this mystic, spiritual (in a sense) goal that the Vikings sought to affirm in their feastings. The sagas suggest, and the commentators often insist, that the orgies were religious in nature. As was the Viking obsession with games, and with possessions.

Of their love of property there is much evidence. Anyone who owned a piece of land watched jealously over its boundary lines. He entered his storeroom as a devout believer enters a chapel. His share of the Danegeld was a point of honor immortalized on a rune stone. The bard Egil hoarded two chests of silver like Wagner's dragon guarding the gold of the Nibelungs, and in his old age he dropped them underwater, nobody knows where. Another Icelander hid his silver one night in a thick fog so that it would never be found by anyone, including himself. Such stories are reported not satirically, but with undertones of admiration for the miser. Riches are never disparaged in Nordic literature. They are considered desirable for their own sake, for the happiness they ensure, and as a visible sign of the gods' favor; hence the lavishness of Viking hospitality, which proved the host to be a man of rank and substance, and therefore clearly a favorite of the gods. There is an Icelandic story about a rich landholder's steward who took in the crew of a wrecked ship and fed them for a whole winter. After the departure of his guests in the spring he went to his master and explained, "I wanted to show what a great lord my master is, when his servant can be so generous without needing to ask." Proud and pleased to be so well understood, the master gave the man his freedom and some land of his own.

The Wisdom of Odin

And yet there is another side to these blood- and death-obsessed Nordics, ravening after honor, vengeance, and immortal fame: a cool, calculating, sober realism. These independent landholders who declined—to cite Tacitus on the ancient Germans—"to sweat for that which they could win by shedding blood" nevertheless praised hard work, industry, thrift, and early rising. "The early riser is well on his way to riches," is one of their sayings. The sagas praise not only the hotheads and fighting cocks, but also the man of few words, the peaceable, prudent, cautious man as well. Much good advice is contained in the *Havamal* (Sayings from On High), which is attributed to the god Odin but is actually a compendium of prosaic folk wisdom, quite without pretensions to literary qualities, and all too humanly full of opportunist, cynical, worldly counsels:

> Let whoever opens a door make certain there are no enemies hiding behind it.
> Praise the day after sundown, a woman after she is dead, a sword when it has proved itself.
> Confidences made are too often regretted; too often a man's tongue has cut his throat.
> A man should be wise, but not too wise.
> Better not seek to know your future, if you want a more carefree present.
> Be a steadfast friend to your friends, but do not befriend your friend's foe.
> A sleeping wolf seldom gets a thigh-bone, a sleeping man seldom wins a victory.
> A lame man can ride a horse, a man who has lost a hand can watch a flock, a deaf man can kill.

The sayings cover every phase of life: food, dress, manners, conduct of daily affairs, loyalty to friends and clan, and so on. They advocate an ethic of expediency full of circumspection, moderation, sobriety, compromise. It is the wisdom of industrious settlers and merchants rather than the heroic, fire-breathing, death-defying stance of a pre-feudal warrior class of empire builders as reflected in the sagas. Viking society was of course made up of both kinds of men.

Loyalty to the Clan

Adventures of a God on Earth
Men Without Rights
Hard Heads—Stiff Backs
The Clan First and Last
Norse Polygamy
Little Women
"Obedient Always to His Father's Word"
The Viking Woman
The Death of Aud
Pirates, Warriors, and Henpecked Husbands

Adventures of a God on Earth

The god Heimdall decided one day to leave his home in the heavens and have a look around the world of men—so we learn from Rigsthula, one of the poems in the *Poetic Edda*. The narrative of his travels on earth under the pseudonym Rig reflects the classes and customs of Norse society.

The first habitation Rig came upon was a miserable shack in which two wretched-looking creatures, male and female, crouched over a poor fire in the center of the earthen floor. He entered, introduced himself, shared their meal of bread and soup, and spent three nights with them. Nine months after his visit the woman bore a son she named Thrall. He grew into a homely but strong, hardworking man, married a girl like himself, and became the forefather of all the slaves and serfs.

The second house Rig found was well-built and had a proper hearth. The man of the house, Atti, wore his hair and beard neatly trimmed, and was busy carving a loom, while Amma, his wife, in a white linen headdress and necklace, was spinning. Rig shared their dinner of roast veal, and shared their bed for three nights as well. Amma's son was called Peasant; he was a lively, strong, red-cheeked boy who learned to break in oxen, plough the fields, build houses and other skilled work. He married a girl in a goatskin tunic and fathered all the tillers of the soil.

Last and best, Rig came to a handsome mansion where the master of the house was twisting a new string for his bow as the lady, a beauty with "breast and neck whiter than snow," was occupied with dressing and adorning herself. Sumptuous foods served on a linen cloth and silver platters included browned meats, game birds, fine light wheaten bread, all washed down with plenty of wine. The handsome boy born in due course after this visit was named Jarl (Earl, meaning prince) and wrapped in silks from birth. Rig returned later on to teach him to read the runes, and ordered him to conquer the world.

Young Jarl soon conquered his way into vast possessions and a lordly life, married a fair-skinned beauty named Erna and with her founded the race of jarls. One of his sons, the strongest and bravest, named Konr (King), not only had the strength of eight men but supernatural powers as well. He could blunt an enemy's sword by rune magic, "quell storms, save men from the sea, douse fires, ease sorrows." He also understood the language of the birds, and so heard a crow one day in the forest challenging him to go out and win more victories in war.

At this point the *Rigsthula* breaks off its lively, informative tale, which in effect declares the structure of Viking society to be god-given, that is, unalterable: there were the slaves, the free landholders and tillers of the soil, and the princes, among whom the king was *primus inter pares*, first among equals.

Men Without Rights

The thralls or slaves were easily distinguishable from the free; their hair was clipped short, they bore no weapons, the clothing for both sexes was made of rough, undyed wool. They did all the heavy menial labor. They looked after the cattle, carted dung and fertilized the fields, cut peat, felled trees. Their women milked the cows, did the cooking and washing, ground corn, helped to bake the bread, nursed their masters' children, were servants to the ladies and concubines to the men.

Viking slaves were chattels, bought, bartered, stolen, re-sold; the thrall was looked down upon as a soulless nonentity—stupid, cowardly, treacherous. To be called a slave was one of the worst insults for a free peasant. To die at the hands of a slave was the worst disgrace that could befall a man. When a slave named Kark brought to King Olaf Tryggvason the head of Duke Haakon, on which a high price had been set, Olaf not only refused him the reward but had him beheaded on the spot for having dared to lay hands on one of his masters.

A free man could beat, imprison, or kill his slave as he pleased. No distinction was made between low-born slaves and the free-born who had been won as booty in battle. Their loss of freedom meant the loss of all human status, the loss of personality. If a freeman killed his neighbor's slave, he merely had to pay sufficient compensation to buy a replacement. A freeman of course had unlimited rights over female slaves, whose offspring were welcome as an addition to the labor force but enjoyed no social privileges. If a free woman bore a child to a slave, she was disgraced and the child became automatically a slave. A slave's blood, so ran the inevitable myth, was tainted with stupidity, cowardice, and insensitivity to honor, from generation to generation. Slaves were buried, if at all, in unmarked graves. According to Ibn Fadlan, Varangian traders along the Volga threw their dead slaves as fodder to the dogs.

Yet in practice a slave might be well treated by a master concerned for his reputation, and to maintain the value of his "goods." Free and slave children, who often had the same father, grew up together. Slaves were their nurses, governesses, and as such might mingle with the family. Slaves could rise to be stewards and overseers; to stand *in loco parentis* while the owner was away; and, if they were helpful in a family feud, especially to the extent of killing an enemy, they might be given their freedom.

The legal position of slaves improved in proportion to the value of their labor, though this varied from district to district. In Iceland, a slave could not own, inherit, or bequeath anything, while in Sweden he could have a hut and cattle of his own, and even sell any surplus of what he grew on his tiny plot of land, possibly to earn enough money to buy his freedom. In some parts of Sweden a slave could give legal witness and be legally married. In Norway, a slave who found his woman or daughter in bed with a lover was permitted to pour a bucket of water over them.

Also, slaves were not always condemned to that status for life. About 1100, the Norwegian Erling Skjalgsson of Rogaland encouraged his slaves to save enough to buy their freedom, and indeed freed many of his slaves. The Viking law books contain many references to the freeing of slaves. Peasants of western Norway were obliged by law to free one slave each year. In Skane, Sweden, only the son of the freedman counted as fully free. In Iceland, newly freed slaves had certain obligations to their previous owners, and a man could be deprived of his newly won freedom for cause. There were special rules for the freeing of slave children fathered by free men.

Detailed laws on the subject date mostly from the late Viking age, the result not only of economic change but the increasing conversion to Christianity, which gradually improved the lot of the slaves. Slave children might no longer be exposed to die, or slaves deliberately killed or refused Christian burial—an important concession, since with it the slave ceased to be a soulless nothing. Denmark and Norway had largely done away with slavery by 1250; it took Iceland another fifty years, and Sweden a hundred years more.

Hard Heads—Stiff Backs

The independent, individualistic spirit of the Viking freeman is well illustrated in Dudo's history of the Normans, where he reports the following dialogue between native Franks and Viking invaders on the lower Seine:

"Where do you come from, what do you want, why have you come to our country?"

"We are Danes and we intend to conquer your country."

"Whom do you obey, who is your leader, and what is he called?"

"We have no leader, we are all equals in rank."

This was not strictly true, since they knew that their Duke Rollo, for one, was "more equal" than his men. But their answer did represent the way they felt about themselves; if a man rose to authority among them, it was by their choice and consent, and in theory they could depose him whenever they chose. When the same Danish invaders were asked later if they would enter the service of the Frankish king in return for high rewards and favors, their answer was an unequivocal no; they would serve no one, they were not accustomed to trade for privileges, but to get what they wanted by fighting for it.

When Duke Rollo in the end agreed to recognize Charles the Simple as his king, in exchange for being made Duke of Normandy, he balked at part of the ceremony; he would not kiss the king's feet. When pressure was brought to bear, he ordered one of his men to stand proxy for him—but that man refused, too. Instead of falling on his knees as instructed, he merely bowed his head slightly, snatched at the King's foot and brought it up to his mouth, causing King Charles to fall on his back, thus receiving the homage of his new vassal in a horizontal position, to the great delight of both sides.

Dudo may be a teller of tall stories here and there, but even if they are not literally true, they reflect the Viking's fanatical love of freedom and independence, his inability to knuckle under to anyone in authority, his jealous guardianship of his rights. One reason Norwegians left home to settle in Iceland was to escape the new regime of an empire-builder, Harald Fairhair, who was beginning to tax them, among other forms of harassment. The free landholders of Norway to this day represent the special character, the attachment to land and tradition, the inimitable flavor of Nordic ways. They held their own for centuries against the upper classes' efforts to subjugate them, though they did not actually form a sharply delineated, self-contained caste. However, all were not truly equal; an individual's status varied according to the rank and dignity of his ancestors, his property, and his success.

Prominent landholders set the tone at the Thing, and were often strong enough to prevail over the nobility. A king could be outvoted and deposed in early Viking times, not only if he lost a battle, but even if a poor harvest, a hailstorm, a flood, was taken as a sign that nature was against him. On such occasions the Thing might debate openly whether to depose him or have him killed. One historian, Snorri Sturluson, reports a speech by the landholder and lawman Torgny addressed at a Thing in Uppsala to King Olaf Lapking: "If you will not do as we peasants say, we will rise up against you . . . as our fathers did before us, when they flung five kings as arrogant as you into the well at Mulathing."

The Vikings were, in fact, the earliest great individualists, anti-authoritarian loners and defenders of personal freedom in the history of Western civilization.

The Clan First and Last

A man's first allegiance was to his family—his clan, which included all blood kin and kin by marriage. Since a man's life was as nothing—he surely had to die, and death in action was better than useless old age—the clan's life counted in a sense as his personal immortality. It could and should go on forever. To injure one member of the clan was an inexpiable crime against all. Blood ties were holy, to be served and defended at all costs; all vows in their interest and in that of the clan's peace and well-being were sacrosanct; infractions were threatened with the most terrifying punishments. Even the gods faced extinction because they had not avenged their clansman Baldur as they should have done.

The clan was a man's master, and to be expelled by the clan for cause was to be outlawed, exiled, worse than dead. Only a slave had no clan, and consequently was not a member of society, for it was through the family that a man became a member of society. The family was in fact, the only social reality; there was no such thing as society, or public affairs other than the land and language community of families and clans. Laws and public morality existed only insofar as they served to protect and ensure the continuation of the clan.

Norse Polygamy

When King Harald Fairhair married Princess Ragnhild of Jutland, he first had to divorce nine wives. Prince Haakon of Norway, victor over Sven Forkbeard, continued to stock his harem with the kidnapped wives and daughters of his free peasants far into his old age; after a while he would send them home again. Even St. Olaf kept himself surrounded by pretty concubines; it was only his excessive devotion to them that was held against him. Irish chroniclers commented on polygamy among the Danes who had settled along the Shannon. Adam of Bremen wrote that the Danes and the Swedes knew no moderation with regard to women.

But the most colorful stories about sexual habits come from Arab travel reports. Amin Razi, for example, speaking of the four hundred men attached to the King of the Rus, wrote that "when they were overcome by lust they would have sexual intercourse in the presence of their king" with the slave girls they owned. Since it never occurred to the king that there was anything wrong with doing likewise, this is hardly any wonder. "He had forty concubines for his nightly pleasure," during which "he did not even descend from his throne." According to Ibn Fadlan's famous account of the Rus merchants and their customs, Viking traders in young slave girls held demonstrations of the quality of their "goods" in large wooden barracks by the river, each holding from ten to twenty people. Every merchant had a bench for himself and his female merchandise. The bench served as a couch for showing off each girl in action. "It often happens that they are all at it in full view of one another, and if a buyer arrives at such a moment he just has to wait until the owner is done with his demonstration." The devout Muslim found the performance most impressive, and was repelled only by the fact that the Nordic traders did not bother to wash their hands afterward.

Abstinence was not a highly esteemed virtue among the Vikings, who tended to follow their instincts. Scandinavian authors today still take pride in the biological vitality of their ancestors and their consequent freedom from moral conflicts, neuroses, and marital instability. They also trace today's liberal attitudes toward sex in the Scandinavian countries back to the Viking social structure and naturalness, the traditional Norse freedom from shame, regrets, and prudishness in regard to sexuality.

The sagas seldom deal with romantic passions and adventures; when they do, it is with a certain detachment suggesting that sublimated emotions did not play much of a role in Viking lives, or at least did not constitute much of a problem. Icelandic poets did touch on romantic themes from time to time. One of the best known sagas, that of Gunnlaug Snakestongue, tells a strongly spiced love story with a tragic ending. In the *Havamal*, too, one comes across insights about love and passion; even homosexual love was recognized though not approved of, and tacitly tolerated at least on long all-male expeditions; sex with animals was not unheard of. Ancient Viking law concerns itself with sexual offenses, seeking to protect women against unwelcome attentions; one Gotland code lists fixed penalties for touching even a young girl's elbow or calf against her will, not to mention fondling a breast or a virginal thigh.

It is clear from the sagas and the law books that it was customary in the North, as indeed throughout the Indo-European world, for a free man to keep a number of concubines in addition to his legal wife. Such arrangements spared a man the necessity of going through the ceremony and expense of bride-buying more than once, and were so customary that they were called marriage Danish style *(more danico)* in the Frankish chronicles. The concubines were either the daughters of family slaves, or foreign women captured from the enemy in war or in raids, or even bought on the slave market, where they brought a high price. They enhanced not only a man's life style but his social status as well. The concubine was considered a second-class wife and enjoyed quasi-legal status and protection, even a chance to rise to the position of a first-class wife. However, she had no rights of ownership. Wives insisted that the concubines live outside the house, at a respectful distance from the marital couch such as, perhaps, a neighboring farm; otherwise, they tolerated the concubines whose children, being chattels, were a valuable addition to the property. The legal wife had sole charge of the household and, during her husband's frequent and long absences on campaigns, of all the property and servants.

Little Women

A Norse girl was not, however, brought up to command; on the contrary. Perfect obedience to the family, the clan, its authorities and needs, was instilled in her from the first. She was brought up to run a household and a farm, while exercising control over her own conduct and safeguarding her reputation until married; her family kept jealous watch over her virginity as well. Boys lived under no such restrictions, needless to say. Marriages were arranged by the family, subject to economic, political, eugenic, or other rational considerations. A man married to increase or secure property, wealth, social status. There was no close acquaintance between man and maid until after the marriage contract was signed, or at least before the official betrothal. Romantic love, courtship, passionate declarations of feeling such as we know and consider natural and normal did not enter into it. A father concerned with his daughter's reputation could demand a high fine from a young man who dared to serenade her. Seduction, or trying to get out of a marriage contract, brought the laws of blood vengeance into operation. The marriage contract was drawn up by representatives of the two families, as in peasant families the world over, with the usual diplomatic haggling for advantage, and with no thought for the wishes of the principals. Not until Christianity was widely established did it become accepted practice to make the agreement conditional upon the acceptance of the future couple.

But even then a girl could not marry against her parents' will. If she eloped her bridegroom was considered a seducer and could be killed with impunity by any member of the offended clan. The giving of a girl in marriage is well illustrated in *Njals Saga*; the heroine of the story is the beauty Hallgerd, whose shining mane of hair was so long and thick that she could wrap herself in it from head to toe—the same who would not save a husband's life by giving him a few strands of her hair for a desperately needed bowstring while he was under enemy attack. A suitor named Thorvald asked for her hand in marriage, and was warned that she was a high-minded, obstinate girl by her own father, Høskuld. Thorvald persisted, certain that he could bend the girl to his will, and the two men came to an agreement. Hallgerd protested bitterly against the marriage, and accused her father of not valuing her properly. But it did her no good; Høskuld declared that he could not let her pride interfere with his business, and that it was his decision that counted. And so she was married.

Once a contract was confirmed by handshake between the parties concerned (usually the fathers), the ceremonious betrothal took place, and not more than a year later, the wedding: a festivity to which all relations, unto the third degree, were invited. The bride's father, as host, was obliged to spare no expense, for the honor of his clan; the feasting lasted several days, presided over by the enthroned bridal pair.

"*Obedient Always to His Father's Word*"

Once married, the couple was expected to produce offspring in quantity. Children were put to work early, helping to make the family more prosperous; their presence ensured the future of the clan. Judging by the explosive growth of the Viking population, the absence of romantic love did not seem to interfere with fertility. Birth control, if any, took place after the infant was born, if for some reason the father chose to find the newborn baby unacceptable when they brought it to him for inspection. If it was misshapen or weak or seemed unfit for life in the harsh northern climate and on the high seas, the father could order it exposed to the elements. Parents were permitted to kill their newborn offspring in times of acute famine or other emergency. Chances are that girls were sacrificed more often than boys. Hints here and there in the literature suggest that girls were deliberately kept in short supply; they could then be married off to better advantage. Old maids or maiden aunts do not occur in the Icelandic sagas.

The custom of exposing unwanted newborn infants seems to have continued quietly till long after the North was nominally Christian, but usually as a last resort.

Once the father accepted the infant, however, he lost the right to expose it. Acceptance was a formal, legal procedure consisting of three ceremonial acts: the father had to pick up the babe off the floor and put it on his knee; sprinkle it with water; and give it a name. Naming the child was most important. Usually the chosen name was that of a friend or relative who enjoyed conspicuous success, and the father bestowed it by reciting a traditional formula expressing the wish that the same good fortune enjoyed by the name's present holder go with the name to the child. It was believed that a person's name was imbued with his qualities, which were thus transferable. Once the newborn had a name it was as if reborn—by virtue of the new life accruing to it, it brought new life to the clan, the only "immortal organism."

Relations between parents and children were as devoid of emotional display as those between marriageable men and women. Even mothers were careful not to wear their hearts on their sleeves; it was considered improper to express affection even in the intimate family circle. At most, a father was permitted to take visible pride in his growing sons. A son had to regard his father as a paragon of virtue, an authority beyond criticism. Among the family tragedies found in the sagas, such as mothers sacrificing their children to the laws of vengeance, or brothers, cousins, or brothers-in-law taking up swords against each other, there are none involving father-son conflicts. Father and son had to pull together for the survival of the family, the clan, the natural order of things.

One of the few literary texts in which family feeling is expressed, Egil's lament for his drowned son, defines the ideal father-son relationship—typically, from the father's point of view:

> Well do I know my son was a man of the best,
> Always obeyed his father, no matter what others might say;
> Helped in my house, and strongly supported my cause.

There was no formal schooling outside the home, nor inside it for that matter, unless one were to count the oral family tradition, maintained chiefly by story-telling. Strength, toughness, skills in the arts of war were fostered above all; self-confidence, fearlessness, a fanatic regard for family honor were the highest virtues. At twelve a boy was practically considered an adult. At fourteen he could keep a slave girl, attend the Thing, take part in the clan's interminable feuds to prove his manhood. By the age of fifteen at the latest he was off on his first long voyage.

The Viking Woman

A girl was raised to be married, and marriage was the institution for the good and the advancement of the family which saw to it that she had the right husband, from the family point of view. She neither chose her own husband, nor could she choose a lover; if discovered with one, she could expect to be killed with full approval from the community. There are no romantic heroines in Viking literature. Female hatred, ambition, arrogance, and vengefulness, on the other hand, are well represented. But on the whole women play a minor, background role in the literature; even Valkyries and Viking Amazons are seldom in evidence there. A rare exception is the "Red Maiden," a mixture of Valkyrie and guerrilla leader who, with her band, ruled northeastern Ireland for a time.

Woman as a character in Viking literature is most likely to be the loyal, hard-working, dependable housewife, a man's helpmeet, his "companion in stress and strife," as Tacitus has it. She keeps a cool head, keeps the peace, smooths over disagreements that could lead to serious fights, attends to everybody's needs while the men drink, gamble, and fight, and is not as dedicated to blood vengeance as her rowdy spouse brooding drunkenly on his honor. Most of the work was on her shoulders; she had to be capable, especially when left to run things during the man's absence at sea or at war. It was a hard and often lonely, dangerous life, much of it spent waiting, full of uncertainty; a life that made the women stern, silent, unapproachable, undemonstrative, controlled. The sagas pay much tribute to these women's strength of character, their poise, their steadfastness and equanimity in the face of disaster.

The Death of Aud

The *Saga of Icelanders* presents this ideal Viking woman in the person of Aud, the wife of a Norwegian general in Ireland, who reigned like a queen on the Orkneys and Faroe Islands after her husband's death in northern Scotland. In her old age she took possession of some land in Iceland and gave it to trusted men of her clan. "At this time Aud was already so afflicted with old age that she never rose before noon and went to bed early . . . but answered in anger when asked how she felt."

But when her youngest grandson was married, Aud insisted on receiving the guests and greeting them "with joy and dignity" on his wedding day. At the wedding banquet she rose and said, "I bequeath this farm with all its household goods to my grandson Olaf as his property." Then she took her leave of the guests, encouraging them to stay and do justice to their beer, while she retired to her chamber. As she left the banquet hall with stately steps, her head held high, "the men remarked to one another how handsome a woman she still was."

The next morning, when Olaf went to his grandmother's bedchamber, he found her sitting upright against her pillows, dead. "Then the men marveled at Aud, a queen to the last. And so it was that Olaf's wedding and Aud's burial feast were celebrated at the same time."

Aud clearly represents a model for the conduct of all Viking women, with her noble bearing, her readiness to take charge and, as the oldest in the clan, to set standards of propriety, dignity, and capability. Aud also followed her husband to Ireland, acted as the head of a newly settled family in Scotland and the Atlantic islands, built a farmstead in Iceland; she did a man's job, like other women who took part in colonization, and received the same consideration as men in the distribution of land. Women had equal rights of inheritance if there was no male heir, and could bequeath their property to a daughter. Widows were sought after as wives, especially if they were independent property owners.

Pirates, Warriors, and Henpecked Husbands

The Viking woman, then, was not without resources, though her social position was stronger than her legal one. She was often independent, honored, even autocratic in the domestic sphere, even though the men dominated public life. At home, the boldest seafarer and fighting cock was quite likely to be ruled by the woman of the house. It was after all the women's dependable control of the home front that made it possible for the Scandinavians to go off on their piratical expeditions.

"Viking culture, our only truly domestic culture," says the Dane Henrik Hoffmeyer, "had many matriarchal traits." This view is supported by archaeological findings. The placement and furnishings of tombs testify to the equality of men and women—indeed, the most sumptuous tomb to be uncovered was a woman's: the Oseberg ship burial, which probably contained the remains of the Norwegian Queen Asa. Many of the rune stones mention women in authority, often widows who had set up memorials for their husbands, but also wives and mothers memorialized by grieving men. Mortality was naturally higher among the men, so that women tended to reign longer and retain their authority in the house and with the family even in old age, when the rare man who achieved it had long since retired. A Viking who was no longer young, strong, and powerful, no longer able to go on a long overseas expedition and hope to survive it, was relegated to limbo, yielding place to a younger man. Meanwhile mothers, grown gray in honor, could fulfill their social and domestic functions to the end of their lives, like Aud. An old man led a pitiable life, largely ignored unless he made a nuisance of himself, and lucky to be tolerated at all, except perhaps at the Thing where his experience of life and knowledge of precedent may have secured him a certain standing. That the early crude warriors' ways in time gave way to a moral order may have been partially the result of female dominance in the home and family, which in all its ramifications performed a part of the social function which later became a function of the state.

Runestone from the Swedish Uppland area.

Blood Brothers

"Man's Greatest Joy Is Man"

A Viking was subjected not only to the family's social demands and code of honor. There were also the specifically Teutonic traditions cited by Tacitus; loyalty, duty, and affection owed to friends, blood-brothers, followers. Such bondings had their vital place somewhere between the private and the public sphere. They formed naturally and early among men who spent months together on voyages, in distant lands, in warfare, and in trade relations over the years. Perhaps the loneliness of life in the high North lent them a depth and intensity unmatched elsewhere.

Friendship was a theme that raised even the frosty temperature of Icelandic literature by several degrees:

> If you have a friend,
> Faithful and firm,
> Go often to see him;
> Thorns overgrow
> And weeds will smother
> The path untrodden too long.

A similar note is struck by another poet from Thule:

> Once I was young,
> Went on my lonely way,
> And nearly went astray;
> What happiness it was
> When my companion came:
> Man's greatest joy is man.

The exchange of gifts was recommended for tying the knots of friendship in this down-to-earth peasant world.

Even deeper and stronger a bond than friendship was the institution of blood brotherhood. By means of a ceremonial mingling of their blood—whether by dipping their hands in animal blood, drinking blood drawn from their own veins, or mixing their blood to sprinkle it on the ground as a fertility rite—two or more men could become blood relatives by choice, as it were; blood brothers had to support each other like members of a clan. The younger obeyed the older in this fraternal association.

Then there were the bands of men attached to a chieftain or prince as retinue, bodyguards, or fighting troops, and who were bound to their lord and each other by oaths of fealty. Though they were often described as a mixed rabble of rowdy fighting cocks, they lived subject to strict discipline, as described in the *Jomsvikinga Saga*, the story of the founding of the fortress Jomsburg, or Jumne, by the Danes. The chieftain had sole responsibility, right of command, and jurisdiction. To keep his men well-disposed, he provided gaming, banquets, and frequent distribution of presents and honors. Their part of the bargain was to fight to the death for him. Tacitus reported that "In battle the men and their chief vie in valor and it is a lifelong disgrace to have given ground after the leader has been killed." They fought for booty and reward, for honor and for glory. As a co-operative they were especially attractive to the clanless man, the voyager, the warrior. Eventually such bands of military adventurers became economically effective as well. The first Viking trading companies in Iceland can be traced back to the year 900; these in turn were the forerunners of the medieval guilds; all had their source in the primitive Nordic cult of friendship, fraternity, followership.

An Arena For Fighting Cocks

Vikings had no ties or duties other than these familial or private, quasi-familial ones. Words like nation, fatherland, civic responsibility, patriotism, were not in their vocabulary. The Thing, the regular gathering of armed freemen in council, began as a court for settling feuds between clans and quarrels between neighbors, not as a parliament in our sense of the word. The word itself, Thing, means a court of judgment, in fact. If the sagas make it appear as an arena for fighting cocks and quarrel-seekers, they may not be doing it full justice, but they are not entirely misrepresenting it.

Viking law, unfortunately, remains conjectural; the texts in existence all date from late medieval times. Iceland, according to Adam of Bremen "had no king but was subject to general law"—common law based on oral tradition, presumably. Since the Icelandic Thing, founded c. 930, was modeled on the Norwegian, it may be regarded as representative of the way Viking justice was administered. The island was divided into twelve, later thirteen, administrative districts, each of which had a meeting of its Thing twice a year; the general council or Althing met once a year, presided over by a Speaker of the Law elected for a three-year term. At the opening of each meeting of the Althing this flesh-and-blood *corpus juris* reminded all present of the traditional legal formulas by reciting them in full, though he was assisted from time to time by two other Speakers. This law code was not committed to writing until 1118.

The proceedings at the Thing rested on the basic assumption that might makes right, and were closer to staged battle scenes or comedy than our conception of court procedure. The two contending parties faced each other like troops about to engage in battle, each side having collected supporters not on the basis of their being acquainted with the facts, but of knowing the litigant to be a man of honor. Each side openly sought the support of the rich and influential. "The accuser does not present a case to an impartial judge, he hurls accusations at the defendant, who responds by demonstrating the absurdity of the charge, and so on. The objective is not to bring out the truth, but to represent the facts to the opponent's disadvantage. The men supporting each disputant are already committed to a verdict in his favor, and will not be influenced by the judge on cross-examination. All the judge does is to . . . pronounce judgment," according to Felix Niedner's account in the introductory volume to his Thule edition.

Justice was done, for the most part, on the principle that wrongs could be righted with money. Even a free man's life could be atoned for with a payment in gold or silver, sheep, cows, horses, even with Frisian cloth. Physical injury was paid for at varying rates. A hacked-off nose, for example, rated compensation equal to that for a man's life; so did hands, feet, and the male genital organ. But an eye rated only half that, an ear only a fourth. There was a long list of carefully graded penalties, so that the Viking penchant for hair-splitting was given free rein in legal proceedings. A superficial wound rated less than a flesh wound, a healed wound less than an unhealed one; visible mutilations, especially face wounds, were worth more than body wounds or inconspicuous ones. Insults, too, were precisely classified. To ask a free Viking male when he had last given birth or to call him a whore or a pervert was a crime subject to heavy penalties—if the injured man had not already taken the more manly and honorable course of taking blood vengeance in person.

The greatest punishment in Nordic law was exclusion from society: the convicted was pronounced an outlaw, an enemy of the people, whom no one could shelter, whom anyone could pursue or kill. His property was forfeit and distributed, his wife and children renounced him, his clan blotted out his existence. The outlaw became a fugitive from men, hiding in the forests or the stony wastelands, like a wolf. He was given time to get out of sight, however, and could go out of the country. If he killed another outlaw or brought early warning of an impending enemy attack he could even be rehabilitated. In Norway his family could restore him to society by paying additional reparations. In Iceland, the period of exile could be limited, as in the case of Eric the Red, who used his three years of banishment to discover Greenland.

In ambiguous cases, the court might hand over the decision to an anonymous body of men who would try the accused by ordeal, such as making him carry red-hot irons, or meet his adversary in single combat. Such a duel usually took place on a promontory or a lake island, a so-called *holm*, hence it was called a *holmgang*, a word imbued with much heroic glamour by bards and balladeers of the North. The place was carefully chosen and then marked by sacred hazel switches. The gods were asked to make a decision where the court had failed. That the victory usually went to the stronger man only confirmed the accepted ethics.

Whatever the judgment, and however arrived at, the execution of the sentence was left to the accuser; the council had no executive powers, no police, no hangman. The Vikings entered history with only the most rudimentary concept of a state or a public interest; what there was existed by the will and for the interests of those in power, whose well-being was the well-being of society as then understood. "What's good for General Motors is good for the country" is clearly a Viking principle reborn.

"Understand That You Are My Man"

According to a ninth-century story, King Eric of Sweden once said to a settler on Värmland, "Understand that you are my man." Ak, the settler, replied: "I need no reminder, for I also understand that you are my man." Ak's Viking spirit cost him his life, for the King proved his point by killing him on the spot.

The story depicts both the beginning and end of internal developments within the Norse countries. On one side were self-assured, independent freeholders who insisted on their rights; on the other side an arrogant clique of empire-seeking leaders who had no second thoughts about stepping on these men's rights. On the one side the yeomanry, determined to make even the king do their will, and not afraid to sacrifice him whenever a ruined harvest or unsuccessful voyage demonstrated he had lost the favor of the gods; on the other side trained and ruthless chieftains and princes, who were convinced of their own might and made brutal use of it. A dramatic conflict—the free peasants who championed the principles of democratic equality against an avowedly aristocratic class who deliberately disregarded the equality principle . . . and ended up on top.

The existence of a ruling class never fit in well with the ideal propagated by the romanticizers of the Teutonic image, the nineteenth-century historians. They painted a picture of peoples living in a sort of primevally democratic state, represented by the mass of common free men who incarnated both biologically and politically the life force of the Germanic Folk. This idealized image accorded no special meaning to the aristocracy, who were regarded as leaders elected for a certain term of time, after which they would step back voluntarily.

But historians with cooler heads started emerging after the First World War who began to correct this picture. Perhaps most influential was the historian Fritz Kern, who flatly called the Teutonic kings and princes "robber chieftains with aristocratic pretensions" and "political entrepreneurs" who outgrew and dominated their less ambitious brothers back home, from small freeholders to rich landowners of good family.

Early Teutonic society was not a static, self-contained, purely peasant culture. It included a dynamic, warrior ruling class. This ruling class retained its rustic character. Even kings remained large farmers, moving their retinues from farm to farm to maintain them in the style to which they felt entitled.

It was just such haughtily led hordes of brigands that conquered Europe— usually after long practice on their own countrymen.

Iceland—Democracy or Oligarchy?

There was no aristocracy in Denmark, Norway, or Sweden at the beginning of the Viking era. There were only some clans among the freeholders who enjoyed esteem and fame for riches acquired by luck and enterprise, without as yet forming a sharply delineated ruling class. The others could either make their way upward or fall behind, depending on circumstances, abilities, and luck. The members of the upper crust had no special rights; it was merely harder, riskier, and costlier to kill them. Once such a family had reached a certain eminence it began to concern itself with its family tree and foster a legend of its "reaching back to the gods," like the Danish Skjöldungs or the Swedish Ynglings from whom the Norwegian Vestfold kings were descended.

Members of these "great families" of the North, possibly descended from the prehistoric Battle-axe People, were buried in luxuriously furnished tombs, traces of which are an indelible part of the Scandinavian landscape. They established warlike principalities in northern and eastern Norway before the beginning of the Viking raids on Europe, equipped their ships for long trading voyages as men-of-war, and accumulated immense riches, using chiefly slave labor. They engraved their names and deeds on runestones of granite and, according to the *Rigsthula*, feasted on white bread, chicken-broth, and roast veal. They called the Council, appointed the Speakers, through them proclaimed the law or their version of it, and controlled religious institutions as their own private property.

The great families also ruled "democratic" Iceland, which proudly calls itself the oldest republic in the world; there they developed an exemplary symbiosis of wealth, state, and religion.

The smallest unit of this nearly perfect power complex of land magnates-lawgivers-priests was the so-called *godorp*, a "society of men headed by a *godi*, a chieftain-priest, owner of a temple." Theoretically, any free Icelander was eligible for the position, but in practice these temple owners were limited to thirty-nine, the number of districts having been set up in 965. Since the position was hereditary and could be passed on or sold only when the clan died out, it was in fact permanently held by the thirty-nine oldest and best-established Icelandic families.

This clique of ruling families held all power in Iceland. Their *godar* were in charge of the districts and their Things, which they called into session; they made the laws and appointed the Speaker who, during his three-year term, was chief executive and magistrate of the island. During the assemblies the leading families sat on raised wooden or stone benches while the other free and independent Icelanders followed the proceedings standing up. The *godar* pronounced judgment in court. Anyone who killed a *godi* had to pay three times the fine exacted for killing an ordinary man. The power of these Icelandic families was well secured, and their self-glorification was boundless. Iceland was, in fact, an Aristotelian oligarchy, not a free, democratic society or state.

Chieftains and Kings

The same pattern prevailed in the Scandinavian countries of their origin. In Norway, too, the temple priests convoked assemblies, appointed the lawmakers, controlled the councils, and the heads of the ruling clans "sat" in council, while the "people" kept a respectful distance, standing, and learned to acclaim the decisions of their betters. Nevertheless perfect harmony seldom prevailed, because the leading families each had their supporters in the audience, so that vociferous disagreements could arise—whenever, that is, the leaders failed to agree among themselves.

On the other hand, if the leaders were in agreement, they could make life a burden for the king by backing up their demands with the joined forces of their private armies. Only a strong and determined personality could hold his own under such pressure from below, applied by chieftains who ruled their own territories like absolute princes. A king had to learn early to keep an eye on his chieftains, "their meetings with each other, their attempts to court popularity, their alliances through marriage, their victories in battle. . . . Even his own sons were not above suspicion." King Harald Bluetooth, for example, was seriously wounded and "had to flee to Wollin after the battle with his victorious son Sven Forkbeard."

However, as a rule, most young heirs waited patiently enough for their turn at the wheel, while making sure to deal in time with any brother ambitious enough to have an eye on the throne for himself. Younger sons often emigrated to set up their own colonial kingdoms. South Jutland, for example, was ruled by Swedish kinglets who tried to consolidate their positions by marrying the right local girls, like King Knuba, the middle one of three such regents, who married the daughter of the Danish chieftain Odinkar.

A king's private army was another source of concern. The men's death-defying devotion was not self-sustaining but had to be stoked repeatedly with generous gifts, good food, and a copious flow of good mead; otherwise even the most loyal of vassals could become dangerously mutinous. The cost of maintaining them in style, together with their restlessness when unemployed, combined to exert constant pressure on the king to lead them out on dangerous adventures. But they were, of course, indispensable to the king's hold on his royal power and his ability to pass it on to his sons. During the two-and-a-half centuries of the Viking expansion, monarchic power clearly encroached upon and grew at the expense of democratic institutions. Hereditary kingship as a family perquisite meant the establishment of a ruling class holding the reins of power more tightly with each generation. By late Viking times the former vagabond armies on the move had become standing armies, lodged in permanent barracks, whose presence asserted the ruler's power to make his will prevail.

While a Nordic freeholder was still king on his own land, his civic rights kept melting away before the steadily growing power of the kings. By the ninth century the fate of the Swedish freeholder Ak signalizes the end of *de facto* democratic equality; the king had learned to think of himself as the equal of gods, not men.

Satanic Realists

This trend toward monarchic statehood is borne out by the growth of administration in the Scandinavian countries and their Atlantic satellites.

A typical Viking settlement would be a collective of about twelve villages headed by the *hersir*, who was elected and could be dismissed at any time by the Thing, to which he was accountable. In Uppland near Lake Mälar in east central Sweden, for example, there were three districts, one consisting of ten, one of eight, and another of four such collectives. Thus a district might consist of 50 to 120 villages, depending on the number of collectives in the district. These districts were ruled by jarls, a title originally meaning simply a man of respected position, which in time took on the meaning of administrator, as the word hersir did, too. In early Viking times a jarl had come to mean a chieftain of those innumerable petty kingdoms which at this time covered the Scandinavian peninsula like a patchwork quilt. This layer of regional chieftains supplied most of the Viking generals who led their pirate flotillas to raid the Atlantic islands and European coastlines during the ninth century. At the same time they were carrying on their share of private feuds on the side, which petty clan warfare led to further concentrations of power. As a result, the three Scandinavian kingdoms eventually emerged from the original crazy-quilt of petty principalities on the two peninsulas. Norway was the first to be unified, c. 872, by Harald Fairhair; Denmark followed in 950, under Gorm the Old; and the unification of Sweden is credited to the Ynglings in the course of the tenth century.

The consolidation of the three kingdoms radically changed the traditional administrative structure; gradually the people's elected representatives were replaced by royal officials, the heads of the village collectives by royal bailiffs, the jarls and petty kings induced to surrender their independence by the lure of important positions at court—and centralized, authoritarian government had come to stay, even though the struggle for traditional individual rights went on far into the fourteenth century in outlying mountain districts of Norway and Sweden.

The speed with which the three Scandinavian kingdoms and their satellites became well-run states is a tribute to the political abilities of the Scandinavian peoples, their self-discipline, their ability to plan, organize, get things done. Iceland, once a mere colony of malcontent emigrés, was a strong, well-administered state by the year 1000. Within two centuries northern Europe evolved from an anarchic wilderness into a community largely run by magisterial courts of justice. Today's historians count Normandy as the most strictly administered European state of the times, where "crudity, cunning, disloyalty . . . evolved into a gift for creative politics." England owes to the Norman Conquest—to the descendants of Viking pirates, that is—innovations in statecraft that remained effective for centuries, some of them to this day. Even Normandy's Mediterranean satellites rank as the first modern states which, according to the historian Hans Freyer, "boldly bypassed medievalism, as their Viking ancestors had the constriction of Carolingian . . . Europe."

It was in the Mediterranean Norman dukedoms of Apulia and Sicily that "the modern European state was born or at least anticipated, with its rational, ruthless pursuit of power and wealth, its worldliness and tolerance, resting its claims on its own strength alone.'' Modern history credits the Vikings not only with explosive energies, physical strength, toughness, and phenomenal recklessness vis-à-vis the unknown and death, but also their immense flair for politics, diplomacy, management and, above all, their remarkable sense of and adaptibility to the realities wherever they found them.

Part Four
Viking Life

Throne of Hardwood: Peasant Kings at Home

*The restored Gokstad ship, frontal view.
A functional ship whose elegant lines
embody the excellence of the Viking
shipbuilders.*

Idyll vs. Reality: the Everyday Life

The image of the Viking freeholder has been gilded and romanticized by Scandinavian and German historians: blue-eyed, proud, and high-minded he strides across his fields. He tends his ancestral lands and rules his family like a king, though he works hard to make the meager northern soil yield a crop; he is a chaste husband, benevolent father and master, upholder of his rights at the Thing, always ready to fight. These historians reacted against the established fright-inspiring portrait of the Vikings as pirates, savages and terrorists; but they erred in the opposite direction by suppressing the unpleasant aspects hitherto over-emphasized. The basic realities of Scandinavian country life then need no more whitewashing than they would today.

Freemen's Hall and Servants' Barracks

The farmsteads were scattered over the land at a respectful distance from each other. With fences like palisades and strictly marked boundaries, each freehold formed an autonomous world unto itself, self-assured, reserved, taciturn. In early Viking times large settlements were rare in Scandinavia. Apart from small, newly hatched trading centers, settlement was limited to individual family country properties, wherever nature and the climate offered a chance of survival. Jutland, with its fertile moraine soil, was the most thickly populated of Danish lands; Norwegian settlements clustered along the mild, damp, grassy slopes near the fjords; in Sweden, the fertile, accessible south was the location of choice then as now. As the population kept growing, however, it became necessary even in pre-Viking times to clear the forests and push northward along the coastlines.

Archaeologists have explored the areas where traces of Viking farmsteads were found, in Scandinavia, on the Baltic coasts, and on the North Atlantic islands. The number of objects examined is rather slight, since the ancient settlements are mostly covered today by thickly populated towns and villages and therefore inaccessible. However, relatively few digs and lucky finds have been enough to throw light on a number of technical and structural problems.

Raw materials varied according to the locality; whatever there was was used with great resourcefulness. In the wooded areas of Sweden and Russia, the wooden buildings were either log huts, made of horizontally placed round logs joined at the corners, or plank huts, made of vertical posts connected with horizontal planks, or stave huts, with vertical plank walls, according to the historian Johannes Brøndsted. In tree-poor localities the Norsemen resorted to frame-built wattle and daub structures. There were houses made of planks covered with sod on the outside; houses with mud walls and reed thatch; houses with roofs supported by free-standing posts, houses with walls made of a wooden framework with wattle daubing. The combination of wood and clay was preponderant, at least in the western part of the Viking world.

Other styles and variants were to be found, however. One jarl's house on the Shetlands consisted of parallel stone walls, the space between them filled with earth. On Iceland, too, boulder walls with earth fillings were common, with reed thatched roofs reaching down to the ground. Eric the Red's house in Brattahlid was made of stones and turf. The design of the whole farmstead was affected by the materials available; where wood was in abundant supply, there would be a large number of small buildings. With stone and clay, posts and turf, farmsteaders would have to put up fewer, larger buildings.

The Teutonic stave longhouse with its posts and thick wattle and clay walls established itself in the far north in pre-Viking times as a common shelter for both man and beast; its classical form was discovered in Germany during digs on Feddersen Wierde between Bremerhaven and Cuxhaven. By the eighth century, however, a tendency to separate housing for man, beasts, and even servants began to emerge. The original communal dwelling gradually evolved into a cluster of buildings consisting of a main house and outbuildings such as servants' quarters, workrooms, barns and stables. A classic illustration of this trend is supplied by the archaeological findings on Lindholm Høje, Jutland. Here two longhouses over eighteen yards in length, built in early times, were later replaced by a settlement consisting of a square farmstead with four wings, surrounded by a dozen subsidiary buildings, one of which showed traces of bathroom facilities. There are many other instances of similar developments on the Shetlands, on Iceland and Greenland.

Fresh Furrows—Ploughed 900 Years Ago

Crop rotation was determined by a winter sowing, spring sowing, and fallow year, in other words the traditional three-field system, introduced to the North probably as early as Carolingian times—at least on Fyn, Zealand, and Skane, praised by Adam of Bremen as the most fertile regions in Scandinavia.

The usually charred remains or clay impressions found in archaeological digs have revealed the Viking program of cultivation. Rye, with its resistance to cold and hardship, formed the staple diet; oats were prized as horse fodder; barley, fermented, made the indispensable home-brewed mead. Many place names on

The cemetery of Lindholm Høje, near Aalborg.

r 700 Viking graves are many in the shape of boats.

Iceland confirm the popularity of these varieties of grain on the Atlantic islands. On Greenland, the settlers succeeded in naturalizing barley and dune grass.

The onion was a prized product of the kitchen garden, not only for its pungency but its healing powers; peas and cress were grown where possible. Fruit was scarce. Only apples ripened in the Northlands, in good years as far as Greenland.

Fertilization of the fields with dung is mentioned in the *Edda* stories as well as in the collections of Icelandic laws. The manure sledges used for this in Norway as late as the nineteenth century were troughs, secured to the skids by willow-twigs. A variety of ploughs was in use, simple implements with traction and steering levers and a downward-cutting point or blade, probably of iron. The Bayeux tapestry shows a wheeled plow drawn by oxen, with bent shares probably made of wood mounted with iron.

Whichever kind of plough was used, the process of ploughing was performed with great ritualistic care, with a suggestion of fertility magic. Unexpected proof of this was provided by the Lindholm Høje excavation, where a freshly ploughed field of late Viking times was uncovered. A sandstorm had apparently surprised the man with the plough in the midst of his work and covered the tilled field with a layer of sand about a foot in thickness. When the sand was carefully removed layer by layer in 1955, according to Oscar Marsen, "the original humus emerged looking like an enormous washboard, each furrow as distinct as on the day it was preserved under its sudden burden of sand. The sand even preserved the traces of the two-wheeler cart in which the farmer had driven home across the fields for shelter from the sand typhoon that must have surprised him at work."

Other implements for working the soil, such as iron-mounted wooden spades, hoes, or poles, were part of every farmstead's inventory. The Oseberg grave contained wooden clubs that might have been used for smoothing over hard clods of earth. On the Bayeux tapestry, next to the ox-drawn plough, is a horse-drawn harrow. Sickles and scythes, rakes and threshing flails were used, though mostly made of wood, iron being scarce.

Cattle rearing was important, engaged in with enthusiasm by such dedicated meat-eaters as the Vikings. Adam of Bremen notes with respect that even the notables in Norway and Sweden were keen cattle breeders. Their cattle were small, rather stunted. Only their dogs and horses might have come up to current standards. Dogs were a farmer's constant companions, as guard- and sheepdogs and trained hunters. They probably had their military uses, too, for a dog, like a horse, would accompany his master into the grave; dog collars and leashes have been found as often in Viking graves as harness, spurs, stirrups and saddle trappings.

Horses were kept primarily for riding, but they also drew the plough and cart, as illustrated in the Bayeux tapestry and on the Gotland picture stones. Horses were status symbols, cows stood for wealth, and in early Viking times they were a kind of currency. A farmer's wealth was reckoned not by the size of his property but by the number of cows he owned—respectability began at about ten oxen, but the average for a medium farm was nearer to twenty. Eric the Red had four cowsheds, with room for forty cows. The Bishop of Gardar on Greenland had room for a hundred cows. Large flocks of sheep were the pride and joy of Icelandic farmers; flocks of a thousand or two thousand were unexceptional. During the summer they were driven up the mountains, as herds are still driven to high pastures in Alpine country, to graze in preparation for the upcoming winter. In the extreme north of Norway, near the vegetation line, a farmer's rank and standing was measured by the size of his reindeer herd. Ottar, King Alfred's Norse friend, had "600 tame deer, also called reindeer" in addition to twenty cows, twenty sheep, and twenty pigs.

Winter fodder was the chief problem of cattle breeding. The interminable northern winter called for immense stores of feed—roughly 5,500 lbs., or 2 3/4 tons, of hay for one cow per winter, those two hundred dark days of the northern year. For a herd of twenty oxen, that meant fifty-five tons of hay to be stored, in an estimated 3,000 man-hours, given the equipment available. This means that on a medium-sized farm, it would have taken ten men ten hours a day for a month to mow, dry, and bring in the winter fodder for the cattle alone, without allowance for horses and sheep.

In Iceland this was done between June and September, depending on the farm's location. The meadows were often damp and stony, many slopes grew more thistles than grass, and if there was no sun the hay went rotten before it could dry. Supplies lasted only in good years. Usually the hay had to be supplemented with dried leaves, fish, and ground fish bones. Even so, emergency slaughterings were the rule in winter, and the surviving cattle were often so weak by early summer that they had to be carried out to pasture. It was a hard life, especially in the polar regions.

Viking Whalers

The constant gnawing of hunger forced Viking farmers into hunting, bird-trapping, and fishing. Hunting equipment found in seventh- and eighth-century graves suggest that the mountains of eastern Norway provided good game. Small game was usually trapped; deer, bears, and wild boar were hunted with bow and arrow.

Fishermen used oyster baskets, lines, and nets; they caught salmon and trout in the inland waters, cod and herring in the sea. Larger fish, as illustrated by a Gotland picture stone, were harpooned or speared; seals and walrus were harpooned or killed with heavy wooden cudgels. Walrus meat was eaten, walrus skins used in the manufacture of ship's ropes. Whales were hunted most probably as they still are on the Faroe Islands: first they were driven onto the beach, then slaughtered there.

Birds were trapped mainly on the Atlantic islands and in the polar regions of Scandinavia, where there are still widespread and thickly populated bird colonies. The men of the Faroes still climb, from the land side, the cliffs that tower up over the sea. Then a man suspended on ropes can catch the birds, nesting on the narrow ledges, with a longhandled net. Feathers and down are collected by hand.

The saga of the Icelandic farmer Skallagrim, who settled on Borgarfjord, testifies to all these everyday activities in the north European farmer's life: "He ordered his men to go out in rowboats to fish, to hunt seals and collect eggs. . . . He always had a number of men around him with whom he searched eagerly for whatever necessities of life might be found in the area. . . . There was everything in plenty, including driftwood that could be taken home. At this time whales were often beached and everyone was free to harpoon them. Hunting was easy, for the game had not yet been made shy, not having seen men there before."

The Self-Sufficient Homestead

The country squire Skallagrim was also a model of Viking self-sufficiency on the land, being adept at many skills and crafts. At his burial his sons put his blacksmith's tools in his grave with his horse and weapons. Every such household-er had to wield hammer and axe as expertly as he did his farming tools and his weapons. Every large farm had its own forge. The Weland saga and the Gotland picture stones bear witness to the ancient tradition of Norse wrought iron work. Digs, particularly in Norway, have brought to light many kinds of hammers, tongs with straight or bent nozzles, files, chisels, many small anvils of iron, which were in wide general use in addition to large stone anvils. Iron bars, hidden away as they were gold, for iron was precious and rare, dug up in modern times and analyzed, reveal that iron was mined chiefly from bog iron ore, at least in Denmark. Here is Ole Klindt-Jensen's expert description of the smelting process:

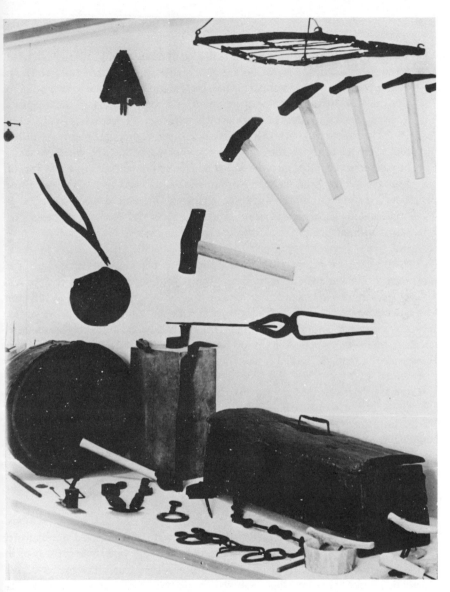

Equipment of a Swedish craftsman of the Viking era who lost his box of tools in a bog on Gotland.

The blacksmiths were highly skilled at building strong, chimney-like furnaces on a wooden framework dressed with clay. In it they fired a mixture of charcoal and bog iron ore at the precise temperature needed to make the iron ore absorb exactly the right amount of charcoal, so that it crystallized as a spongy mass that could be worked by hammer.

The following work was done in the forge: There were hammers and tongs, anvil and water troughs, the forge with two bellows by which air was blown on the charcoal through a clay nozzle, to fan up the fire. As protection from the intense heat, the man working the bellows and his tools stood behind a curved stone shield with a hole for the nozzle. The shield was often ornamented. The apparent simplicity of the tools and weapons conceals much brilliant technical skill that was unique in its day.

While each farmer was likely to be his own blacksmith, there were also professional blacksmiths, at least in the larger settlements, trading centers and towns, working as independent craftsmen for the open market, or as itinerant free-lancers boarding with their employer for the duration of the job. As a rule, they did the more complicated work, such as door locks, iron kettles, swords, harness, armor. One such itinerant left his box of tools at the bottom of a lake near Mästermyr on Gotland. When it was dug up a thousand years later, 150 different tools came to light: axes and saws, tongs and files, chisels and augers, an assortment any master to this day might be proud of.

Digs have also unearthed a great variety of carpentry and joinery tools near Viking farmsteads. Bertil Almgren lists the most important: T-shaped broadaxes, scraping irons used for planing wood, coarse files suitable for working horn as well as wood, metal saws like our padsaws, knives of all sizes, precision augers.

With such equipment, a man could clearly build his own house.

A Man's Home Was His Hall

Viking architecture has not made history. Houses were of the utmost simplicity in construction, and offered the minimum of comfort. They were basic shelters from the extreme rigors of the climate, no more. The Viking architectural flair and love of ornamentation went into their beloved ships, it seems. The Norse longhouse with its straw or shingle roof sheltering man and beast together disappeared from the scene during the Viking era, when oxen, sheep, and pigs were relegated to outbuildings, though their warmth was probably missed in the main house. Yet the majority continued to be content with an undivided, hall-like interior. Only kings and chieftains indulged themselves in partitioning off space for kitchen and bedrooms. In some cases the bedrooms were relegated to a separate structure, a sleep house.

The hall-like "longroom" was divided into three parts by two rows of pillars. The two side aisles were slightly raised, and served as places to sit or recline in, with wall benches supplied in the better houses. In the center of the south aisle, "opposite the wind-eye in the roof through which the sun shone" the owner sat on the famous "high seat," holding court like a king even if he was not a rich man. The throne of each freeman was supported by wooden posts decorated, if he had the means, with magic signs and figures.

If a family emigrated, these carved props went with them. Tradition has it that upon reaching the new shore, these seat posts were thrown overboard, and the ship then landed wherever they drifted on land "by the will of the gods." The Icelandic *Landnamabok* relates that the first Norwegian immigrant, Ingolf Arnason, had to search along the coast a long time for his seat posts, to find them at last on a spot on the southwest of the island, favored by nature with hot, steaming springs. Ingolf Arnason called it Reykjavik, or Smoky Bay, and the name stuck to what has since become the capital of the Republic of Iceland.

Facing the master's ceremonial seat was a smaller raised seat for close friends and valued guests. Between these two rustic thrones, in the center of the main hall, a fire was laid on an oblong hearth made of stone or clay. This fire was the spiritual hub of Norse family life. It was also the main or only source of illumination in the house, since windows made of pigs' bladders or the shiny parchment skin of unborn calves did not come into use until the Middle Ages, and the primitive oil and whale-blubber lamps gave little light. Though the scene has atmosphere, there were many real hardships involved. In many areas, as on the Atlantic islands, wood was scarce, while turf and dried cow dung emitted billowing clouds of biting smoke that must have been hard on eyes, bronchia, and mucous membranes.

Such houses of wood and wattle construction can still be found on the Orkneys, the Shetlands, and the Hebrides, linear descendants of the ancient Viking homes, so it is not hard to visualize those interiors. "The sooty thatched roof covers a room in semi-darkness, smoke rises fro the open hearth in the middle of the floor and makes your eyes smart . . . it forms a thin haze in the room and billows out when the door is opened. But the room is warm and cozy and keeps the wind out."

Queen Asa's Kitchen

There was not much in the way of furnishings, other than benches, which served
not only as seats, but as couches and beds, in the typical Viking countryman's
home. The upper-class domicile was another matter, as the opulent ship burials
have revealed.

The queen found in the Oseberg ship slept under an eiderdown, on a warm,
soft mattress, in a bed 52" x 72", with posts ending in carved gargoyle heads,
fierce guardians of her slumber. The rich man of the Mammen grave was buried in
similar comfort, in a well-made bed with luxurious bedding.

Tables tended to be long, low, and narrow. The table from the Horning grave
in East Jutland, for instance, resembling "a long chest on four legs" is only about
a foot high. The chair from the Oseberg grave, a wooden cube with a backrest and
rush seat, is about four inches higher. But the Bayeux tapestry shows chairs with a
backrest of wooden rods, and handsomely carved animal heads. The Buttle picture
stone on Gotland shows blocklike seats. There are, in short, indications of
considerable variety in this area as well. Other kinds of furnishings found in graves
include many chests and coffers, well proportioned, mounted with silver and
decorated with wood carvings, some with the most ingenious locks, suggesting
that they might have been used to hold valuables. Beautifully made jewelry cases
have been found in the women's graves; the most magnificent of them, now part of
the Bamberg treasure in Germany, belonged to the Empress Kunigunde, spouse of
Henry the Saint and a daughter of King Canute of Denmark.

Women's work, especially making clothes and cookery, is well represented
by the requisite tools among grave goods. Implements for beating and hackling
flax, yarn reels and warp weights of clay or soapstone, shears and long-toothed
combs for the wool weavers, wooden boards for ribbon weaving, and looms and
other implements needed for rug making, were all found in profusion. Spinning
and weaving were highly developed even on the smallest freeholds. Queen Asa's
ladies-in-waiting did complicated tapestry work.

Kitchen utensils included wooden troughs and pails, tubs and vats, often
reinforced with iron hoops, spoons and ladles. From the forge came iron axes and
knives, grilling forks and roasting spits, kettles and pans. Most pans, however,
were made of soapstone chiefly quarried in Norway. Soapstone was durable and
easy to work, which is possibly why it eventually edged out the art of pottery in the
extreme North during the Viking age.

Judging by the Oseberg grave goods, a Viking prince's kitchen and household was hardly smaller than that of a medieval castle in Germany and France.

Among a whole battery of kitchen utensils at Oseberg were three iron kettles and an iron tripod, four troughs, ten vats and a barrel, even a millstone, so that the Queen could grind her own grain in all eternity.

What They Ate

What do we know of the gastronomical habits, the culinary arts of the European North? They tended to be self-sufficient, from field to mouth; cereal and meat, milk and eggs were home produced. Corn was ground laboriously in handmills, and was likely to contain a sediment of stone dust and pebbles that in the course of time would be hard on the teeth and the stomach. Barley or oatmeal porridge was a regular part of breakfast, though dismissed as servant fodder in the sagas. Of the many varieties and qualities of bread, the coarse, hard barley bread predominated, judging by the over sixty pieces of bread that have come down to us from the Viking age, almost all containing stone dust. Many were supplemented with ground field peas, some with ground pine bark—bitter and indigestible, but its high vitamin C content was probably valued for medicinal reasons.

Bread was baked on long-handled iron trays on which were made crusty flat loaves, a kind of rusk that lasted well on long voyages. They also had round clay ovens "and a beehive-shaped framework of wattle," which heated quickly, but were fragile and had to be frequently replaced.

Second to bread, the Vikings consumed vast quantities of meat. Meat and mead were twin joys of life, indispensable ingredients for any sort of occasion, social or ritualistic. Ibn Fadlan called them pork eaters, with a Moslem's distaste presumably, and considered them virtually addicted to meat eating. The oft-cited Bayeux tapestry shows a whole series of illustrations of an opulent banquet, opened with trumpet blasts, the main course a truly mountainous array of meats and fowls. The fallen heroes of Valhalla enjoyed the flesh of castrated boars, not only as a delicacy but, according to the folklore, one that inspired courage and high spirits in those who dined on it.

While the permanent residents of Valhalla ate boiled meats, the Normans on the Bayeux tapestry are clearly feasting on well-browned meat roasted on an open fire. But boiling and stewing were probably more common than roasting. The average Norseman's daily diet was most likely a one-pot dinner of soup with cooked meat, or a stew, prepared in semicircular vats of four- to six-quart capacity, suspended by chains over an open fire. For open air cookery there was a collapsible tripod on which to set the vat, with sturdy legs, frequently ending in birdlike claws.

Another method, described by Ole Klindt-Jensen, who cites the Icelandic sagas as well as archaeological evidence in support, is that of the roasting pit. Such a pit, about 28" deep, was found in the house of Sogn in Ardal, Norway; its bottom was full of cracked stones. Putting pieces of meat, fish, or poultry wrapped in leaves or clay to roast between hot stones preserves the juices and vitamins. "To judge by the number of these pits, they were very popular."

Viking housewives knew how to preserve foods for a period of time, to see families through those long winters, or equip husbands with provisions for their long voyages. They knew how to dry, smoke, and salt meat and fish, as well as *skyr*, a curdled milk which, salted and soured and stored in large vats, would last through the winter. Sour milk was also a popular staple.

The scarcity of vegetables and fruits has been mentioned. They had onions, leeks, and field peas; apples, and honey—the only sweetener and a luxury, since it was also needed to make mead, that barley wine spiced with aromatic herbs celebrated in the sagas.

At table, they used knives—a man always had his knife with him in any case—and flat spoons made of horn or wood, and of course their fingers. Wooden plates and trenchers completed the table setting. Tablecloths were in use, according to the *Edda*:

> Then mother took a patterned cloth
> of bright linen,
> laid it on the table.

Despite the scarcity of greens and fruit, the diet seems to have contained all the necessary vitamins. Vitamin A was obtained from the fish, whale and seal meat, sea birds, milk and butter, and animals slaughtered in the fall. The B vitamins could be found in the coarse flour, in liver, eggs, fibrous meat, and dairy products. Vitamin C was a problem, but onions and berries, apples, and the aforementioned pine bark apparently supplied enough to prevent scurvy, except perhaps on long sea voyages. Fish livers and several of the foods mentioned above are rich in vitamin D.

All in all, it was a varied, vigorous, protein-rich diet that fueled these extraordinarily dynamic men of the North.

Sea Kings
in Dragon Ships

Viking Ships

Ever since Adam of Bremen's first ecstatic reports of Viking ships struggling against maelstroms on the abyssal deeps of the oceans, the Scandinavians' obsession with the sea has been widely romanticized. They were, of course, as familiar with the sea as they were with their fields at home. Ships are the chief theme of the Gotland picture stones; swords and gold ornaments are decorated with their image; the Bayeux tapestry devotes a whole sequence of pictures to the building of the Norman invasion fleet. Kings and princes were buried with their ships. Adventure at sea is a dominant theme of the sagas, and the vernacular contains more affectionate and imaginative epithets for ships than for any other kind of object. Writers, too, tend to grow eloquent on the theme. Swedish historian-archaeologist Count Eric Oxenstierna calls his ancestors' ships "the swift greyhounds of the oceans," Bertil Almgren, "the clippers of their time," and Winston Churchill wrote that "the souls of the Vikings were in their ships." Wheaton estimates that at the start of the ninth century, more Danes were voyaging at sea than the number of those who had stayed home. The title of "sea king," borne by Viking leaders, says Mordal, was greatly coveted.

Even historian Johannes Brøndsted's prosaic style takes wing on the subject of Viking shipbuilding: "Ships embody the high point of the Vikings' knowledge and technical skills. . . . Their ships were their means to power, their joy, their most prized possessions. What temples were to the Greeks, ships were to the Vikings."

The nature and position of their countries forced Scandinavians seaward from the first. The sea was the easiest route to Europe, but they had already learned to use it for internal traffic on the fjords and between their own islands.

How the Ships Began

It is not known when the first log canoe appeared in northern Europe, when the first boat was built, when the first ship was launched. But the world-famous rock drawings of Sweden and Norway prove that travel and trade by sea must have played an important part in the early Bronze Age, 3,500 years ago. The Norwegian A. W. Brøgger, who researched the Vikings' voyages to Vinland, speaks of "the great millennium of seafaring," of trading fleets, shipping companies, new routes and regular lines. There is much information even in the schematic diagrams of ships and their equipment on the rock engravings. The ships are always shown with double sterns, even then ornamented with carved animal heads; they had rudders and were powered by oars probably attached by loops. Brøgger believes them to be the best built ships in Europe during the Bronze Age. Toward the end of that era, an appreciable deterioration of the northern climate led to much modification of ship design. The hull and framework had to be reinforced, stern and sides had to be raised to prevent flooding during storms; such changes were made gradually, in the course of centuries.

Still of the Bronze Age is the Alsen boat, excavated in 1921-22, and dated by its contents as fourth century B.C. It is about fourteen yards long, six and a half feet wide at its center, and only about two feet deep. This oldest ship extant has the characteristic double stern of the rock engravings. Made of limewood planks and hazelwood ribs, the Alsen boat is remarkably light and slender, as though its design might owe something to the primeval hide boats. It was probably a swift rowboat for maneuvering in Danish territorial waters, not suitable for the open sea.

The Nydam boat, dug up in 1863 north of Flensburg, and dated about 300 A.D., or seven hundred years after the Alsen boat, shows some remarkable advances. The Nydam boat was clearly capable of weathering storms on the high seas. It is an impressive clinker built boat made of oak, eighty-one feet in length, nearly twelve feet wide, over a yard deep, partly nailed, partly riveted, caulked and joined by means of woollen and bast-fiber cords. There was room for eighteen oarsmen on each side; when fully equipped, it could hold at least fifty armed men with their tents and provisions. The most significant technical advance on the all-wood Alsen boat is the riveting of the overlapping strakes, like roof tiling, and the attachment of the oak stern to the reinforced decking.

The next stage in pre-Viking shipbuilding, a century later, is marked by the Kvalsund ship, found near Sunnmoer in Norway. It is about sixty feet long and is distinguished by its two elongated crescent-shaped stern posts which point toward the center of the ship, an innovation which made the vessel much more stable fore and aft. No traces of a mast were found on the Kvalsund ship, but the body is so strongly made that it could have been equipped with a pair of sails. Though linguists have considered the Germanic word for sail, *Segel*, to be of ancient origin, the use of sails in northern Europe has not been proved until post-Roman times. The Celtic Veneti sailed around the west coast of Gaul in Caesar's time, using skins for sails. But in Scandinavia sails do not appear until centuries after the great migrations.

But this does not preclude their having been used earlier. Norse traders could have used sails as early as the second century; there are indications that traders rather than fighting men initiated advances in shipbuilding. By the seventh century at the latest, sails were commonly used for transporting crews in the northern countries. The ships had one mast and rectangular or trapezoidal yardsails. Ships that could be rowed and sailed both were most in use.

Of the great Viking ships found along the Oslo Fjord, the Tune ship was the first to be excavated, in 1867; it came to light in fragments. No stern posts or upper board planks were found, and the rest was greatly damaged or deteriorated. Nevertheless, the shape and framework were clearly discernible. Made of oak and sixty-five feet long, it appeared to have been well made, with so strong a mast and keel that it undoubtedly was a seaworthy vessel, with eleven pairs of oars. Naval architects date it as of the ninth century.

This first excavation of a Viking ship did not create much of a stir; the fragmentary nature of the finds did not make for a vivid image. But only a few years later Norwegian archaeologists lucked upon a find that continues to excite specialists to this day. The Gokstad ship, discovered in 1880, inside a sixteen-foot-high grave mound previously plundered, was embedded in and filled with potter's clay. It was a complete Viking ship, a masterpiece, yielding much precise information. Its nobly curved prows have become emblematic of the Vikings' love for the sea.

The massive tapered keel, made from a single tall straight fir tree which must have grown to at least eighty feet in height, forms the backbone of the ship, which is much the same size as the Tune ship, about seventy-eight feet long by seventeen feet wide at its widest point and five feet nine inches deep at midkeel. The keel forms a shallow arc between bow and stern, so that the depth at midship exceeds that fore and aft by about ten inches. Both the elegant body posts fore and aft are made of one piece each, and joined by two short connecting pieces to the keel in such a way that the overlapping, diagonally cut broadsides are riveted together as well as quasi-welded together by wooden nails. The sixteen clinker built strakes are treenailed; nine of these are under the waterline. Willow thongs join the strakes to the ribs, tarred woollen strips provide the necessary caulking. This kind of construction gave the powerful, elegant ship extraordinary elasticity, which stood it in good stead on stormy seas. Such a Viking ship, with its handsome carved figureheads and fine sea-bird curves must indeed have looked like a mythical sea creature as it rode both rough seas and smooth.

Sailing the Viking to America

The beauty of the Gokstad ship inevitably moved someone to make a faithful copy and try it out on an Atlantic crossing. In 1893, Captain Magnus Andersen sailed this ship, named *Viking* of course, across the ocean, with a crew of experienced sailors. It flew over the waves "light as a seagull" and so impressed even seasoned sailors that they were moved to cries of admiration at the grace of its movements. Deck and keel were able to move flexibly with the hull without springing a leak, more like an organism than a construction; as if, indeed, it were alive. (The principle at work is reminiscent of Frank Lloyd Wright's famous Hotel Imperial in Tokyo, built to rock and move with an earthquake rather than resist its movement with the usual rigidity of such edifices, and crack.)

A further surprise was that the square sail sufficed to give the Gokstad replica *Viking* the speed of a cargo steamer. The *Viking* achieved the peak of her performance on May 15-16, 1893, when, with fair weather, she covered 223 sea miles, averaging 9.3 knots (a replica of Columbus's *Santa Maria* sailing the same year achieved only 6.5 knots).

Magnus Andersen, the old sea lion, was particularly delighted with the side rudder to starboard.

> "This rudder," he noted in his account of the expedition, "must be considered indubitable evidence of our ancestors' vision and skill in shipbuilding . . . it's a brilliant idea. In my experience, with this kind of ship, a side rudder is vastly preferable to the usual rudder at the stern; it is totally reliable . . . and can be steered with ease by one man in any weather."

When becalmed, the Gokstad ship was rowed with pinewood oars about seventeen feet long, out of sixteen round holes about twenty inches above the water line. In port, and perhaps also on the high seas, the crew hung two shields each over these oarlocks, alternating black and yellow, with both decorative and awe-inspiring effect, which incidentally added quite a bit to the height of the sides.

It was a strong, sturdy, sound ship, capable of carrying about nine tons of cargo—for instance, a crew of seventy men weighing 175 lbs. each, 900 lbs. in weapons, 5,500 lbs. of provisions and water, and 1,100 lbs. additional cargo. A serviceable vessel of medium size, functional to the last rib, well designed, combining solid craftsmanship with technical perfection. It was built early in the second half of the ninth century, at the height of the Viking era. As Anders Hagen wrote:

> This is what most of the ships must have looked like . . . setting out in the spring, freshly tarred and well outfitted for their war or trade expeditions to unknown shores. . . . It was ships like this one, alone or in convoy, which made westward for Iceland and Greenland, braving storms, wind, and fog; headed southward to the Mediterranean, and eastward, by way of the great Russian rivers, as far as the Black Sea.

Queen Asa's Royal Yacht

The Oseberg ship, found just forty years after the Gokstad ship and not far from it on the Oslo Fjord, proved a difficult dig. When Vikings piled earth atop the ship to form the barrow, the ship itself was filled with tons of rocks, and these ended up literally breaking the ship apart into innumerable fragments. Fortunately all these bits of wood were in an excellent state of preservation, thanks to the airtight covering of grass sods on the bed of clay, so that the patient toil of modern experts succeeded, over the decades, in putting the Oseberg ship together again.

Like the Gokstad ship, the Oseberg ship was a large open boat, a skillful combination of sailing and rowing ship, and yet very different. Not designed to withstand the open sea, it was a luxury yacht meant for the quiet coastal waters. As wide as the Gokstad ship, and over six feet shorter, it nevertheless appears lighter, slimmer, more elegant—a handsome royal galley with billowing purple sail and extravagantly carved figureheads, enough to illustrate a whole textbook on Viking

The Oseberg ship during excavations.

art. It must have been a splendid sight with the Queen aboard, setting out on a pleasure jaunt. It is considered unsurpassed in the grace and purity of its lines.

Norse archaeologists made many important ship finds after the three Norwegian ships had been unearthed, finds that considerably extend our knowledge of Viking naval architecture. In Sweden especially they often came across rows of rivets as all that was left of a completely decayed ship. This allowed for mental reconstruction at a desk, but it was nothing to rival the Gokstad or Oseberg ships. Neither the burial grounds of Old Uppsala nor the Vendel field in Uppland yielded up a complete ship anything like the Norwegian ones.

Better results were obtained by the pharmacist Paul Helweg Mickelson in 1935-36, at Ladby on the Kerteminde Fjord on the Danish island Fyn. He, too, had little more to go on than nails and impressions on the ground, for the ship had virtually fused with the surrounding earth. But the sparse remains sufficed for a quite exact description. The Ladby boat was about seventy feet long, nine feet wide, and thirty-one inches deep—a very slender, long, narrow boat, and with its sixteen pairs of oars something of a sea gazelle, though not likely to have gone out on the open sea. It may even have been built solely as a burial ship, as some experts believe also of the Gokstad and Oseberg ships; namely, that they were never in actual use.

There was all the more excitement, therefore, when submerged Viking ships were discovered in German as well as Swedish and Danish waters following the Second World War. In recent years, then, it is the submarine archaeologists who have come up, literally, with important finds of Viking ships.

Submarine Uses of the Fire Hose

In 1953, submarine archaeologists found a late Viking ship grounded in the harbor of Hedeby near Schleswig. It has not yet been salvaged, and it will probably take a while yet before it is properly raised; the cold murky waters of the Atlantic coastal sea are not the easiest terrain for excavation, and costs are high. Nor have the Viking ships found and photographed by amateur divers in the summer of 1959 in the Bay of Landfjärden, twenty-two miles south of Stockholm, been dredged up as yet. We know only that there are at least three ships. One of these, an open vessel of medium size, has "riveted sides of pine (not oak), a mast, and some equipment." Eric Oxenstierna suggests that the site fits in with an account of ships sunk in the sea battle near Sotaskär in 1007.

News of the Landfjärden find was barely off press when a flotilla of submerged Viking ships was discovered in the Roskilde Fjord, about thirty-five miles

Aerial view of the excavation island in the Roskilde fjord, from which Danish archaeologists salvaged five well-preserved Viking ships.

east of Copenhagen. This flotilla has been preserved by a salvaging project which is the most spectacular feat of submarine archaeology to date.

The project began in 1957 when Danish frogmen, experts on the staff of the National Museum in Copenhagen, began to explore the wreck of a ship known to have blocked the navigation channel near Skuldelev, one of the fjord's narrowest passages, since time immemorial. It was called Queen Margarethe's ship, after the queen who was credited by folklore with ordering it sunk around 1400, to keep pirates from entering and sacking the cathedral town, which happened to be the first capital of Denmark.

The obstructing wreck told a rather different story. The object found, stated

Olaf Olsen's 1960 report, "was not like a ship at all, but emerged as a huge pile of stones about 55 yards long and 15 yards wide athwart the navigation channel, covered with shells and seaweed." This pile could not be raised but needed digging. But spade, trowel and brush, archaeology's traditional implements, were useless here, since they began by stirring up the mud and by making the water opaque, destroying visibility. Instead, the excavators turned to the fire hose, which blew sand, shells and other obstructions from the surface to be uncovered. Bit by bit, the fire hose washed the mound of impacted stone clean and uncovered not one, but a total of five ships!

The next step was to free these ships of their cargo of stones, which had been used to sink the ships to block the harbor of Roskilde against we do not know whom. Some of these boulders weighed over three hundred pounds! Partly by hand, partly with tongs, the Danish frogmen brought up all the rocks and pebbles for re-dumping into deeper waters. Slowly and laboriously the wrecks were cleared and "their oakwood fragments, as it turned out, found in an excellent state, of preservation."

The remains of a ship in the mud of the Roskilde fjord.

View into the interior of the Viking ship hall in Roskilde where the five ships are being restored.

The first few fragments confirmed the supposition that the Skuldelev barrier was laid down in Viking times, centuries before Queen Margarethe.

Underwater topographers bounded off the site with steel cords and spent months taking measurements and charting the position and size of each ship. The entire area had to be drained during salvaging. Piece by piece, often lying on their stomachs only seven inches above the dried-out seabed, the diggers heaved the wreckage up out of the iridescent black ooze, mostly barehanded—the human hand turned out to be better than the most sensitive archaeological tools in this case.

Over 50,000 fragments were salvaged in this way, packed into numbered, water-filled plastic bags, and taken the same day to the National Museum's laboratories, there to be treated with polyglycol and preserved.

The Five Skuldelev Ships

Two of the five Skuldelev ships have now been reconstructed; the rest are taking shape gradually. A good deal is known about all of them, as to dimensions, construction, designation and such. There are two warships, two cargo boats, and one small coastal sloop.

The larger of the two warships is the largest Viking ship found hitherto anywhere. It is about five yards longer than the Gokstad ship—about ninety-two feet—held fifty to sixty fighting men with their gear, had a mast and sail, and was indubitably one of those fearful longships with which the Danes attacked England. The second warship is smaller, lighter, almost a twin of the slender Ladby ship, with a profile like those of the ships Duke William readied for England, as seen on the Bayeux tapestry. Constructed of oak and ash, it accommodated twenty-four oars. The upper planks made of ash had evidently been "cannibalized" from another ship.

The larger of the two cargo boats is almost fifty-five feet in length and over two yards high. Its capacious interior boasted a quarter deck fore and aft, separated from the cargo space amidships. It was clearly a seaworthy merchant vessel, a typical Atlantic boat for trading voyages to England, Iceland, and Greenland.

The second, much smaller cargo vessel may have been used for trade across the Baltic. Cargo was stowed amidships under skins, while the crew of four to six men on the quarter decks were exposed to the sea and the weather. This cargo boat could be rowed and sailed, and was the first to show that "supporting ropes had stretched from the tip of the mast to the front and sides."

Finally, the small coastal vessel, made of oak, birch, and pine, with mast and sail but no oarholes, has been provisionally designated as a fishing or ferry boat.

The Skuldelev ships, emptied of all usable contents and attachments and then filled with rocks, were sunk between 1000-1050 in the Roskilde Fjord, in the Peberrende, twelve miles north of the town. This makes them two hundred years younger than the Oseberg royal yacht. Between them they mark the beginning and end of the best of Viking times, while being visibly offspring of the same family, their basic similarities being much more striking than the variations in details.

This means that Viking naval architecture had reached a high degree of maturity already in Carolingian times. These clinker built rowing and sailing ships with keel and mast, equally useful as vessels of war, trade, and leisure, could hardly be improved upon, though in the course of their development three tendencies are interesting to observe: the refinements in craftsmanship, the tendency to make bigger ships of every kind once the technical problems were solved, and the progressively stronger differentiation among the different types.

Cross-section of the Roskilde freighter or cargo boat.

Purple Sails and Dragon Heads

Shipbuilding probably began as a communal activity of seafaring coastal peoples. We know that it was a public duty in Viking times. The coastal areas of northern Europe were divided into shipbuilding districts all the way north to the Norwegian salmon line. Each district was obliged to maintain a warship with twenty to thirty oars, depending on its size and resources. Towns or scattered large settlements also had to provide the king with a fully equipped boat for his far-reaching war expeditions.

By the time towns began to develop, shipbuilding passed into the hands of trained and paid professionals, and even specialists. The Norwegian Gulathing Law of the tenth century, for instance, specifies joiners as responsible for keel, stern posts and ribs, i.e., the architectural framework, and strake workers for the planks, the exterior, the "skin" of the ship, considered easier and therefore paid at only half the rate for joiners. The *Olaf's Saga* names a master builder responsible

for the making of the *Long Serpent*, as well as the nailsmiths and tree fellers expert in cleaving and preparing the logs. The Viking wharf on Öland suggests that a shipbuilders' guild might have existed there, and even the Bayeux tapestry testifies to the presence of skilled labor squads at work on the expeditionary fleet.

Most ships were made of oak, but failing that, sycamore, lime wood, birch or beech, ash or aspen and pine were also used, but only for the less important sections. The preference for oak is understandable; it is the hardest wood of these latitudes, and can also be cleaved crossways. The logs were hewn with broadaxes; to keep them steady they were rammed into the fork of a tree branch, as the Bayeux tapestry shows. The keel, curved slightly outwards, was made first, preferably of one piece, since it had to support the weight of the whole ship. Then the stern posts were made, consisting of three sections in the larger ships: the submerged section joining the keel, the *bard* or central portion extending above the waterline, and the vertical upper end terminating in a decorative head- or tailpiece.

The body work was next, the lower strakes nailed and riveted before the ribs were built into the body. The keel was then fastened, and the strakes joined together with round-headed iron rivets hammered through both planks and then secured inside with a small square iron plate. All the joints were caulked with cowhair. The tow was made of loose threads of thick woollen yarn soaked in tar, then laid in a ridge on the lower edge of each strake, so that the planks were firmly pressed together during the riveting. Keelwater that seeped in despite these precautions was shipped out with ladles, and the aid of two buckets hung, as in a well, over a pulley. The ribs were fastened with spruce root lashings, a fastening which could give without tearing or cracking, which made for greater flexibility under sail, and for lighter weight.

By the time the Gokstad ship was built, the Vikings knew how to fix a powerful mast to support full sail in a stiff breeze. Sails were usually made of white woollen fabric, more rarely of sailcloth, and often had colored vertical stripes or, in the case of luxury craft, appliqué work of a figurative nature. Purple sails were part of the pomp of kings and chieftains. Ships were tarred once a year, usually before being laid up for the winter, and were often painted above the waterline with red and white stripes or, in the case of the Normans, black, red, gold, blue, and sea-green stripes. There was also lavish carving and decoration where the upper strakes joined the stern posts, well illustrated by the Oseberg ship where even the inside of the stern posts was ornamented with carving and gilded. The headpieces atop the stern posts were usually serpentine or snail-shaped. Often they were carved in the shape of animal heads, usually dragon heads but bear, dog and bison heads as well, or cranes or hawks.

These figureheads were invested with magical powers. An Icelandic law even forbade ships "with monsters or dragons with gaping jaws" to approach the island's shores, lest they offend the peaceable spirits of land and field. Sailors solved the problem by taking their monster's head off, literally, when approaching land without warlike intent. There was magic in names, too, and a ship would be given a name of some potency, it was hoped, generally for the fabled beast on its prow.

These ships were regarded as living creatures, cared for like pedigreed horses, loved as much for their beauty, strength, and temperament as for their uses, with a kind of breeder's pride and paternal affection. The incessant competition for making and owning the most perfect and loveliest ship was not the least factor in producing the Vikings' admirable tradition of craftsmanship.

Out of such rivalry came the most famous of all Viking ships: Olaf Tryggvason's *Long Serpent.*

Cruisers, Liners, Dreadnoughts

In the year 999 King Olaf sailed his *Crane*, a swift, powerful thirty-rib boat, to Halogaland in northern Norway. There he encountered Chieftain Raud on his *Little Serpent*, a ship that outdid the *Crane* in size and beauty, despite its modest name. Immediately on his return home, the King ordered a new, larger ship built for himself during the winter. It was ready for its maiden voyage in the spring, proudly named the *Long Serpent* by King Olaf.

It was a splendid dragon ship, about 164 feet long, with thirty-five oars on each side, that entered the sagas with its owner. Centuries later, according to Snorri Sturluson, Iceland's country Homer, the master shipbuilders of Trondheim knew the dimensions of the *Long Serpent* by heart.

Such heroic dimensions, however, were disadvantageous in battle against ships of the more maneuverable Gokstad size, as King Olaf found out when he sailed his Norwegian fleet to meet a joint Danish-Swedish armada at Svold. The *Long Serpent*'s descendants did not fare much better: Harald Haardraade's ship *Mariasuden*, with seventy oars and only five yards shorter than the *Long Serpent*; Magnus Lagabøters *Kristsuden*, a medieval giant over twice the size of the Gokstad ship; and largest of all, King Canute's royal sixty-rib vessel, almost half again as long as Olaf's dreadnought, for example. Twelve admirals' ships were modeled on the *Long Serpent*, according to Eric Oxenstierna, but though they were praised and admired, the sagas report no great feats of them. They were royal prestige ships, huge and showy, but better for a parade than for battle or the open sea. The ships the Vikings used for their expeditions were smaller, more mobile, more of the Gokstad type. The sagas name three kinds:

a. slender, swift ships with about twenty pairs of oars and a crew capacity of a hundred men, analogous to modern cruisers *(schniggen)*;

b. somewhat larger ships, with twenty-five pairs of oars, higher body posts and better fittings, analogous to our liners *(skeidh)*;

c. dragon ships, the Viking dreadnoughts, with dragon heads and at least thirty pairs of oars, wider than *a* and *b*, with higher sides and better sails *(draken, drakkare)*.

However, when applied to actual ships restored, the correlation is only approximate, and often fluid, depending on changes in fashion, as with Harald Haardraade's *Mariasuden*, which is referred to as a *skeidh* in one place and a *draken* in another. The emphasis in the sagas must be on men o' war, too, so that other kinds of ships are not even named in them.

These Viking warships were unrivaled in their time. With their minimal draught and curved keels they could land on any beach, and penetrate far into the interior by way of the rivers. Their great swiftness and adaptability made surprise attacks possible and effective, though the ships were light and the crews large. Adaptability was also furthered by using the fighting men for the crew as well, so no space was taken up by noncombatants. The speed and tactical expertise of this cavalry of the sea helps to explain their successes along the west European and Mediterranean coasts and their own island waters all the way to polar regions. But they were too light for the North Atlantic. On the high seas, the cargo and merchant ships were far superior to even the greatest of the Viking *draken*.

The Gokstad ship was not yet specialized; it could be used as a warship, but also take enough freight on board to make a profit in overseas transport. But at the millennium, specialized merchant ships were in use, as borne out by the larger Skuldelev cargo boats. Built according to the same general pattern, they lay deeper in the water and were presumably steadier than the birdlike skimmers described. They tended to be shorter, wider, more capacious. Their planks were not lashed to the ribs but treenailed, sacrificing the flexibility of the framework for greater strength and seaworthiness. They were called *knorr* or *knarr*, and their full roundness of form is alluded to in an Icelandic saga's reference to the *knorrbosom* of two evidently healthy-looking peasant women. Such a *knorr* held about fifty men, though normally fifteen were sufficient, and could hold forty tons of cargo.

A smaller, slighter version, the *byrdinge*, with a crew of about ten, was also used as an escort vessel accompanying war fleets; though usually confined to coastal service, they might go as far as Iceland.

Navigators Without Compass or Chart

Whether the Viking sailors were out for trade or plunder, conquest or colonization, wherever they went they were always risking their necks. Not only their achievements, but even their survival may be considered miraculous, considering all they lacked of those aids to navigation we have come to take for granted. No maps, no charts, no lighthouses, no compass, no foghorn, no direction-finders. They had to rely on various natural and manmade landmarks for coastal voyages: mountains, bays, islands, isolated trees, crosses, or memorial stones. On the open sea, the sun, moon, and stars made extremely unreliable guides, all too often hidden behind massive cloudbanks. Experienced sailors could chart their course with the help of wind direction, currents, and waves up to a point, but a long stretch of bad weather, sudden fog, or storm left even the most resourceful of them to chance and their native wit.

Recent investigations have turned up a few navigational aids developed in late Viking times: a wooden dial with a vertical needle for indicating the position of the sun, and a horizontal needle for pointing the course, for example. There are also the *sunstones* of ancient fame, a mineral that indicates by a change of color the presence of sunlight even when the sky is overcast—possibly the grayish-yellow calcite found in Norway and Greenland which turns bluish when held against the sun. These may have functioned like the "twilight compasses" of modern aviation to indicate the position of an otherwise invisible sun.

Lack of instruments forced Viking navigators to hug the coast wherever possible, or go "island hopping." Every experienced captain was undoubtedly a walking compendium of information, of a kind largely untransferable, having become a species of acquired instinct. But not all of this knowledge was intransmissible; descriptions of such courses can be read in *The Greenlanders' Saga*, the Icelandic *Landnamabok*, and even in Adam of Bremen. The following instructions were provided for Hennö's voyage from Norway to what is today Cape Farewell, the southern tip of Greenland:

> The course to take is one passing the Shetlands so far to the north of them that they will be visible thence only on a clear day; then onward past the Faroes, far enough south of them so that only half the height of their mountains can be seen on the horizon, and so far to the south of Iceland that birds and whales will accompany the ship all the way from there.

In Case of Storm . . .

Helpful as such shared knowledge was to the experienced, it would be of little use, even in the fairest weather, to those without a high degree of acquaintance with seafaring, the necessary acquired instincts, the eyes of a hawk, and keen quick senses in general—preferably those of migratory birds—to take over when all else failed. The best described signs and signals could desert the voyager and often did when most needed. Whales and birds did not necessarily appear in formation on cue, and even if you brought your own birds, like Captain Fläki, who released crows on a voyage from the Shetlands to Iceland in the hope that they would guide him in the right direction, there was no guarantee of success.

A seaman had to have "the weather" in his blood, be able to sense approaching rain or thunderstorms before they became dangerous, "smell out" gathering storms in time to swing out of their path. If that seaman's sixth sense failed, there was a standard drill to be followed. Walter Vogel has described it:

> Sails were reduced, a man put to each rope, faulty tackle renewed, the dies raised amidships by means of washboards. If the mast swayed dangerously, it was lowered or cut down. There are several references to preventing the planks from splitting by lashing them horizontally, i.e., by drawing ropes under the keel amidships and winding them around the hull, like a belt, which was tightened by twisting them with the help of sticks.
>
> Sailors near the coast escaped the storm by beaching the ship, while those on the open sea tried rather to avoid landing too forcibly, so they kept away from the shore and allowed the ship to drift, with lowered sails and mast, using the oars to prevent capsizing. But if it was too late to escape the breakers and cliffs, it was preferable to steer the ship resolutely landward in the hope that a controlled wreckage would give the men a better chance to escape with their lives than blindly fighting the odds.

But even when there was no immediate danger, life on board was strictly disciplined. Duties—attending to sails, bailing, standing guard—were assigned in rotation even when in port. The captain had supreme authority, but he informed his crew of his decisions in a kind of standing conference at the mast, when he might even put to a vote a decision as to which course to take.

Viking sailors preferred to spend the night on land wherever possible. Ships were pulled up on the level beach or anchored near the shore. They carried tents which during war expeditions were pitched on deck, one on the forecastle and one on the bulwark. The two Oseberg tents and the remains of the Gokstad tent indicate that the tents consisted of a wooden frame over which blankets or skins were thrown. The Oseberg princess and the master of the Gokstad ship even had collapsible beds, field cots that took up little space and could be instantly assembled and set up. But most of the men slept in sacks made of skin, sometimes doubling up. Daytimes, these sleeping bags could be used to store weapons and utensils and sea clothing made of skins for rough weather. Warships carried sea chests instead of sacks, which served as rowing benches.

There were no galleys on board; any cooking was done after landing for the night, using huge thirty-five-gallon vats suspended on a collapsible iron tripod. Porridge or stewed meat was likely to make up the staple diet even so, unless there was fresh fish. On board they made do with cold food: flat bread and butter, dried cod, ham or pickled meats, washed down with water, mead, or whey stored in skin bags of a kind still in use today in the Mediterranean countries, for wine.

Rather scanty fare in all, and indeed many of these Viking raids were nothing more than foraging expeditions, mostly for fresh meat.

Three Days from Denmark to England

And yet, in open boats barely the size of a fishing smack, they achieved the unbelievable: the invasion of Western Europe, the piratical expeditions to the Mediterranean, the opening of the Baltic Sea and Russian rivers, voyages to Iceland, Greenland, and America.

The distances they could cover per day have been reliably estimated as follows:

from	to	no. of days
northern Scotland	Hebrides Islands	two days
Orkney Islands	Faroe Islands	two days and two nights
Denmark	England	three days
Statt, Norway	Horn, east Iceland	three and a half days
west Iceland	Greenland	four days
Skane	Birka	five days
Birka	Russia	five days
Bergen	Greenland	six days
North Ireland	Iceland	six days
central Norway	Iceland	six days

For voyages from Norway to Iceland, an average speed of 6.6 to 8 sea miles has been suggested. In crossing the North Sea from Denmark to England, Viking ships did not exceed an average of 5 knots, so that this voyage took three days and three nights. From the mouths of the Oder or Neva, fourteen-day voyages are on record. When King Alfred's friend Ottar sailed from Norway in the spring, he needed seventeen days to Skiringssal in the Oslo Fjord, and five days more from there to Hedeby. But he must have spent the nights on land.

A good cargo boat could do 150 sea miles per day nonstop, or about seven miles per hour, quite a feat for a single-sail vessel only sixty-five feet long.

Of course they took a high quota of losses, especially in the grim North Atlantic. Eric the Red lost almost half of his fleet on the way to colonize Greenland. That this was no catastrophic exception we know through a story of a man named Lodin, called Corpses Lodin because he salvaged bodies that had drifted into caves and gorges on Greenland, off shipwrecks and ice floes.

These Northerners were hardheaded realists, not inclined to take needless risks, all the heroic myths about reckless romantic daredevils notwithstanding. They did not seek out danger, they merely regarded it with defiance as part of the natural obstacle course between them and what they sought, whether it was simply fresh forage or all the gold of Constantinople. But all the obstacles and dangers, especially their life-and-death struggle with the sea, seem to have acted as a stimulant. Still, they always began by seeing it soberly for what it was. Or lyrically, as in the lines of the bard Egil describing a raging storm on the Atlantic:

> The storm with mighty blows
> whittles away at the ship's prow.
> Violent waves seething and hissing,
> Icy breath from a monster's maw
> roars round the bow
> blasting all to destruction.

Viking Warfare
and Statecraft

By Sail and Sword
Cavalry of the Sea
Master Guerrillas
Odin's Raven
Men Like Ravening Beasts
The "Trojan Coffin" of Luna
Wolves and Sheepdogs
From Danework to Trelleborg
Professional Soldiers and Foreign Legionnaires

By Sail and Sword

In 1000, by Snorri Sturluson's account, King Sven Forkbeard of Denmark, King Olaf of Sweden, and Jarl Eric of Norway banded together against Norway's King Olaf Tryggvason, the "greatest fighting cock of his era." They assembled a powerful fleet at Øresund, he set out to meet it halfway with his own, and the two armadas met at Svold, where Olaf Tryggvason, against the advice of his council, instantly prepared for battle.

His fleet advanced in formation. The ships closed ranks and roped their stern posts together to form a floating dam, with Olaf's magnificent *Long Serpent*, gilded fore and aft, in the center, flanked by the *Little Serpent*, not much smaller, the *Crane*, and many more. The men took their places. The king stood on the poop deck, a picture-book hero with golden helmet and shield, a short purple tunic over his breastplate. Horns sounded the call to battle, the royal flag fluttered from the mast.

> The plash of oars
> the clang of swords.
> Shield clashed
> with shield.
> Old songs of war
> rang in the air.

It was a breath-taking spectacle.

The first round went to the royal hero. His tall dreadnought went crashing into the center of the enemy formation, his men tossed anchors and boathooks into Forkbeard's ship and soon had the advantage over Sven's men, many of whom fell before the enemy's superior—literally, as their ship was lower—position. The Swedes also suffered heavy losses at the hands of Tryggvason's men.

Then Jarl Eric attacked Olaf's flanks—and the luck of battle turned. Eric came alongside the outermost Norwegian ship, boarded it, hewed his way across the deck, and slashed its ropes. Then he attacked the next one, and the next, in the same way; the crews of the smaller outside boats were driven to retreat on the larger ones toward the center, while Járl Eric slashed the ropes of each cleared ship, cutting it loose, until only the royal flagship was left in the center, still resisting.

Spears flew from ship to ship; soon "the hail of spears and arrows was so thick" that the king's crew on the crowded flagship could hardly stand up against

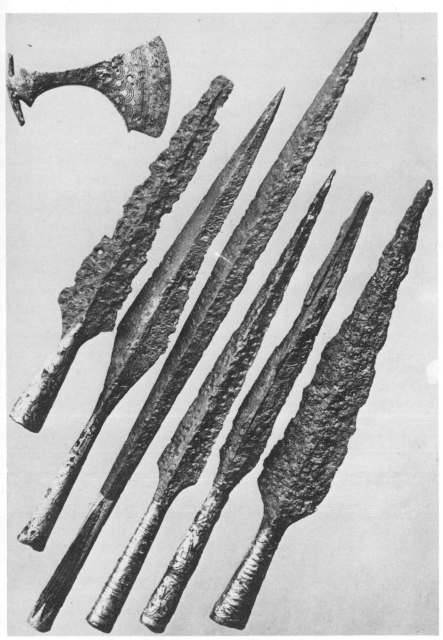

Beardaxe and lance-heads from Sweden. Weapons with rich decoration.

the attackers, though Olaf Tryggvason fought like a bear. Arrow after arrow sped from his bowstring, he hurled spears with both hands at once, and wielded his sword until it was blunted, whereupon he opened a chest of fresh swords for all his men.

It was no use; Jarl Eric's men boarded the *Long Serpent* too. Snorri continues: "Then all the defenders went aft to join their king . . . but so many of the Jarl's men were now on board . . . while his ships harassed the royal flagship on all sides . . . strong and bold though they were, most of the king's men fell." Many leaped into the water, rather than be cut down by the enemy's sword. In the end, Olaf Tryggvason, too, leapt overboard, in full armor, "and when they tried to seize him, he flung his shield over his head and drowned." It was an ideal Viking death, an exemplary end for a great warrior, extolled by poets and bards for a long time after.

Other great sea battles, as recorded in the *Egils Saga* or the *Jomsvikinga Saga*, followed a similar if less dramatic course. These sea battles were not fought on the high seas, of course, but only in bays and inlets or fjords; they were boarding battles which ended in hand-to-hand fighting, rather like land battles on floats. The Viking sea wolves did not ram or sail each other down, nor strip oars, nor engage at sea, nor have running fights.

When enemy ships engaged for battle, the sails were lowered, the crews put up breastworks as shields against missiles, the oarsmen took their places and rowed for their lives. The encounter proceeded more or less as described by Snorri, though the excerpt quoted does not mention stones, used as missiles, as part of the armamentarium.

Since the hand-to-hand fighting concentrated to the fore of the ship at first, a raised forecastle was an advantage. When in 897 King Alfred's virgin navy won its famous victory over the Viking invasion fleet, the fact that he had shrewdly built ships higher than the enemy's greatly helped his cause. However, if the deck was too high, the oars would need to be dipped too low. In late Viking times small turrets were erected to the fore of the ship, to provide raised positions for fighting without adding hardship for the rowers.

Meanwhile the rest of the crew, assembled in the rear around their chieftain, fought with bows and lances until, like Tryggvason at Svold, they too had to take up axe, sword, or cudgel. Even scythes, sticks, and flint catapults were used in maritime close combat.

Tactically, the Vikings, for all their obsession with the sea, had not yet discovered the sea as a battleground. Viking sea battles play only a minor role in the history of sea wars. Their method of sailing in formation to attack was effective enough, as it was impossible to break through such a phalanx of ships roped together, and the crews became exchangeable on such floating fortresses. But the subsequent lack of mobility rather offset the advantages. The danger of exposed flanks is made evident in Snorri's exemplary account. Nevertheless, it was the Vikings who perfected a basic maneuver of sea warfare: the surprise attack on enemy coasts, the blitz raid.

Cavalry of the Sea

The best example, as well as the first recorded, of the Viking blitz raid is the Lindisfarne maneuver, reducible to three elements: to show, to hit, to blow. (Gangster terms for gangster methods? Why not, if it fits? It's not really necessary to make the Vikings respectable guests for the Bishop's tea party, as Scandinavian writers so often seem to think it is.)

The pirate fleets that fanned out to sea every spring on their treasure hunts tended to approach their target stealthily, moving up the coast, looking for a good place to land, a beach or wide river mouth above all. Since the continental population had no ships, or few if any, there was no danger of meeting resistance—the coastal settlements were helplessly exposed to any decisive attack. Once the men had swarmed ashore, everything happened with lightning speed. "Only a few minutes," Bertil Almgren wrote, "passed between the moment when the Viking ship was seen to appear out of the North Sea mist and the moment when the pirates leapt on to the land, ravaging and murdering in the coastal towns and villages. By the time the defense had rallied, the marauders had long disappeared with their booty."

Such isolated flotillas from the North battered the continental coastline for centuries, arriving like a summer storm and overpowering their victims by the unexpectedness and swiftness of their assault alone. It was done on the same principle as the lightning raids on horseback of the Eastern Steppes peoples, who also shook Europe to its foundations in their time. Like the Huns, Magyars, and the hordes of Genghis Khan, the Norsemen attacked the continent, perhaps even more boldly, swiftly and fiercely. Horsemen of the sea, omnipresent but elusive, able to win enormous victories and treasure with relatively small units, they had the special advantage of getting clean away on "mounts" no one else had. If they could not be stopped, they could certainly not be pursued.

For the first time in history the Vikings proved that power at sea is superior to far greater strength on land, so long as it does not meet the enemy on his own ground. When they transferred their tactics to land warfare, they revolutionized it, for the slow-moving land armies of Europe were no match for their mobility. Moving inland on Europe's great historic rivers, in their shallow, supple ships that could be sailed, rowed, towed, and beached with such ease, their mercurial cavalry tactics worked well for them everywhere. Where the water became too shallow, they used log canoes they could produce almost overnight.

Master Guerrillas

In 1806 such a Viking canoe was dredged out of the mud of the Seine near the Pont de Jena, over eight yards long, only twenty-six inches deep. But even their regular ships were so light they could be moved cross-country on rollers, as they did in 886, when they rolled their fleet two thousand feet past the city of Paris which was refusing them access to the Seine. In the same way they penetrated Hamburg with their ships, navigated the Rhine all the way to Mainz, the Somme as far as Amiens, the Marne as far as Meaux. On the Loire they ''marched'' via Tours to Orléans, on the Garonne they reached Toulouse, and from the Rhone delta they made their way to Arles and Lyons.

Their shallow but immensely adaptable boats enabled them to winter in enemy territory. They could moor the boats in the middle of a river and be secure from attack, or use a river island as headquarters. Their ships could glide easily over mud and sand, in waters inaccessible to enemy craft. Once in 860 they were bivouacking on the Seine island Oiselle, only a few kilometers from Paris, roasting fresh steaks at their campfires, while a large Frankish force assembled on both sides of the river to drive them off and could only look on, helpless without water craft.

When the Norse invaders went out on forage from these strategic points, they would requisition the horses of the local peasantry and ride cross-country in bands of ''small flying squadrons.'' Though they fought on foot, they secured all the advantages of mobile warfare, moving like the independent panzer divisions of World War II, though they were out for booty rather than control of the land. They would avoid walled towns, fortresses, or any encounters with sizable enemy forces, and after a full night on the road, might appear in the gray of dawn before a cloister or castle to greet its inhabitants with a rude awakening.

They were brazen, skilled in the use of every trick and tactic of guerrilla hit-and-hide warfare. They first made their own camps secure with guardposts, and initiated broader actions only after familiarizing themselves with the terrain, through reconnaissance. If forced into a quick retreat, they vanished in the thick of forests. They made expert use of the terrain, choosing the most favorable, sheltered positions for bases, moving stealthily through ditches and behind hill-ocks, scattering and rejoining according to the nature of the ground, finding the dominant hillcrest, with the sun at their backs, before battle.

Even when they had to operate in larger units, mobility remained the ace up their sleeve. They never stopped, but moved and acted constantly, shifting their forces overnight, dissolving into thin air at the approach of overwhelming force, to reform where the advantage was on their side. And always they had the advantage of the sea, as well as the rivers and the islands inland. They could cross the Channel and come back when least expected, leaving their landbound adversaries stunned both times.

Odin's Raven

We know their arsenal of weapons: axe and cudgel, spear and lance, bow and arrow, and the noble sword, their cult of the sword which they made and wielded superlatively well, thus indeed endowing it with magic powers. Seven times the *Edda* praises Sigurd's sword Gram that gleamed like fire and could sever a wisp of wool floating in the river, so sharp was it. It was onlh one of many mythic swords about which tales and poems grew. The Vikings reveled in the gory poetry, with its erotic overtones, of the beloved sword, and in fact slept with it beside them.

Two thousand of these swords were found in Norway alone. Archaeologists have so far classified them in twenty categories, but they all have a straight, pointed, usually double-edged blade with a shallow indentation down the center. The best blades came from the Frankish Rhineland, home of Europe's best swordsmiths, especially in the so-called iron triangle between Cologne, Solingen, and Siegen. The Rhenish armorers made high quality steel and had learnt the art of damascening by way of the trade routes from the Middle East. James Mann has described the elaborate process of crafting these fine blades by welding together several strips of metal, superimposed, cut into thin layers and hammered until, with beating and bending, the strips formed a pattern that permeated the whole piece.

The Norse forges could not compete with the Rhenish creators of such gleaming, patterned, resilient blades. They imported and embellished them with accessories and ornaments. Their speciality was the handles, consisting of four parts: cross guard, branch, grip, and pommel, which they richly ornamented, depending on the buyer's wealth and status, by engraving, damascening, silver-ing, gilding, and inlaying. A Viking's dream sword, then, consisted of a Rhenish blade and a Norse handle. Those who could afford it had the triangular bronze straps on the upper part of the sword sheath decorated as well. The sheaths were of wood trimmed with leather, and were fastened with straps and buckles. Suspended from a leather belt was also a single-edged iron knife—a man's last resort in hand-to-hand fighting.

What the sword was to the rich and noble, the axe was to the common man. Easy and cheap to make, useful in peace and war, at home and on the move, this long-shafted, broad-bladed weapon, for which the prehistoric Battle-axe People have been named, had a new flowering in the Viking era. To the monks who wrote the chronicles it became a symbol of heathen bloodlust.

The archaeologists distinguish between two main types: the beard axe, with a "blade drawn downward like a goatee," in use as early as the eighth century, and the broadaxe with its splayed-out cutting edges, not in use until about 1000. Spear and lance continued in use, as did bow and arrow. The most indispensable defensive weapon was the shield, mostly in the form of a yard-wide flat wooden disc, often covered with leather. The pointed oval shields of the Bayeux tapestry belong to the Norman cavalry. Viking round shields had an iron boss in the center to protect the hand of the man inside; the shields were often painted. The 64 shields of the Gokstad crew, for example, were painted alternately black and yellow.

Helmets, like swords, were expensive, and for this reason alone the prerogative of kings and chieftains. But many men of high rank were content to wear pointed leather morions, probably designed on oriental models. However, the conical helmets of the Norman invaders of England recall the Gothic buckle helmets admired by the Franks.

The Bayeux tapestry also shows the mail shirts worn by the Normans, made of linked iron rings, some of them reaching to the knees and with a headpiece. The Oseberg wall hanging illustrates, among other things, white-painted ringmail shirts that cover the whole body. Such iron robes must have been exceptional, however, if only because they cut down on the wearer's mobility enough to cancel out their protective value. The Norsemen of late Viking times also wore protective leggings fastened at the back of the calf, as well as stirrups and pointed spurs based on oriental models.

On the whole, however, their weapons and gear, while well-decorated, were strictly functional and serviceable. The traditional encumbrances of continental land armies went against the grain of these fleet sailors accustomed to the spare, strictly rationalized and functionalized life aboard ship where every inch and every ounce is either essential or excessive.

Viking armies carried standards, usually white banners with fierce fanged monsters to demoralize the enemy. They were referred to in the Fulda annals as *signia horribilia.* On Ragnar Lodbrok's banner, embroidered by the king's own daughters, Odin's black ravens fluttered, foretelling the doom they brought. The invasion army at Hastings carried wind-inflated dragon-shapes overhead, looking fearfully alive. Part of the psychological warfare were the deep-toned horns that signalized the start of battle with a noise that went through the marrow of the listeners' bones, providing the accompaniment to the blood-curdling Viking battle shrieks and wolfish howling with which the attackers hurled themselves upon their adversaries.

Men Like Ravening Beasts

They went *berserk*—the word has entered our vernacular, meaning wild, out of control, crazily violent. It derives from the Norse *berserksgangr*, i.e., bearskin-wearers, bearshirts. Such bearshirts play a mysterious, terrifying part in the Icelandic sagas that may have its origin in shaman-like sorcery. They are evildoers who take on the shape of beasts after dark and wander through woods and moors setting fire to farms, ambushing travelers, and ravaging virgins until, at daybreak, they are transformed back into their harmless, good-natured daytime selves, indistinguishable from the rest of the population. Such terrorists probably existed in fact; every society has its outcasts and criminals, and once the legend was established, it may have served actual robbers and murderers before and after the deed.

The Vikings on the warpath openly adopted the berserk style, partly psychological warfare, partly temperament, and in any case an effective aid to their business. Snorri describes them in the *Ynglinga Saga* as "raging, half-mad, insensate," as quasi-mythological beings who "went into battle without armor, like mad dogs or wolves, biting their shields, strong like bears or bulls, mowing down everything in their path, immune to fire or iron."

It has been suggested that they stimulated their berserk rage by eating toadstools containing muscarin, a poison and psychotropic drug producing effects similar to a bad LSD trip. Artificial or natural, the Norse bearshirts are among the human models of Norse society and certainly of Viking warfare; their raving violence was not merely sanctioned, it was idealized.

The poets and bards never missed an opportunity to give enthusiastic descriptions of this crazy violence. The *Heimskringla* tells the story of King Harald Haardraade (the Ruthless) at the Battle of Stamford Bridge, overcome by such fury that "he rushed far ahead of his men, hewing down everyone in his way with both hands with such force that no helmet or armor withstood his weapons and all nearby fled before him." Later, when an arrow had mortally wounded Harald the Ruthless, the followers of the Norwegian Eysten Orri were seized with such fury that they did not bother to shield themselves as long as they could stand up. In the end they even shed their shirts of mail, so that the English could mow them down without effort, some of them being so exhausted that they fell down dead though not wounded.

This berserk element in Norse psychology—extreme savagery, suicidal trance, ecstasies of fury leading to total collapse—comes most to the fore in the inordinate cruelty of their warfare. Contemporary accounts are brimfull of stories about their frightening brutality, perhaps embellished by the monks but not invented by them. A few samples:

When the Norse marauders took Nantes by storm in 843, "they started a senseless bloodbath, slaughtering men and women alike, and then in sheer exuberance tossed infants to each other as if they were playing ball, to catch on their spears."

Ragnar Lodbrok, next to Olaf Tryggvason the most admired hero of his world, had 111 captives hanged or axed on a Seine island in full view of the horrified Franks watching from the river bank near Carolivenna, twelve miles from St. Denis, in 845. A few years later Ragnar Lodbrok was murdered on King Ella of Northumbria's orders, using poisonous snakes. Ragnar's sons evened the score by opening King Ella's chest with hot irons and tearing out his lungs.

Adam of Bremen, too, has Viking atrocity stories to report, such as the one of the Sea King Ivar Lodbroksson, who lashed the Saxon monk Edmund with whips, then had him beheaded, and threw his body to the dogs. In the summer of 994, a Danish force that had come as far as the banks of the Elbe is reported to have cut off the hands, feet, noses and ears of their prisoners. Among the mutilated were "some noble lords who stayed alive for a long time, looking hideously pitiful, to the deep humiliation of their kingdom."

East Vikings were no different than West Vikings in this regard, to judge by a comment of Ibn Fadlan's about the dreadful Northerners: "Men like ravening beasts."

The "Trojan Coffin" of Luna

Viking atrocities, however, were not all the contemporary chronicles dwelt on in such tones of lament and execration; another inexhaustible subject was the malicious cunning of the Vikings. Confirmation of enemy complaints and allegations comes straight from the accused: the Norse sagas and Norse poets extolled every

Viking act of treacherous cunning, sneak attack, and calculated malice, and historians confirm that such treachery added to the perpetrator's honor.

One flagrant instance of Viking duplicity, the sack of Luna, south of La Spezia in Italian Riviera country, is most thoroughly reported by Dean Dudo of St. Quentin, 150 years after it happened. In his account a coffin plays the role of the Trojan horse.

> The authorities of the town of Luna, terrified by the suddenness of the dreaded attack, quickly arm all citizens, and Hasting [the Viking commander in the Mediterranean] realizes that the town could not be taken by force of arms. Consequently . . . he sends a messenger to the Duke and Bishop of the town . . . with the following declaration:
>
> "Hasting, Duke of the Danes, and all those whose fate drove them from Denmark, send you greeting. You know that, drifting over the stormy seas, we reached Franconia. We penetrated this territory and in many battles we subordinated their land to our chief's kingdom. We then wished to return to our native land, but first a North wind, then unfavorable West and South winds have exhausted us, so that against our will and by the skin of our teeth we have reached your coast. We beg you to permit us to buy food supplies. Our Duke is ill. Harassed by pain, he wishes to be baptized here, and if he were to die, he beseeches you in your charity and piety to accord him burial in your town."
>
> The Bishop and Duke reply: "We will make everlasting peace with you and will baptize your Duke into Christianity. We will permit you to buy whatever you wish." They signed a peace treaty, and active trading began at once between the Christians and the faithless heathens. The Bishop, in the meantime, prepared the baptismal font, consecrated the water, lighted the candles. Hasting, the deceiver, is brought on a litter, baptized, and still shamming serious illness, carried back to his ship. There he gathers his churls around him and lets them in on his vile scheme. "Tomorrow night you shall tell the Bishop and the Duke that I have died, and ask them, in tears, to let me be buried in the town. Promise them my sword and clasps and all I have as a reward." No sooner said than done. Lamenting, the Norsemen hasten to the city elders. Upon returning they report the success of their falsehood. Joyfully, Hasting gathers the chiefs of the various clans and says to them, "Quickly now make me a bier, lay me out on it like a corpse, but with my weapons beside me, and you surround me as mourners. The other men must then raise great lamentations in the streets, in camp, and on our ships."

They do as he commands. The Norsemen's laments echo far and wide, while the bells ring the townsfolk to church. . . . Hasting is carried from the town gate to the monastery by Christians and Norsemen to the place where the grave is being prepared. Ceremoniously the Bishop begins to celebrate mass, piously the people attend to the choir's hymns.

Suddenly all the Norsemen rush toward the bier, calling to each other that the Duke must not be buried. The Christians stand there, thunderstruck. In a flash Hasting leaps from the bier, snatches his gleaming sword from its scabbard, and hews down the luckless Bishop and Duke, while his henchmen encircle the defenseless Christians at the church door and proceed to strangle and murder them. This done, they tear through the streets and cut down all who oppose them. The sailors, too, come rushing in through the wide open city gates and join in the furious fighting. At last the bloody work is done, the Christians almost all killed, the rest dragged to the boats in chains.

Dudo's report rests on a lively oral tradition, and on the testimony of half a dozen other writers of his time who gave similar descriptions of the events recounted.

The Nestor Chronicle reports analogous feats of cunning. Helgi, a Norse leader related to Rurik, at first made his men hide inside the boats when he moored them at a settlement near Kiev. When the first curious settlers approached, the Norsemen, pretending to be merchants, enticed them on to open ground and killed them. Harald Haardraade (the Ruthless) did much the same to a Sicilian town. Robert Guiscard ("The Wily") took possession of a Calabrian monastery by using a funeral cortege escorting a coffin full of swords. Such stratagems had probably become part of the tactical repertoire of a seasoned Viking army faced with the well fortified settlements and city states of the Mediterranean and inland along the Russian rivers.

Keeping faith with the enemy simply was not part of the Viking code. Only the strong and cunning had rights, and only to the degree they were able to win them, every time, by strength and cunning. Treaties and promises were made to be broken at the right moment, when they had served their purpose of putting an adversary to sleep. The point was to win; to harbor scruples about the means to that end implied unmanliness, if not mental weakness.

When, in 845, they handed over Paris for 7,000 pounds of silver, they gave their sacred oath never again to attack the Franconian kingdom. This vow, made upon their own sacred swords, they broke on the homeward voyage not long afterward.

Wolves and Sheepdogs

Nevertheless military historians feel fully justified in praising the soldierly qualities of the Vikings. If one made allowances for an ethic that did not apply outside the family, the clan, the leader and the team, then such qualities as bravery, self-control, disdain for death, a great capacity for discipline and organization, a readiness to subordinate themselves to the common goal and leader, and the ability to set up a hierarchical system of command and adhere to it fixedly were in fact military and even social virtues. Tacitus praised the Teutonic fighting man's reliability, rooted in the mythical soil of the vassal's allegiance to his chieftain. A man who deserts the battle after the death of his chieftain leaves himself open to lifelong contempt; the chieftain fights for victory, the men for their chieftain. Delbrueck asserts that they loved war for its own sake, preferably hand-to-hand, man-against-man combat, ideally in the front lines, for all to witness.

This Teutonic love of a fight produced neither a Hannibal nor a Caesar—neither of whom probably loved war for its own sake. It was a matter of temperament, perhaps, for the bards loved most to sing of those inspired Viking attacks that rage through the enemy lines like a scythe in a cornfield. Franks, Anglo-Saxons, Scots, and Irish learned to fear eternal hellfire alone more than they did these crushing Viking attacks. In his lust for combat or booty, a Norseman might get so far ahead of his own troop that he would suddenly find himself surrounded by the enemy; in this way, many Vikings lost their lives.

In defense, they formed themselves into a hedgehog of bristling spears and shields—as Swiss peasants centuries later—a live, barbed fortress, impregnable while it held its formation. However, if this was breached, and deteriorated into each man fighting for himself against a numerically superior enemy, they suffered great losses in battle. For the badly wounded there were, of course, no organized field hospitals. The nearest thing to any kind of care for the wounded mentioned in the literature is Snorri's story of the wounded bard Thornod, who dragged himself to a hut where an old woman was bandaging the wounded. On the floor of her hut a fire was burning, and on it a large kettle with hot water for cleansing the wounds. The old woman also had cooked leeks and onions in a stone pan, and fed them to the sick in order to diagnose which wounds were mortal. It was believed that wounds through which one could notice the smell of an onion escaping were incurable—a belief probably based on experience with stomach wounds. In any case treatment could not go far beyond hot or cold compresses and the herbal lore of shepherds and old crones. A serious wound meant quick or lingering death, and many men were lost in warfare on both sides.

Viking generals learned to combine the fleet and their land forces in battle as though they were "the two arms of one body." They also learned the complicated art of laying siege to a fortress or walled town. By the middle of the ninth century they had learned to dig trenches and attack with battering rams and missile engines. In 885-86 they set up movable protective walls in front of Paris, and built a threefold battering ram—but this was never completed, because of the inventor's untimely death.

By the ninth century they had also merged a number of small rival units into a sizable army capable of concerted action. After Godfred's early invasion of Frisia, involving a landing operation with 10,000 men, the first "great army" was formed in Scotland, consisting of 20,000 men. The army that besieged Paris in 885-86 was 30,000 strong, and its achievement must be judged all the more remarkable in that they operated without supply lines from home, without communication with their families, armories, or reinforcements, even as they penetrated deeper into enemy country. It took high discipline and organization on the basis of a strict hierarchy of command.

The dual character of the Norse people, their alternation between ecstasy and sobriety, was necessarily reflected in their kind of warfare. The wolves were transformed into obedient sheepdogs under their commanding masters. As Adam of Bremen put it, "They all enjoyed equality at home, but when they set out to battle, they gave their king inviolable obedience." But even small groups were highly organized and disciplined; infractions were ruthlessly punished. When Viking strays lifted a few things from a looted church treasure, they were quickly condemned to death and hanged.

Obedience was expected even at the top of the hierarchy. The first great army in Scotland was led by eight kings who had agreed to accept the leadership of one of their number. Twenty jarls served under the eight kings, with each jarl in command of about 1,000 men led by their chieftains, each of whom had about a hundred men (or one or two ships at sea) to control. The domestic territorial structure of village collectives and districts was reflected in the army hierarchy. The Norse ideas of clan and family were automatically transferred to the organization of Viking armies with marked success. Rule by oligarchy proved itself at war abroad as well as at home.

In late Viking times these civilian armies were superseded by the regular troops and highly trained mercenaries with which Sven Forkbeard and the great Canute conquered England. Chief evidence for the existence of these mercenary armies are the impressive military camps dating from the time Denmark was a great power.

From Danework to Trelleborg

The Vikings built strong ramparts and fortresses, and were much admired for it in the ancient literature. One of the most famous is the Danework, a complicated and extensive system of ramparts between the Schlei and Treene rivers, on the Jutland peninsula between the Baltic and North Seas. Begun under Godfred, it marked the southern border of Denmark at the time, but is now in the German state of Schleswig-Holstein. Many earthworks outside Scandinavia have been credited to Norse builders, among them the Irish fortresses at Limerick, Cork and Waterford—"eyries on a rocky coast affording distant views across the sea"—as well as the fortresses at Lincoln, Nottingham, Stamford, Derby, and Leicester which dominate the Mercian landscape like "rooks on a chessboard." Some scholars are skeptical and urge caution in such attributions, even in the case of many *burks, camps,* and *dykes* linked to the Danes by linguistic reasons. Even the joint Danish-Swedish digs of 1951-52 at the Hague Dyke, an earthwork which runs through the Cotentin Peninsula in Normandy, left important questions unanswered. The finds unambiguously point to the military function of the headland dyke, including traces of fires suggesting the use of powerful fires in the long trenches for defense. The site seemed almost to smell of Norse sweat, but as no datable objects were found, it remained inconclusive.

The Danish military camps, on the other hand, offer incontestable proof of their date of construction. Three of them, Trelleborg, Fyrkat and Nonnebakken, date from the last decade of the tenth century, while Aggersborg dates from the first half of the eleventh. Judging by Trelleborg and Aggersborg, they were masterworks of precision, superior to anything of the kind found anywhere else, and must therefore be described in some detail.

In 1934 the Trelleborg site (on west Zealand, *not* modern Trelleborg, which is in Sweden) attracted attention because someone wanted to turn it into a motorcycle race track, suggested by a perfectly curved slope that would have been suitable for a grandstand. Trelleborg, object of intensive investigation until 1941, turned out to be the site of a military encampment which dated from the time of Sven Forkbeard, on a wide spit of land between the mouths of two rivers that poured their waters into an inland sea that has since dried up. This afforded a navigable connection with the Great Belt, the strait between Zealand and Fyn, about two miles away, so that the boats of the camp fortress could be moored within sight. The main fortress is to this day surrounded by a circular rampart six and a half yards high and eighteen yards wide at the base, originally fortified with palisades. Four openings in the rampart, with wooden gates, pointed in the four directions of the compass. (See illustration on p. 160).

The renowned Trelleborg on Zealand, with the layout of the barracks ma

cavators. To the left (near the farm), the restoration of the Viking house.

The inside circle was divided into four parts by plank walks leading from gate to gate: two perfect diameters crossing. Each of the four sections held four elliptical houses forming a square around an open courtyard. Another fifteen houses stood side by side between the inner and outer ramparts, like firmly anchored ships. The whole camp was a geometer's dream of precision, based on a unit of 29.33 cm. (within 2.5 millimeters of a Roman foot) which appears in the most varied combinations. The houses were 100 feet long, those in the outer fortress, 90 feet; the width of the rampart was exactly 60 feet. The radius from center to rampart measured 234 feet, as did the distance from inner to outer moat. As Oxenstierna says, architects and surveyors must have been at work here with lines of sight, exact measuring instruments, with a pedantry no one would have expected of the temperamental, wild Norsemen.

The Trelleborg houses, or barracks, were identical chain products and

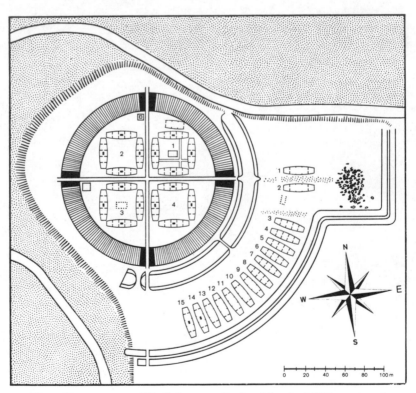

The military camp of Trelleborg on Zealand (end of 10th century).

apparently corresponded in every detail, except for the difference in length of 10 feet between the inner and the outer barracks. About 8,000 full-grown trees must have been needed for the thirty-one houses. A reconstruction—based on structural similarities with two small jewelry caskets from the Cathedral treasury of Bamberg and Kammin, both in the shape of houses with concave horizontal walls and straight gable walls—indicates that each barrack was divided into a large central hall, and two smaller lobbies, each taking up one fifth of the total length. The lobbies probably served as store rooms, the central hall as living and sleeping quarters, with two doors leading to the inner courtyard; one door each led to the lobbies, four in all. At the exact geometrical center of each house was a square stone fireplace. The benches along each side wall held room for about fifty men; probably each building housed the crew of one longboat.

The main rampart was protected by streams and marshes on three sides, and on the landward side by a huge moat spanned by two bridges. Rows of posts which ran around the convex, boat-shaped barracks were later found to have been slanting planks identical with the roof rafters, to take the weight of the roof off the walls. It meant being able to use much thinner wood for the building itself. How to

The Fyrkat circular rampart in Northern Jutland.

economize on wood was a major problem confronting the master builders responsible for so extensive and expensive an undertaking, probably only one of several planned simultaneously. We do not know who the master builder of the Trelleborg camp was, but he enjoys a place of honor in the history of Danish architecture, and deserves one in the history of communal architecture anywhere.

The Fyrkat camp in northern Jutland proved to be similar in essentials to Trelleborg: also situated on a peninsula, protected by streams and marshes, with access to the sea, and a rampart as circular as that of Trelleborg. It was smaller, did not have an outer rampart, its houses were four feet smaller, but in most respects it was essentially the same kind of construction and built at the same time.

Both the Danish military camp at Nonnebakken near Odense, investigated toward the end of the 1950's, and Aggersborg, studied earlier in the late 1940's, (the latter larger than Trelleborg) confirmed the impression of rigorous planning, mathematical precision, clever use of space and resources, respectable technical workmanship, above all in the construction of the barracks, and functionalism comparable to that of a Roman military camp. Such camps presupposed a strong central power and a smoothly functioning executive.

Professional Soldiers and Foreign Legionnaires

Under Sven Forkbeard and Canute the Great, then, Denmark was a highly centralized monarchy possessing military strongholds at home—reminders of the power and prestige of the king even when he was away, and serving to dampen the ambitions of regional chieftains. The camps also served as training centers for such military enterprises as the frequent invasions of England. The majority of the men were drawn—perhaps *drafted* is the word—from the general population, who had to serve as vassals of the king, though the earliest written service order found dates from the times of Valdemar the Victorious (1202-41). Its most important features were probably in operation under Canute. It required one out of three owners of a farmstead to serve. The execution of the royal conscription order lay with the tax collectors who came in person, "with horse and armor" to build the obligatory boat "from the contributions made by the peasants" and were in command of the crews. One of these is known by name, "Eirik, a brave warrior" who fell at the Danish siege of Hedeby in 983. Thorulf, one of Forkbeard's men, had a runestone memorial.

The kings of the Danish North Sea Empire also hired mercenaries, mostly from Sweden, as the runestones indicate. Members of this foreign legion probably formed the cadres of reservists permanently stationed in the Viking camps; some of them came to serve in the royal bodyguard at Constantinople. That these camps were permanent garrisons is further proved by the cemetery at Trelleborg, where women and children had been buried, along with spinning and weaving equipment, so that at least the families of the permanent crews must have lived there, or nearby. The barracks outside the main rampart but enclosed by the outside wall may have been family housing, in fact. As the grave goods include forge implements, ploughshares, sickles and scythe blades, the troops forged their own weapons and cultivated the fields.

On Denmark at least, then, the old seasonal pirate gangs, marauders, daredevils, terrorist killers, and whatever else the outraged monks of the chron-

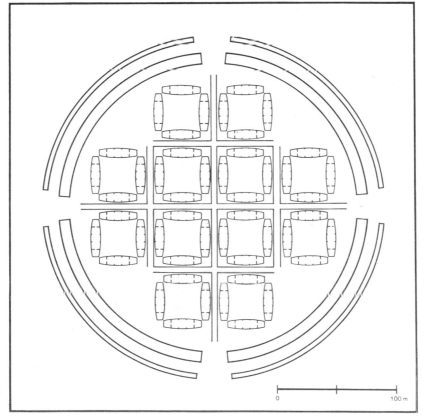

Plan of the Aggersborg camp with its 48 barracks (first half of the 11th century).

icles had called them, were transformed into a professional army. The existence of such an army, and of the centralized state it presupposes, can be expected to mean the end of the ancient democratic, egalitarian individualism as a political fact in Viking lands.

But economically, as traveling merchants and world traders, the Vikings were among the most enterprising, boldest, craftiest, and successful individualists still. Their historical achievement created more stir throughout Europe than even that of the Viking fleets and armies.

Part Five
Trade

Viking Trade
Makes History

Part of the silver treasure of Värby,
southwest of Stockholm. Above,
pendants with coins. In the foreground,
two ring brooches and a disc brooch
with masks and animal decorations.

Pioneers of Viking Trade

The Norwegian tradesman Ottar, according to King Alfred's account, lived farthest north of all Norsemen, on a long, narrow, coastal strip of northern Norway called Halogaland. It was wild, rocky country, habitable only along the coast which narrowed from a width of sixty miles in the south to three miles in the far north. East of this stretched vast bogs and moors, some of them so wide that it took two weeks to cross them. These were inhabited by Finns, who paid tribute to Ottar, each according to his rank, in the form of animal skins, birds' feathers, whalebone, and ship's ropes made of whale and sealskin. The highest-ranking Finn had to pay fifteen marten skins, five reindeer hides, one bearskin, ten buckets of feathers, one bear or otterskin jerkin, and two ship's ropes sixty ells long (over thirty yards).

Ottar himself went fishing and whaling, and was a successful seal hunter. Actually he felt more at home on the sea than on land. Once he sailed northward along the coast for three days, open sea to larboard, to "the furthest point whale hunters go" (well inside the Arctic Circle). Then he kept going north for another three days, until "the land turned eastward, or else the sea came into the land, he was not quite sure." For nine days he waited for a west wind and crept eastward along the coast for four days, until at last a vast bay opened up to the south. For five days he sailed southward until he reached the mouth of a great river where he found fishermen, bird-catchers and hunters who "spoke almost the same language" as his own Finns. From them he bought walrus tusks, some of the best specimens of which he later gave to King Alfred.

Evidently the intrepid explorer had made his way around the North Cape into the White Sea in that open sailboat of his. Ordinarily, on his annual trading voyages, he sailed southward from Halogaland to a port he called Skiringssal. This voyage also took about a month, with a favorable wind, and on it he left the mountains and bays of Norway behind him. South of Skiringssal he came to a large sea, which he crossed in three days and three nights, to reach the northernmost point of Jutland. It was another two days to Hedeby, where he traded his goods.

The merchant Wulfstan, also a regular at Hedeby, gave King Alfred a detailed account of a voyage to Truso (probably Elblag, now in Poland) which he reached in seven days from Hedeby "if the sails were hoisted all the time," i.e., if he went nonstop. This port was situated somewhere in the Vistula delta that, according to Wulfstan, separated the Wends from the Ests.

We know the stories of Ottar and Wulfstan because Alfred the Great of England, when he was translating from the Latin Orosius's *History of the World*, decided to slip into his translation the adventures told him personally, and not in

Latin, by the two Norse merchants—thus enriching the Latin historian's work by unheard of vistas of the far North, and incidentally our own knowledge of early Norse exploration and trade.

Another merchant mariner, Thorolf Kvedulfsson, named in the *Skallagrimsson Saga*, was a vassal of Harald Fairhair, and like Ottar, a chieftain in Halogaland. He hunted seals, commanded a fleet of cod and herring fishermen, and a task force of egg collectors in the bird colonies of northern Norway. On his trading voyages, mostly to England, he sold fish, hides and furs, for cloth and wines, grains and honey, or even cash.

All three of these men, Ottar, Wulfstan, and Thorolf, merchant mariners around 900, spent winters at home on their land, but set out each spring on a new voyage, driven as much by their restlessness and zest for adventure as by the hope of quick profits. Those long dark winters in the frozen North, huddling around a smoking fire, might have been quite enough to catapult healthy men out and away from home in the spring.

These rural traders, who when the situation allowed were always ready to take part in a little banditry on the side or at least to dictate the prices for their goods with their swords, were the pioneers of Viking trade. Typical of the Teutonic peasant aristocracy, embodiments of the dynamics of the Viking era, they were the most enterprising traders of their time; clever, daring, and handy with their weapons. With the Arabs and the Frisians, they developed the bartering systems of the early Middle Ages, opening new regions and new trade routes.

Trade Routes North and South

For the origins of trade contacts between southern and northern Europe one has to go back to prehistoric times. By Roman times, and with the help of Roman military roads and organization, a great stream of goods flowed down the Rhine, and by way of the North Sea coast into the mouths of Weser and Elbe, but also northward up the west coast of Jutland to southern Norway by boat. They might also cross the Jutland peninsula at the level of Ribe, reach the Danish islands and from there establish trading points in Sweden.

Another much used trade route went from Aquileia in the Isonzo delta, on the Gulf of Trieste via Carnuntum, today's Carinthia near Vienna, through the March Valley and the Moravian gateway to the amber markets of the Baltic—the famous Amber Route. A third route led from the Black Sea to the Baltic, by largely unknown roads of the time.

During the great migrations, roughly between the third and the sixth centuries, the two eastern routes lay almost fallow, put out of use for long stretches of time by the sudden arrival of nomadic horsemen in wild unpredictable hordes. The route along the Rhine was the only dependable trade link, north to south, for lengthy periods, and continued as such after the departure of the Roman legions. The Rhenish manufacturers did a flourishing trade as a result, and some maintained their superiority in the market—if we think of those Viking swords, for example—long after the Rhine route slackened off, about 500, probably because Franconia under Clovis I and his sons was turning southward.

The role of the Rhine route was taken over by the ancient Amber Route, the Aquileia line, which was fairly secure again after the collapse of Attila the Hun's empire and the establishment of the Ostrogoths in Italy. Streams of gold went up the Danube and all the way to Sweden, where it led to the great flowering of Norse luxury, jewelry-making, and art. But the death of Justinian ended the Byzantine Empire's brief renaissance under his rule, and the onset of the attacks from the Avars storming westward from Central Asia, put an end to the Aquileia route about 565.

After the Avars came the Slavs. From the small territory on the central Dnieper where they had lived surrounded by Finnish and Turkish nations, they first percolated into the depopulated areas between the Bug and Vistula rivers, then moved on to the Oder and finally the Elbe, putting all these rivers out of action for trade between southern and northern Europe.

But in the meantime trade between the Rhine and the North Sea was reviving, largely because in the early seventh century, with the rise of the Carolingians, Franconia's center of gravity had moved eastward again. The areas that profited most from this shift were the Rhineland, the Dutch Lowlands, and the northern Gallic coastal strip. Politically secure, full of new churches and other ecclesiastical centers safeguarding Christian traditions and the civilizing contributions of late antiquity, these regions enjoyed an economic renaissance attested archaeologically by coins, pottery, and fine glassware.

The Heyday of the Frisians

In the middle of the seventh century the Frisians—inhabiting the long sandy stretches of the North Sea coast, and dependent on trade since Roman times, bartering cattle for cereals and other consumer goods—appropriated all trade between Jutland and Ireland. A century later they had also opened the Baltic for the north-south trade, even as the Arabs had taken over commerce in the Mediterranean.

In the Baltic they found congenial partners in the Swedes who had learned to love southern luxury goods, and had to find a new conduit for them since the Aquileia route was blocked by Slavs and Avars. A southward route had to be found in a westerly direction, and here the Frisians seemed the ideal intermediaries. Relations between Frisians and Vikings were cordial from the start. They did not deteriorate until the newly rich Frisian settlements on the North Sea coast attracted Viking marauders at the beginning of the ninth century, after the Lindisfarne coup. But even then, though the trading voyages became more risky, they were too profitable to be abandoned.

So trade continued behind a curtain of "blood and tears." Dorestad, the Rotterdam of its day, was burnt to the ground several times. There were times when all Frisia was ruled by Danish usurpers. Even the thickly settled routes between Hedeby and Birka, within Norse territory, were unsafe. Frisian merchant venturers had to be prepared for attacks in the shoals as well as near the Norse islands and bays.

A typical incident, which took place in the spring of 830, is described by Archbishop Rimbert in his biography of Ansgar. The merchant ship on which the missionary was sailing was attacked midway on its course, and the men repulsed the first pirate onslaught successfully. But they were utterly beaten in the second attack, and lost their boats and all the cargo; they were lucky to make it to shore alive, with whatever trifles they had on them. Imperial gifts on the way to Sweden were lost, as well as their own personal property, on that voyage in the spring of 830.

When in 852 Ansgar made the voyage to Birka again he arrived unscathed, although the voyage itself had been even more hazardous. The law speaker at the Birka parliament, who was pro-Christian, referred to the dangers at sea in his welcoming address:

> King and Assembly of the Thing, hear me! Many of us have heard a great deal about the worship of this god: we know he helps those who have faith in him, for we have often put this to the test on our dangerous voyages by sea and in many another hour of need. To embrace this religion, we have been going to Dorestad. . . . But nowadays there are many dangers lying in wait for travelers along this route. Pirates make the seaways too unsafe. Why should we seek so far off, and at such great risk, what is now offered to us here?

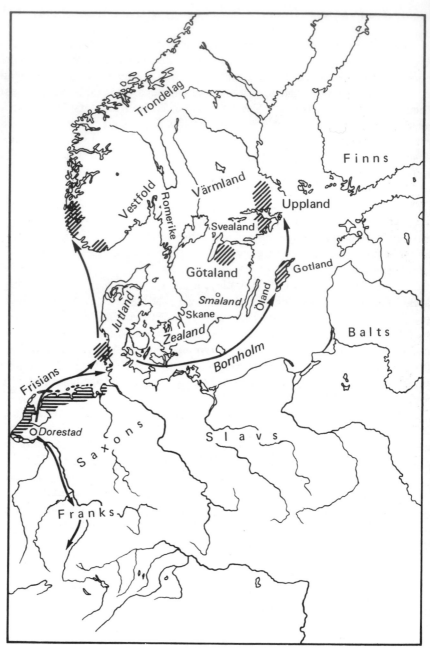

Franconian-Frisian-Norse trade routes in the 7th and 8th centuries.

The risk of death and slavery was part of the traders' occupational hazard. No doubt the mortal dangers they ran were included in the price of their goods. A barrel of Rhine wine may not have been cheap in Birka.

But it was there to be had. Rimbert tells the story of a pious woman called Friedeburg, around 850, who fell sick and "craving the familiar Christian sacrament, had some wine bought and held in readiness in a special vessel" for her last hour on earth. She also charged her daughter to sell all her property after her death and take the proceeds to Dorestad, "at the first opportunity" to give to the poor. Since the daughter was able, according to the Bishop's tale, to fulfill her mother's behest faithfully, we can only conclude that traffic between Birka and Dorestad went on despite all obstacles, and that the Frisian colony in Birka made a comfortable living.

Exactly when Danes, Swedes and Norwegians became business partners and rivals of the Frisians is not known, but the founding of Hedeby in 804 is likely to have increased their share in the Baltic and North Sea trade quite considerably. By the middle of the ninth century they were probably full partners, since the Frankish North Sea coast—called by someone "Frisian Normandy"—was largely ruled by Danes from 857 on. From 900 on at the latest, England, Ireland, and Scotland as well as the North Atlantic islands were included in the Norse trade circuit. The merchants were never far behind the warriors and the colonizers; often enough they were the same people. These were merchants who carried not only their goods to market, but their own skins as well. The graves of this era usually contain swords, spears and other weapons next to the coins and silver scales.

From the Sea to the Steppes

These Norse lords of the seas and river routes came also to dominate the great Russian forests and steppes.

They began by colonizing the east coast of the Baltic, beginning about the middle of the seventh century. The island of Gotland, situated almost midway between Sweden and Latvia in the Baltic, made a natural point of departure for the Svea clan's early attempts to stake a claim on the eastern Baltic and turn it into a Swedish inland sea. Gotlanders took a decisive part in founding the first Norse trading colony in the Baltic, at Grobin near present-day Liepaja. The Svea traders probably began penetrating inland by way of the Western Dvina River. But exploration of the possible markets along the coastal routes was a far more immediate and pressing concern for them.

Early in the eighth century, therefore, they pushed forward from Uppland by way of the Aland Islands to the Gulf of Finland, and on by way of the Neva—past the marshes where 900 years later Peter the Great laid the foundations of today's Leningrad—on to Lake Ladoga. There at the mouth of the Volkhov they established a trading center, Old Ladoga, as a base for further thrusts inland. They sailed eastward over the Svir to Lake Onega, and thence by way of several smaller rivers and lakes to Beloozero on Lake Beloya, until finally they reached the northern bend of the Volga. By means of several other, more southerly routes, the Rus-Varangians had already established a network of trade routes connecting them with the Far East and the Orient in the early part of the ninth century (decades before 852, the year cited as "epoch-making" in the Nestor Chronicle).

The next large reshipment port they entered was Bulgar, on the eastern bend of the Volga, starting point of the famous Silk Road to China. Here Viking longships met with caravans from the steppes of Central Asia and Arab freighters from the Caliph's flourishing eastern provinces, the cultural and economic heart of the Arab kingdom since Baghdad had become its capital c. 760. The Arabs came by way of the Caspian Sea into the Volga, which was deep enough to carry seagoing vessels north as far as Bulgar. Itil, today's Astrakhan, at the mouth of the Volga, had also grown into a port of reshipment of the first importance, a magnet to the Norse traders who were known to have been among the annual regulars of all the great trade centers about the middle of the ninth century. About 860, the Arab Ibn Khordadhbeh even saw Norse traders in Baghdad and Constantinople, selling swords and furs.

Along the Dnieper to Constantinople

There was also the Dnieper route, probably even more important than the route through Bulgar and Itil. Old Ladoga was probably the embarkation point for most of the Dnieper voyages proceeding down the Volkhov, passing Holmgard (contemporary Novgorod), crossing Lake Ilmen, and then following a series of minor rivers until the tributaries of the upper Western Dvina brought them near the Dnieper's source. There they had to transport their boats overland. It was, in fact, a strenuous voyage, demanding exact knowledge of the country, the small tricky river courses, the treacherous marshes full of midges and foul water.

But it took them to another important reshipment center, at the location of today's Gnezdovo, near Smolensk. Its Norse origins are proved by the large burial site. One of the junctions in the network of eastern trade routes, the town was fortified, like Birka and Hedeby, and ruled by a Rus chieftain. Here Norse traders shipped out on the Dnieper, gliding between impenetrable forests on the widening stream three hundred miles to Kiev, another market town that attracted merchants

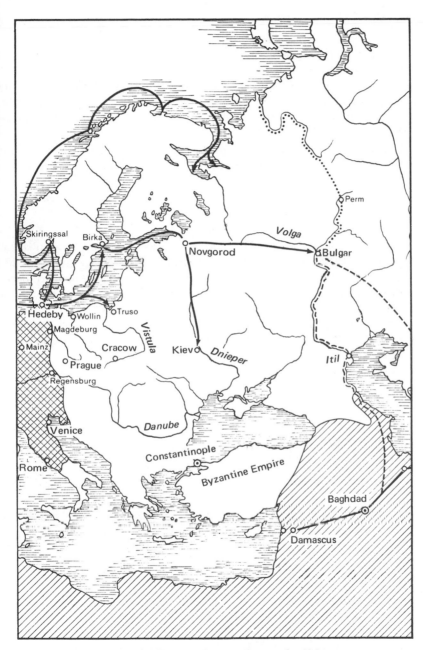

Trade routes to Eastern Europe during the Viking era.

from all points of the compass. The Kiev exchanges and business emporia maintained constant touch with Krakow and Prague, Regensburg and Mainz.

Two other important trade routes crossed the country between Dnieper and Volga; the southerly one, an old caravan route, ran straight across the Ukraine to the Don and on to the Volga near Stalingrad. Nor did the intrepid Varangians fear the lower reaches of the Dnieper, despite the dangerous rapids in the area of today's Dniepropetrovsk. The Byzantine Emperor Constantine Porphyrogenitus wrote a lively description of this dramatic part of the voyage in his government handbook. His account reveals that the greater part of the Dnieper trade was controlled by the Varangian princes long settled in the country. Their favorite winter sport was tax collecting.

Early in November, after returning from their annual trade tour, the Varangian chieftains set out from Kiev to visit the Slav tribes under tribute to them, on either side of the Dnieper. With the goods they collected, mostly slaves and furs, they returned to the metropolis in the spring, after the thaw, smashed up their canoes and bought ships built for them during the winter by Slavic shipwrights, and fitted them out for their annual tour.

In June the "voyagers to Greece" gathered near Wyteczew, then sailed in convoy for mutual protection on the voyage downstream. The worst of it was the seven rapids south of Poltava, where the Dnieper hurled its waters through a fifty-mile-long bed of granite, part of a spur of the Carpathians. Emperor Constantine's account has left us a vivid description of sailing through these cataracts:

> They reached the first waterfall . . . extremely narrow, with steep rock islands in the center; when the current strikes these it falls with a terrifying roar. The Rus do not dare to sail between these rocks, but land the crews, leaving the cargo aboard. Then they go naked into the water, feeling their way gingerly with their feet over the treacherous stones at the bottom. Meanwhile they use logs to push the ships forward, some at the stem, some at the center, some at the stern, crossing the rapids on foot, close to the banks. Once safely out on the other side, everyone gets back on board and they sail on.

The worst of these narrows was the fourth, called Aifor, a nesting place for pelicans.

> Here they all get ashore, unload the goods, and lead the slaves (the most valuable part of the cargo) six miles across the mainland, until they have passed the rapids. The boats too are dragged and carried past the rapids and then put back in the river, to be reloaded for the rest of the voyage.

The rest was relatively smooth going, until they reached the island of Berezany, Birch Island, on the Dnieper delta, where they had built a permanent center. From here they had what seems to have been a regularly scheduled summer route going in two directions, one up the Don in the direction of today's Volgograd (Stalingrad), the other across the Black Sea to Constantinople.

Skulls For Drinking Cups

On Berezany or Birch Island a runestone was found in 1905, erected by a man named Grani ''for his comrade Karl''—the only runestone found in Russia. Grani and Karl both came from Gotland, but Karl died there on the Dnieper delta, on the Black Sea, practically within sight of Constantinople and the East, the Viking merchants' goals.

There are nearly a hundred runestones memorializing a Norseman's failure to return from a voyage to the East or to the distant ''land of silk,'' most of them found in Uppland or Södermanland, which supports the belief that the Varangians in Russia came chiefly from these areas in Sweden. All the runestones intimate an underlying sense of the dangers of these voyages to the East. Though the routes had been made secure by fortified strong points along the way, the risks were high.

> Ingefast had this stone carved for Sigvid, his father. He fell in Holmgard, as captain of his ship, with his crew.

> Torgard set up this stone for Assur, his mother's brother, who died far from home, eastward, in Greece.

> He fell on his voyage to the East with Ingvar, God rest his soul.

These are typical inscriptions.

A Gotland runestone is erected to the sons of Rodvisl and Rodälf, one of whom lost his life in Kurland, while the other was treacherously ambushed and killed by the Wallachians, a tribe inhabiting what is today Romania. Another Gotland stone commemorates Vitgeir, who perished in the marshes of Novgorod (Holmgard). The famed Gripsholm stone is inscribed to Tila's son Harald ''who went to seek gold'' in the south, the land of silk called Särkland, where he became ''fodder for the eagles,'' i.e., his body was left to the vultures, unburied.

The worst surprises seem to have come from the Slavs, subjugated but not subdued, who threatened the voyagers, especially in the area of the rapids, where they had to come on land. At these points, the Byzantine Emperor reports, the Varangians sent out patrols to guard against the Petchenegs ''who were constantly

lying in wait,'' as the Nestor Chronicle confirms. In 962, Rurik's grandson
Svyatoslav "set out for the rapids. There Kurya, lord of the Petchenegs, attacked.
They killed Svyatoslav, made a cup out of his skull, and drank from it.''

Goats for the Gods

Those voyagers who reached their destinations in the East were met by all the
hurly-burly of a market in full swing. The Arabs bear witness that the Norsemen on
arrival celebrated their regular meetings with one another with noisy effusiveness,
shook hands, praised their wares, haggled, invoked witnesses to one's own
sterling honesty, and promised the buyer anything.

If business was bad, the gods were invoked. Ibn Fadlan reports on the ancient
traditional ways of the Russian merchants, whom he encountered in Bulgar about
921-22:

> As soon as their ships were moored, they came on land. Each man carried
> bread, meat, onions, milk, and *nabid* [probably beer or mead] and walked
> toward a tall wooden prop with a human-like face carved on top. All around it
> there are smaller images, and behind them is another high wooden support
> fastened in the earth. The man casts himself on the ground before the large
> figure and says: "Oh Lord, I have come from afar with such a number of girls
> and such a number of furs.'' He then enumerates all his goods and continues:
> "Here is the gift I bring you,'' and lays down the food he has brought. "I
> entreat you to send me a buyer with many dinars and dirhems who will buy all
> I have to sell and will not contradict my words.''
>
> Then he goes away. If business is slack and time passes, he brings
> further offerings . . . or he may give each of the small images a present and
> begs them to intercede for him, saying: "These are our Lord's wives, sons,
> and daughters.'' Then he prays to each little image, one after the other, to
> intercede for him.
>
> If business goes well for him and his goods are sold, then he says: "The
> Lord has answered my prayers, so I must repay him.''
>
> Then he goes and slaughters some goats or cattle. Part of the meat he
> gives away as alms. The rest he cuts up and scatters among the wooden
> images. The heads of the goats or cows he hangs on the large post which is
> rammed into the ground. At night the dogs come and devour everything. The
> man then says, "Truly, the Lord has accepted my sacrifice.''

Such sacrificial offerings were made not only in Russia, however, but in Hedeby and everywhere in Norse trading country. Sometimes the men would join to give a great sacrificial feast together, and this would usually end in riotous celebrating and great drunkenness. The songs they sang on these occasions evoked the following comment from Ibrahim Al-Tartushi of Cordoba, after hearing them at Hedeby: "I have never heard singing more hideous than that of the men of Slesvig, they give vent to sounds like dogs baying, only even more bestial."

Written in Vermilion on Parchment

But apart from native customs and religious rites, trade was based on certain laws designed to give order to the relationship between buyers and sellers. There were trade treaties, agreements among rulers. The treaty of 811 between Charlemagne and King Godfred of Denmark probably contained some trade clauses; three years before, Godfred had shown his concern with the economy of his country by moving the merchants from Reric to Hedeby. In 873, emissaries of Siegfried of Denmark came to Louis the German to negotiate on the issue that "traders of both countries should be able to cross the frontiers, carrying their goods and be permitted to buy and sell in peace."

Varangians and Byzantines, too, made trade treaties with one another; trading privileges, in fact, were part of the objective whenever the Varangians besieged Constantinople in the early days. The Byzantine Emperor Leon VI and Oleg, the Grand Duke of Kiev, reaffirmed in 911 "the long established friendship between the Christians and the Rus" in two documents "written in vermilion on parchment." The delegates of both met once more for friendly talks in 944. The historic agreement reached after many months—the one that records for history the names of almost a hundred Varangian diplomats—contained references to such legal issues as murder, theft, the plundering of wrecks, and a number of clauses on trade law. The merchants of Kiev, who until then had to carry the Grand Duke's silver seal for identification, could now enter the imperial city by showing written identification—an ancestor, presumably, of our present-day passports. They had to enter through a gate assigned to them, without weapons, and no more than fifty could enter at a time. If they bought silks, they had to pay the maximum official price, and their transaction had to pass muster with an imperial inspector. Under these circumstances and rules, they were assured of the Emperor's protection and favor. "When the Rus leave here," the treaty states, "they will be given provisions for their long journey . . . so that they may return safely to their own country. But they must not stay the winter in the sacred city." They were welcome to do business on Berezany and Bieloberezje, another market town on the Dnieper, only during the summer months. "When autumn comes, they must return to Rus country."

This agreement was a sort of complete trade treaty, drafted by expert lawyers, which had the whole weight of the complicated bureaucracy of the Empire behind it. Similar instruments executed between the Norse countries and their Western European allies were probably not as polished or exhaustive, though we know that Olaf Tryggvason himself put Norway's trade relationship with England on a legal footing by an agreement with King Ethelred. Kings and emperors found themselves with more quick riches if they protected the merchants rather than robbed them or let them be robbed and killed. The merchants paid tribute coming and going—official taxes and who knows what unofficial bribes to imperial inspectors, town officials in charge of "protection" and so on. One royal perquisite in Sweden, namely that the king, by the law of Birka, was "to be permitted to buy newly arrived goods. . . . three days before anyone else" helped to make the king of the Svea clans so rich that they were able to consolidate their power all the sooner. In this way the growth of trade, trade centers, towns, and cities aided the growth of monarchies everywhere, at the expense of the old agrarian and feudal orders.

Growth of the Merchant Guilds

The establishment of imperial agents in charge of collecting dues, protection fees, tariffs, and fringe benefits for the rulers from the merchants brought about the organization of merchants' guilds—a sort of protection against their protectors. The guilds are probably not of Norse origin, for they existed in France by the end of the eighth century, but there is no evidence of their having taken root in Scandinavia until the end of the tenth century. Yet it is the Scandinavian guilds that have preserved the original features of the merchants' protective associations, perhaps because they began as part of ancient cult practices there.

The term *guild* in Frisian and in Old Norse signifies a feast or banquet, and refers specifically to the lavish ritual banquets which were the climax of guild meetings, like those of the blood brotherhoods. Just as it was the brotherhoods' function to supply clan-like protection to the clanless man abroad, so the guilds served as a quasi-family for the trader far away from home, a bond without which many an itinerant merchant might have felt lost in an alien and ever-threatening world. The brotherhoods were democratic, egalitarian, unlike the feudal hierarchical order that prevailed in the military and in the increasingly powerful monarchies at home. Even their nominal heads, like the *Alderman* or elder of the Danish guilds, were only the first among equals; things were done by agreement, not by force of executive power. On the other hand, the brothers or guild members had to be prepared to assist each other in every conceivable way, from taking in and caring for victims of shipwreck to ransoming those of their number taken captive and enslaved. They had to stand guard over another guild brother's house and cattle and goods, even if he had blood on his hands. Paragraph 15 of the Flensburg St. Canute Guild reads as follows:

> If it should happen that a brother kills a man who is not a member of St.
> Canute's Guild, while members of the Guild are present, they must help save
> his life as best they can. If near water, they must help him find a boat with
> oars, bailing vessel, firestone, and an axe. . . . If he needs a horse, the brother
> must see that he gets one, or else he may take his brother's horse as if it were
> his own and use it for a day and a night. If he needs it for longer, he must pay
> for it . . . but not more than six marks. If the horse dies in his service, he must
> pay only if he has the money; if not, his brothers must pay jointly.

The first of these fraternal trade organizations seem to have sprung up in Iceland c. 900. A rune inscription regarding a Frisian and Swedish merchant guild in Sigtuna near Uppsala is dated not much later. The Bartholines of Trondheim had their charter recorded about 1100, and there is evidence of an Olaf's Guild in Reykjavik for 1120. A brotherhood of Gotland merchants even had their own guildhall in Novgorod by this time.

The chances are that trade alliances were established in most northern and western European centers by the year 1000. Their members embarked on voyages together, appeared as firmly established groups in the *vics* or market towns, got on well with officials a matter largely of knowing whom to pay and how much for safe conducts, lenient inspections, etc. By this time merchants tended to be full-time professionals, even though they accepted seasonal part-time traders into their guilds. One such professional, an Anglo-Saxon, is vividly memorialized in a biographical account of around 1100.

He was called Godric of Finchale, the son of poor peasants well acquainted with hunger. Godric began as "an itinerant peddler in the smallest possible way" after salvaging enough flotsam for his first collection of trading goods. When he was ready to stop taking his goods to the buyers as a lone peddler, he set up shop in

London and joined a merchant guild, and spent several year more as an itinerant trader in company with his guild brothers. Then he discovered the sea.

As a merchant seafarer, he sailed to Scotland, Denmark, and Flanders, showing great enterprise and business acumen, and rapidly increasing his capital, until he could afford his own ship and even to become part owner of a second ship and third ship. His luck held, and he became a rich man. With that, he ceased to be a peasant, though he continued as an itinerant trader. Unlike Ottar, who spent his winters at home, Godric continued to trade in winter, having lost interest in country life and possessions. He had become a full-time professional business-man.

Hedeby—Babylon on the Baltic

Norse-Frisian Trade Centers

The rise and growth of northwestern trading points made the transition from the lone itinerant peddler to the professional urban merchant possible. The early beginnings of such trade settlements sprouted in two basic forms—either along a main street which was also the only street in the settlement or as a semicircular affair. The form may have depended on whether the warehouses were planted on a river bank, or on an island with a curving beachfront.

At first the settlements tended to be inland, along a busy river route, on a lagoon, or as in the case of Birka, on an island midstream in one of the wider arms of the sea. Here boats could be dragged into the shallows or on land for unloading. The oldest such landing place was discovered in Uppsala in 1907, and it had clearly been divided "into various properties" on each of which had stood a merchant's house or warehouse. Such warehouses were built well on into the thirteenth century. The goods went from ship straight to storage or shop in the simplest, most economical way.

That landing stages were built, as early as the twelfth century, proves that the boats had grown larger and deeper, so that they could no longer be parked on the gently sloping shore. One such quay dates from 1038 in Sandwich, England. They consisted of earth-filled wooden blocks which were built out into the water like piers, and were called "bridges"—which accounts for the name of "the German Bridge" in Bergen, whose oldest remains date back to the twelfth century. There are traces of such landing piers in Birka, built especially for Frisian cogs which in later Viking times replaced the old Norse cargo boats.

One-street trade marts existed in the early Middle Ages in Burgundy and southern Germany, in Ireland as well as Norway and Russia. They may have been based on Gallo-Roman models, but were so natural a kind of settlement to spring up on a river bank as to require no models. The semi-circular towns are not so easily explained, and it is supposed that politics or religion may have had a hand in determining their structure, not only economic or practical necessity. Hedeby and Birka were royal residences and had fiscal as well as economic functions, for example.

Both types, however, came into prominence as market places, and not because they happened to be the inevitable center of their area. They were stations along important land or water trade routes, designed to fill the needs of itinerant commerce as stopping places, storage places, and commercial meeting points.

Vics *From the Thames to the Elbe*

On the North Sea the most important *vics*, as they were called, were London, Quentovic, Domburg and Dorestad, as well as Emden, Bremen, and Hamburg on what is today the West German coast.

London was a flourishing, lively port as early as c. 700. The Venerable Bede calls it "a mart sought out by many peoples on land and sea," with quarters for Frisian merchants as well as the natives. There are traces of a city wall dating from the second half of the ninth century and an independent, growing population, despite constant harassment from the Vikings.

Of Quentovic we know that it was one of the Franconian kingdom's foremost mints, as well as an important stopping place for pilgrims from England on their way to Rome. When threatened by Viking invaders in 842, it was rich enough to buy itself off, and to continue as a mint and market town. Named as a mint of the first rank in 862, it is all the more surprising that we still do not know where it was situated, though French historians opt for the neighborhood of today's Etaples, on the lower reaches of the Canche river.

Domburg, on the island of Walcheren off the Rhine delta southwest of Rotterdam, began as a one-street settlement, about three-quarters of a mile long, early in the seventh century. Domburg was probably a trading point even in Roman times, for commerce with England, which flourished on into the early Middle Ages. Glass, pottery, metalware, Merovingian gold coins, and over eight hundred English silver coins were found in digs beginning in the nineteenth century near the present-day Domburg.

Dorestad, the Rotterdam of the early Middle Ages, situated on a tributary in the Rhine delta, near present-day Utrecht, was also a typical one-street *vic*, about half a mile long, with neat rows of houses for carpenters and other craftsmen. One half of the town was home to its permanent settlers, the other half served transient merchants, chiefly the Frisian traders, but Hedeby and Birka also sent visitors here. "Goods from all countries were traded or transshipped here. The coins commonly exchanged here were not only the local kind but others from Franconia, Mainz, and elsewhere, such as England, Milan, Pavia, Treviso, even from Constantinople. The two rivers served as trade routes from all possible directions. There was also a permanent harbor where vessels could lie for months, especially through the winter."

The settlement, up to five hundred feet wide, was surrounded by a wooden pale, possibly indicating the area within which merchants were legally under the king's protection and which was guarded by a nearby Carolingian fort. The king's

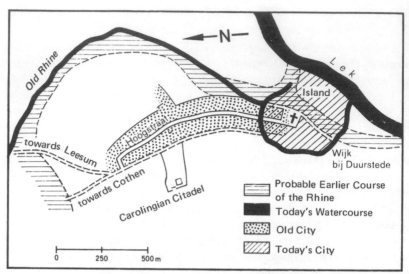

The trading center Dorestad, in Frisia.

protection did not prevent Dorestad from being burnt to the ground by Viking raiders seven times between 834 and 863, whereupon it dwindled to a small, unimportant sailor's settlement, from which today's Vijk near Duurstede inherited its mellifluous name.

Emden, at the mouth of the Ems river, on the Frisian coast near the German-Netherlands border, flourished a century and a half later than Dorestad. It was built expressly as a trading center, called Amüthon, making it the oldest known example of a planned market town in Germany. Emden also started as a single street with neatly serried rows of little wooden houses—perhaps modeled on Dorestad—still clearly discernible as a street in the town plan for 1600.

Today's world harbor city of Bremen was probably also a busy mart at the beginning of the Viking era. It came into being as a ferry and trading station where the Weser shore road cut through a trade route running southwest to northeast, and gained rapidly in importance and stature as a favored site for Church activity. In 787 the Anglo-Saxon Willehad founded the bishopric of Bremen, and in 847, after the Vikings destroyed Hamburg, Ansgar moved the archdiocese Hamburg-Bremen from the Elbe to the Weser. The Bremen Church's missionary activity in Scandinavia went hand in hand with the harbor town's growth as a Norse trading center.

Even more than Bremen, Hamburg was an offspring of the Church. The town's nucleus was the Hammaburg, erected around 825, a sizable fortress on a sandspit between the Elbe and Alster rivers, whose protection attracted civilian settlers, probably of Frisian origins. Their huts stretched as far as the ramparts of the fortress, which was also a place of worship, and worship was good for trade. Here stood Ansgar's first church with its monastery. Hamburg went on growing as a trade center in the second half of the ninth century, after the Bishop's Castle had been destroyed during the Viking attack of 845 and Ansgar had moved to Bremen—in other words, the merchants were tougher than the missionaries. They stayed on to rebuild their booths after the fire, and went on doing good business; by the tenth century, Hamburg's *vic*, its business area, had markedly increased in size, proof of their sound judgment in refusing to give up so suitable a location for the exchange of goods.

The Jomsvikinga Saga *Revised*

On the Baltic, too, trade settlements flourished during the heyday of the European Northwest. Somewhere on the Mecklenburg coast stood Reric, a Slav settlement known only from the Carolingian Annals—it has eluded all other efforts to track it down—as a place destroyed in 808 by King Godfred of Denmark, though it had brought him good tax revenue. Godfred apparently decided he wanted a revenue center closer to home. He founded Hedeby that same year, on the Slesvig, and transferred many of the rights and duties, and apparently also the merchants, from Reric.

Another great "world" trade center of the time may have been Vineta, a Norse Atlantis supposed to have sunk to the bottom of the sea overnight, and still not definitively located. It could have been the mart of Jumne or Jomsborg described by Adam of Bremen:

> . . . the Oder, the most fertile river in Slav territory. Where it flows into the
> Scythian sea, the famed town of Jumne is a most popular meeting point . . .
> really the largest of all towns in Europe, inhabited by Slavs, Greeks,
> barbarians and many other nations, even Saxons who were permitted to settle
> though they may not make open profession of their Christian faith there. . . .
> The town is full of every kind of Norse goods, nothing is missing that anyone
> might desire, nor any rarity. They also have a beacon, called Vulcan's Pan,
> an open flare like the Greek Fire known to Solinus, to light the ships home.
> This town is not far, by rowboat, from the mouth of the Peene . . . from
> whence one can reach Samland, ruled by the Pruzzi [the Prussians]. Jumne

may be reached in seven days from Hamburg, going cross-country along the Elbe; by sea, the points of embarkation for Jumne are Slesvig or Oldenburg.

Other medieval authors, like Saxo Grammaticus, have been interested in this former great city on the Oder. But they see it as primarily a militarettlement. According to them, Harald Bluetooth, driven from his own strongholds by his son Sven Forkbeard, came to Jumne, in Wend country, to build the Jomsburg, a fortress from which he terrorized the entire Baltic with the help of Slavic pirates.

The Jomsburg legend later entered the world of the Icelandic sagas and, in the form of the *Jomsvikinga Saga*, has given rise as late as the twentieth century to a number of romantic misconceptions. According to the sagas Jomsburg was a powerful Nordic military base and Viking colony, with a man-made harbor in which no fewer than three hundred ships could anchor. Behind the thick fortress walls lived a community of warriors sworn to one another, who practiced the strictest discipline, scorned contact with women, were contemptuous of death and loved nothing better than bloody, merciless battle.

But the digs on Wollin Island in the thirties under Otto Kunkel tend to provide a far more sober picture. Jumne, on Wollin, seems to have been a trading center of growing importance from about 900 on, though destroyed many times. Fifteen layers were distinguished in the thirty-five-foot-deep rubble beneath the market place; the final catastrophe, another devastating fire, put an end to the city toward the final years of the twelfth century. By about 1250 a new German settlement adopting the Slavic name Wollin grew up on the site of what had been a city of mixed Norse-Slavic population, with far-reaching connections, much active trade, and many crafts importing foreign raw materials for products also sold in many foreign markets. Planned by men of northern Teutonic descent who at first ruled over the native Slav population and gave the settlement its original character, assimilation took its usual course toward the end.

The modern dreamers of a warlike Norse Jomsburg were greatly disappointed by the archaeologists' findings, which left no room for doubt that there was no warrior fortress, no garrison town at all. Great Jumne, also called Jumneta, from which seems to have come the myth of the sunken treasure-city Vineta in German folklore and poetry, was a great trading center in which Northmen and Slavs lived and did business together and side by side, peacefully.

Where Was King Alfred's Truso?

Another unsolved problem is the city of Truso, which King Alfred's informant Wulfstan claimed to have reached in seven days' sailing from Hedeby. Truso supposedly lay in the Vistula delta near present-day Danzig, in a country governed by Ests, according to Wulfstan a country of many kings and many fortresses. Here the rich and powerful drank mare's milk, the poor drank mead, and it was their custom to let the dead lie uncremated for a month or more while the funeral guests drank and played games—the Ests knew how to chill the body so that it would keep for a long time.

But Wulfstan's topographical information was tantalizingly inexact. Until forty years ago, Truso was assumed to lie on a lagoon on the Baltic. But then the Prussian town of Elblag made a believable claim of being the original Truso. During the thirties digs in Elblag turned up a large Norse burial ground near the railroad station, full of grave goods—clasps, brooches, bangles, swords, lanceheads—dating from the ninth and tenth centuries, i.e., the times of Alfred and Wulfstan.

The Elblag finds indicate that the merchants of Gotland were the forerunners of Norse colonization, followed by Swedes in the later ninth century. Another burial ground, in the Niemen River country in Lithuania, showed traces of Danish Vikings as well as Gotlanders and Swedes, confirming Saxo Grammaticus's report of a Danish stronghold in Samland, dating from about 1000. By this time the Norse invaders had probably been driven from the Courland coast long since.

All in all, too little is known of Norse-Slav trading centers on the Baltic. Lacking town plans, theory rests almost entirely on scattered burial grounds. This is equally true of the Norse marts in ancient Russian sites; the one extensive settlement in Old Ladoga had square plank houses, stone hearths, small stables, square wooden wells—and that is nearly all that has been established about it.

Gotland, the island of buried treasures, did not have a trade center until the end of the Viking era, early in the twelfth century. Until then it was a trade center without a center, though it managed even so to be one of the mainsprings of the east-west exchange of goods for two centuries before and after the millennium. It was "the heart of trade in the Baltic," maintaining connections with Constantinople and Baghdad, the silver center for central Germany and the great goods exchanges of Western Europe. As such, it collected immense riches which in the end made the island into an archaeologist's paradise. For example, over five hundred of the eight hundred treasure finds registered to date by Swedish archaeologists are from Gotland, and still not a year passes without some find of Viking treasure on the island. "There is more gold from the Viking era on Gotland than anywhere else in the North"—jewelry and ornaments in vast quantity. More Viking coins have been found on Gotland than anywhere else in Scandinavia. Of 200,000 coins minted at the time, 100,000 came from Gotland, as well as huge quantities of ready silver. This means that Gotland had to be a treasury for the whole Norse world, in its season. One expert, Bertil Almgren, has calculated that if only one coin out of every 1,000 has been preserved—to be optimistic about it—then the Gotlanders, during their century and a half of flourishing trade, must have collected over 100 million coins. Though the Anglo-Saxon silver coins were called "pennies" each one had a purchasing power of $2-3.00, approximately, so that the total is a quite staggering sum.

Its own production for market was insignificant. The island could provide meat and fish oil, skins and feathers or down. Gotland owed its prosperity chiefly to its favorable position and the flexibility of its inhabitants, who were excellent sailors and shipbuilders as well as farmers. Theirs were the best ships on the Baltic, apparently fast enough to elude both Norse and Slavic pirates. Perhaps they had even worked out a system for avoiding trouble by paying regular tribute—their way to the rich silver mines of central Germany led through Slav territories east of the Elbe.

Nevertheless, no Norse *vic* has yet been proved to exist on Gotland. Probably the island's inhabitants earned the vast quantities of money and valuables, so largely entrusted to the earth, in foreign markets. Gotland did not even have a natural harbor; they must have beached their ships for the winter, probably near their farms.

Not until the twelfth century did the roots of a trade center begin to develop on Gotland, at Visby, on its west coast, looking toward Germany. It was logical that Visby became in time one of the great trade centers of the Hanseatic League.

Helgö Trade from India to Ireland

By 1200 A.D. the fame of Helgö had long faded. This Holy Island on Lake Mälar that had maintained trade relations from the Atlantic islands to the Himalayas during almost the entire first millennium A.D., sank into obscurity before the heyday of the Vikings and was not rediscovered until 1950. By then it was known as Ekerö, a weekend island eighteen miles west of Stockholm. During the construction of a summer house on this vacation island two spiral gold bracelets were uncovered by accident. The archaeologists arrived, and digs began in 1954 under Wilhelm Holmqvist. They are still in progress. "Finds of extraordinary historical significance" were not long in coming. In an area 650 x 1,800 feet, a wholly unknown trading mart with its own industrial quarter was uncovered. In addition to a fortress rampart and two burial grounds, the Swedish excavators on Ekerö found half a dozen farmsteads based on artificial terraces or "dwelling platforms."

There were dug-out houses with sunken floors and ovens, plank houses on level ground, and wooden houses on stone platforms, as well as other hitherto unknown kinds of houses. Some of these farmsteads, continuously inhabited for over five hundred years, contained such a wealth of material that the experts have their work cut out for decades to come.

Swedish archaeologists regard as "absolutely sensational" the fact that these houses of various ages and styles had harbored an equally great variety of metal workshops. Among the carefully sieved waste products were many thousands of mold fragments, even more fragments of crucibles, bellows, bits of gold, silver, bronze, lead, wax and whatever else might be found in metal workshops. Most of the finds dated from the fifth and sixth centuries, a matter of great scientific importance, inasmuch as it does away with the "gap caused by the great migrations" hitherto laboriously "explained" by a number of far-fetched theories, from slave rebellions to outbreaks of grave robberies of epidemic proportions.

In other words, there was no gap. The Ekerö finds prove that the Mälar Lake region was solidly settled centuries before the beginning of the Norse migrations, and that highly skilled craftsmen whose goods were in great demand lived on Helgö.

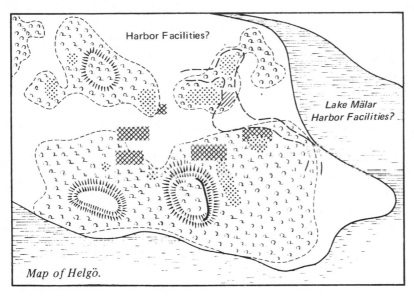

Map of Helgö.

Great excitement was generated when twenty-six couples made of beaten sheet metal were dug up. Such couplings—men and women in intimate embrace—were a Norse specialty, probably made for an unknown fertility rite. This particular batch had been buried for 1,000 years in the rubble of what might have been a special workshop for their production; possibly one of the special products of the island for a market far beyond itself.

Quantities of imports were also found, some of them world famous by now. A bronze ladle, dating from late classic antiquity, of "Coptic" style, indicates an east Mediterranean origin. A Buddha slightly over three inches high, with painted lips and a golden mark on his forehead, was made in northern India sometime during the fifth century. There was also a bishop's crook from Ireland, from the seventh century, and many less spectacular objects such as late Celtic bronzes, Roman dice, east Baltic jewelry, west European pottery, Franconian glass, etc. Silver was found in quantity, mainly in the form of Arab dirhems, gold chiefly in late Roman coins from Milan, Ravenna, Rome and Byzantium.

Since the heyday of Helgö coincides with the era of the powerful, luxury-loving royal dynasties of Vendel and Uppsala, we may assume that the craftsmen and traders of the little lake island did their share in providing the early Svea rulers with the showy finery and glitter they were known for; perhaps even with the wealth they had to spend on their pomp, to begin with, if the clans profited from the Helgö trade directly.

Ekerö finds do not go beyond the eleventh century, but they had begun to thin out during the ninth century, signalizing the rise of Birka.

Birka: Four-Harbor Island

About 845, according to Archbishop Rimbert's Ansgar biography, the Swedish king Anund, driven from his kingdom, fled to the Danes and asked for their aid in regaining his lost power. As bait, he told them of the riches to be gained by such a military expedition.

He described to them the mart of Birka, full of rich tradesmen, vast quantities of every kind of goods and much money and treasure. He promised to lead them to this *vic* himself. They would gain much booty there with very little risk or trouble to themselves. He awakened the Danes' greed for all these riches and the promised presents, and so they manned twenty-one ships in Anund's aid, and set sail with him and the eleven ships he had of his own. So they left Denmark together and appeared unexpectedly at Birka, whose king happened to be abroad.

In the end the inhabitants of Birka succeeded in buying off the Danes with a load of silver, which they managed to collect overnight with ease, leaving the Danes with the extremely irritating suspicion that every single trader on Birka was possessed of more riches than the total of what they'd received. Certainly the archaeologists, who have been kept at work on Birka for the last century, have been able to confirm the island town's astounding wealth. Apparently Birka was,

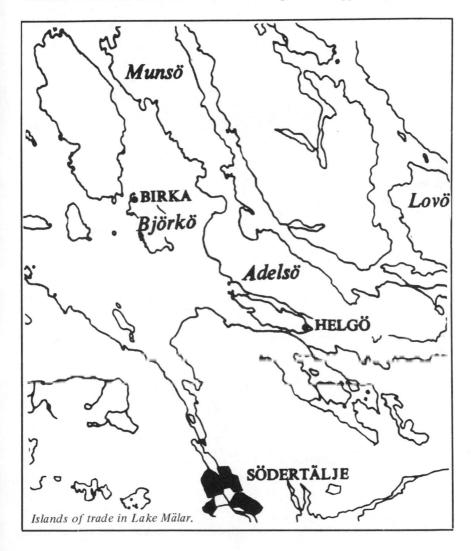

Islands of trade in Lake Mälar.

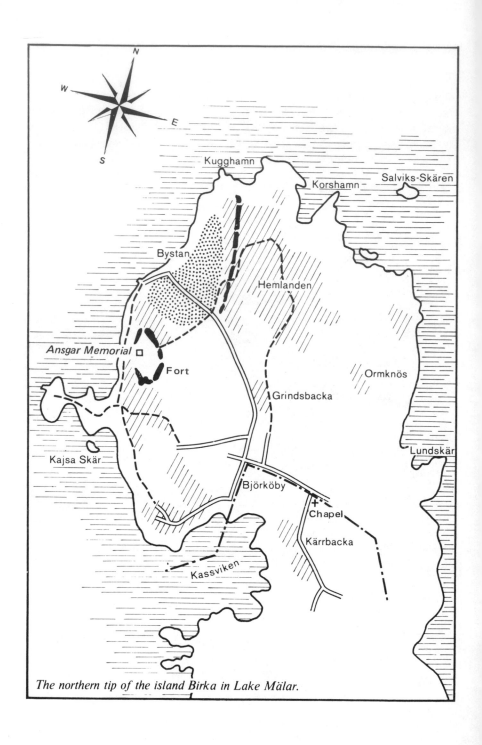

The northern tip of the island Birka in Lake Mälar.

next to Hedeby, one of the busiest Viking trading marts, a *vic* of continental scope, bigger, richer, and more of a world center than medieval Stockholm.

Birka was rediscovered in 1687 by the Swedish State Curator of Antiquities Hardorph. It was situated on the northwestern promontory of the lake island Bjorkö, somewhat hidden away like Helgö, which was only four miles to the southeast (indeed Birka may have been an offshoot of Helgö starting around 800), but in the middle of a huge lake whose many watercourses linked all the important settlements of central Sweden.

Digs on the actual site, which is today a peaceful meadow land, have yielded only a sketchy outline of the ancient *vic*. It was dominated by a fort on a high rocky plateau to the south, dropping ninety-seven feet to the water. The fort rampart and the settlement's stone wall can still be seen from afar. The semi-circular fort had wooden turrets facing in a northeasterly direction. It seems to have been built early in the tenth century, modeled on Slavic fortifications.

The formerly inhabited area is characterized by a darker soil than that of its surroundings. This "black earth" of Birka encompasses twelve hectares, about

View of Björkö, the Viking trade island Birka in Lake Mälar, with its preserved semicircular rampart.

thirty acres of land, fed over the centuries with coal and ashes and every kind of decayed organic remains, a rich humus that has not yet yielded up all its secrets. The trading settlement itself, with its block and wattle-and-daub houses, faced a flat sandy beach running down into shallows suitable for landing.

A few oak posts still stand in this so-called inner port, remnants of landing stages perhaps, or else of a wooden palisade. Birka had three other ports, surmised on the strength of their names to be a port frequented especially by Frisian craft, at the north end; another specializing in grain deliveries; and an artificial, square Anchoring place, a wet dock where goods could be traded directly, without previous warehousing, as in a market place.

Most of what we know about life in Birka we owe to the over 3,000 graves, round, square, triangular, and boat-shaped, of which Hjalmar Stolpe, ethnographer and archaeologist, examined 1,100 in the nineteenth century, enough to fill a museum with grave goods. The others have yet to be excavated, along with the black earth waiting to be explored. But even the fraction available so far is rich enough in remains of Arab silver, Byzantine silks and brocades, Rhenish glass, Frisian cloth, Franconian weapons, precious furs and jeweled stirrups, dice and gaming stones, even Rhine wine, gold, earrings, necklaces, clasps, Chinese silk and bronze ornaments of Anglo-Irish origin, to cast considerable light on the luxury trade and life of this world center. Wherever there is such lively traffic in luxury goods, great craftsmen, foreign and native, are likely to congregate and contribute their share to the enhancement of the valuable raw materials flowing into port. There is evidence for workshops specializing in the manufacture of jeweled or beaded ornaments. Beads of carnelian and rock crystal, as yet unpierced, were also discovered. Half-finished spinning wheels and whetstones of slate, sandstone, and quartz, indicate that much stone work was done here as well.

But Birka also seems to have satisfied the everyday needs of most important Swedish provinces, to judge by the immense number of iron objects found such as knives, scissors, padlocks, files, bridle-rings, nails, and arrow heads. Similar objects have been found scattered throughout central Sweden. It was not only a mobile trade and production center, but also far advanced toward urban status. By comparison Helgö's topography retains a rural character, despite its profusion of metal workshops. Birka was a palisaded garrison town with a fortress, several ports, an institutionalized bureaucracy, communal self-government—it was well on the way to being a city.

How could such a lively, going concern come to an end after only two centuries? The answer is still largely a matter of conjecture. The channel near

Södertälje seems to have dried up; Oriental trade was badly hit by the fall of the Samanid state in Persia, invaded by Turks in the tenth century. Possibly the Swedish royal house was unable to continue to protect its merchants abroad, or the power struggles within Sweden led to catastrophe for Birka as well. We know that no German or Anglo-Saxon coins dating beyond 980 were found on the Birka site. Her successor, Sigtuna, near Uppsala, minted its own coinage. Perhaps Birka's merchants moved on, or were moved, to Sigtuna, although Birka did not cease to be inhabited for a while yet, as a runestone of the eleventh century, decorated with a cross, indicates; and its fame continued into the late eleventh century. Adam of Bremen wrote of Birka "situated in the heart of Sweden, opposite the Slav town Jumne" that it was a *vic* receiving many ships in its harbor of Danish, Norwegian, Slavic, and other Scythian peoples who came there to fulfill their many trade needs. But he also records the rapid decline of the town in his Church chronicle, when he tells the story of Bishop Adelward of Sigtuna arriving at Birka in 1060 to visit the grave of Archbishop Unni of Hamburg-Bremen, who died there in 936. Bishop Adelward found on arrival a wasteland with devastation on every side, and nowhere a trace of Unni's grave.

Rhenish glass vases and funnel glasses from the Birka graves, evidence of the active trade between Northern Europe and Franconia.

Oslo Began with Skiringssal

Helgö, Birka, and Sigtuna count as the ancestors of Stockholm. The history of Oslo begins with Skiringssal, the port and trading town where Ottar of Halogaland stopped on his voyages to Hedeby.

Skiringssal is the only known *vic* of Viking Norway. It was rediscovered only twenty years ago, near Kaupang in Vestfold, as a five-acre area of black earth in a dried up bogged-down bay, an area whose appearance of wooded meadowland did nothing at first to encourage the image of a Norse seaport. But then it was found that the water level had been seven feet higher originally, and gradually the picture of a small natural port behind a protective shield of islands, promontories, and cliffs took shape. Here the merchant seafarer could moor his boat ashore, as an open stall from which to sell his goods directly.

It was a well-built port; a thousand-year-old jetty on pillars secured with stones has been traced, off the black earth potato field where the digs began. It turned out to be the site of "an open, unfortified trading town, a smaller version of the one-street *vic* of the Dorestad type. The remains found consist chiefly of what is left of simple wooden houses and a mass of rubble containing fragments of silver and bronze objects, scrap iron, and bits of slag, attesting to the presence of metal workshops. Imports pointed predominantly to Western Europe. The frequent finds of large Rhenish pottery jugs suggest that wine was a major import. Grave goods were chiefly Anglo-Saxon, Scottish, and Irish. Many of the brooches and ornamental discs found seem to have been Church loot originally, brought to Skiringssal to be "secularized," presumably by Norwegian pirates after raids on the British Isles.

Compared with Birka, Skiringssal was only a little rural market place, small potatoes as it were, a meeting place for peasants engaged in barter, as the noticeable absence of coins suggests. The *vic* lasted only about a hundred years, just long enough for Ottar to have passed through, but not beyond 900. Perhaps it could not compete successfully with the little trading port that was to become Oslo—mentioned for the first time c. 1050—or with the rising star of Hedeby which, with Birka, became the greatest Norse trading center in the tenth century.

The End of Hedeby

The great market town on the Schlei river lay like a spider in the center of the web of marketplaces where Frisian, Anglo-Saxon, and Norse seafarers had their rendezvous.

The chronicler who mentions it for the first time, in 804, in the Carolingian annals, refers to it as a small settlement on the Danish-Saxon border. Four years later, after the destruction of Reric, King Godfred built the great Danework rampart just south of it, to give notice that henceforth Hedeby was exclusively his to tax. The next mention of it occurs in Rimbert's biography of Ansgar: King Horik of Denmark permitted the great missionary to build a church in Hedeby in 849, part of a move to improve relations with the traditional Franconian enemy, with permission to his Danish subjects to choose baptism. Merchants south of the border, i.e., from Bremen, Hamburg, Dorestad et al. could come to Slesvig without fear. "This in its turn caused an abundance of goods and stores to pile up there." In other words, conversion was good for business.

Three decades later King Alfred described the various routes to the now teeming commercial center in some detail, though the town itself did not interest him. In his translation of Orosius's *History of the World* we learn that Hedeby was clearly Danish. But around 900 Swedish kings ruled on the Schlei, an interlude not mentioned in contemporary sources, but confirmed by Adam of Bremen, and by two runestones found near Slesvig, now in the local Museum for Pre- and Early History. They name Queen Asfrid, Odinkar's daughter, who had these stones set up for "King Sigtrygg, her son and Knuba's."

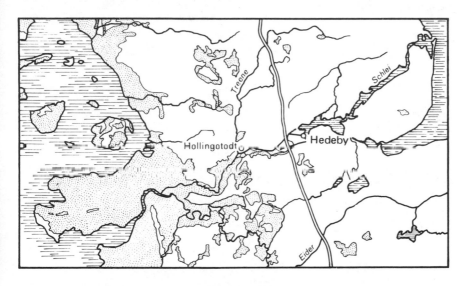

The Hollingstedt-Hedeby isthmus.

This Knuba is also mentioned in the monk Widukind's late tenth-century *History of Saxony*: In 934 Henry I, the first German king of Saxon blood, crossed the border with a large army, conquered Hedeby, and forced Knuba, who had threatened the Frisian coast, to accept baptism and pay tribute to the conqueror—the usual form of submission for the time. Hedeby remained Swedish, however, though under German suzerainty, as a protectorate. In 974 it was finally incorporated into the German Emperor's realm, but only nine years later Sven Forkbeard won it back for the Danes, and set up the Busdorf runestone as a memorial for his vassal Skartha, killed at Hedeby, confirming the date of his conquest.

This reconquest of Hedeby in 983 marks a final turning point in the town's history. Was it Swedes or Slavs who contested the ownership of Hedeby with the Danes (who were rather preoccupied by their struggles with England at the time)? We know that around 1000 Bishop Ekkehard of Slesvig lamented that his bishopric had been laid waste, his town abandoned, his church deserted—and he must be referring to Hedeby.

The tenth century saw the dramatic end of Hedeby. An army led by Harald Haardraade of Norway attacked the trade center on the Schlei and burned it to the ground. An unknown Norwegian bard who saw Hedeby's houses go up in flames described it in moving verses:

> From one end to the other
> Hedeby was burnt down. Fearful
> Fury of strife. Splendid
> Seems the great action, I think;
> Chagrin to the wicked Swede.
> Before twilight I set foot
> On the ramparts to see
> Flames leaping high from roofs.

Whatever was left was destroyed by the Slavs in 1066, the year William left Normandy for England, as reported by Adam.

The Vic *of Many Peoples*

The isthmus between Eider and Schlei, separating the North from the Baltic Sea, was discovered by Franconian and Frisian traders as early as the first third of the eighth century, on evidence found in early medieval graves. Such west-east traffic was bound to create a little settlement at its terminus, of mariners, carters, and bearers assisting in the transport of imported goods. The earliest graves of Hedeby are in fact dated toward the end of the eighth century.

When trading was moved from Reric to Hedeby by Godfred, growth was powerfully stimulated, and the Hedeby graves testify to population growth, mostly Danish-Norwegian, specifically in the town itself, in the first few decades of the ninth century. The newcomers tended to bring their wives, and the settlement flourished. Toward the end of the century its rural surroundings also filled out, mostly with Swedish immigrants who started to cultivate the soil intensively. A third wave of immigrants, this time from Jutland, reached Hedeby and its surroundings after 950, when Hedeby had become an international center second to none in Europe. The social structure of this cosmopolis included a good proportion of solid middle class for its time, in addition to the usual proportion of rich to poor.

The best-equipped graves, probably of Swedish chieftains whose grave goods contained a large proportion of weapons clearly tenth-century in style, point to that century as the highpoint of Hedeby's career, when it must have had 800-1,000 permanent residents on its sixty acres of territory, not counting the dead who also occupied their share of ground, in the "constantly used, crowded cemetery" which was also inside the semi-circular rampart. That rampart, according to Kurt Schietzel, Curator of the Viking section at the Schleswig-Holstein museum, "was built at least a century after the settlement was established." Generations must have worked on it. A section through the north gate revealed no fewer than nine periods of building.

The rampart, eight feet high, begun as a line of demarcation for the market area, consisted of sod-covered earth dressed halfway up with logs. In time it moved forward, with each building addition, until it reached the shallow, trough-like moat around it. Owing to its favorable position, the settlement behind this wall grew steadily as a port and trading center. Gently sloping banks led down to the Noor where two flat sandspits provided a natural landing place. The stream provided a good supply of fresh water and the very sandy soil was suitable for building barracks or tents.

The houses were expertly constructed, but without a trace of provision for hygiene or comfort. They varied in size, especially in the rich merchants' quarter directly on the bay. The largest was about seven by eighteen yards, the area of a medium-sized farmstead, while in the New Town to the west a temporary sort of

Excavation site in the "city" of Hedeby. The wooden remains

...rduroy road leading to the bog, as well as houses and huts.

What part of Hedeby may once have looked like:an ima,
pages. In the backgr

...truction based on the excavation cite pictured on the preceding
...rt secured by palisades.

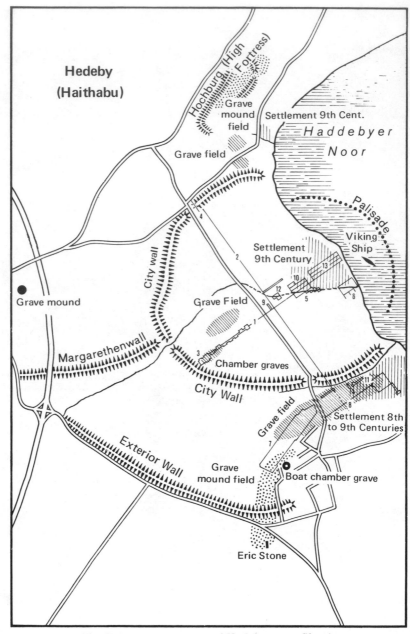

The Viking trade center of Hedeby, near Slesvig.

house about three by four yards predominated. These, like the Franconian houses of Neuwied on the Rhine, built five hundred years earlier, were sunk nearly twenty inches into the ground. They all had the central open hearth and the hole in the roof for letting out the smoke. Windows were unknown, even to the rich. The low narrow doors opened into a small fenced-in yard. The street was a four-foot-wide log road intersecting the stream. Remains of a bridge were found, as well as traces of other wooden and stone paths connecting the houses with the street. There was usually room for barns and stables beside the houses. There were wooden well shafts about thirty-two inches wide.

Schietzel, who completed an eight-year dig in 1970, has found indications that Hedeby was built according to a master plan, possibly one for which King Godfred himself was responsible. To judge by the number of mooring poles in the shallow water, whole flotillas of small cargo boats must have stopped at Hedeby to unload their goods during the season. Many craftsmen must have been at work in the town; casting in bronze was highly developed, and many kinds of ornaments made out of imported raw materials, such as the tortoise-shaped brooches of bronze, clover-shaped clasps, fine pewter ornaments, and filigree work show the influence of southern Europe after 900. One famous mold found here is the matrix of a valuable gold brooch discovered in an East Gotland treasure; another was the source of many small ornamental discs found throughout the Baltic territory.

One of the most significant finds on record at Hedeby is the glass kiln dug up in 1913. Although it was probably only used for the production of glass beads, it signalizes the return of the mysterious craft of glass making "from the woods to the towns" long before it became clearly traceable in the twelfth century.

Many other crafts were pursued at Hedeby. Bone and antlers were made into combs, pins, knife handles, dice and gaming stones. Beads and pendants were made from the amber brought in from the Baltic lands. Many finds of loom weights and hand spindles indicate a lively activity in the making of textiles, and pottery was probably produced for export, according to the historian Herbert Jankuhn. The so-called Hedeby pot appears so often among the debris that it would suffice by itself to prove the existence of a pottery manufacture and trade here.

The Town on the Heath

Hedeby was a settlement built on royal command; a *vic* under military protection, and sometime royal residence; a point of intersection for political and economic interests; a mart, a mission station, a crafts center with highly specialized workshops; a port with breakwater, mooring facilities, trading facilities to serve all Europe—a town with many faces. It had to be an enterprising, active, busy, lively place, prosperous, noisy, international: a little Babylon on the Baltic.

Of all the Norse marts, it came closest to being a world city, surpassing its nearest competitors, Dorestad and Birka. But it never became a full-fledged city. As the name Hedeby indicates, it remained a "settlement on the heath," rootless, not an outgrowth of the surrounding region but only of far-flung mercantile interests that came to their annual climax at market time. Official structures are only vaguely distinguishable from among the uniformly modest buildings, all in the tradition of Germanic wooden houses, with firm plank walls and shingle roofs. Nowhere was there an attempt to create some distinctive "town architecture." Although Hedeby reached the respectable age of 250 years, it never quite cast off its gypsy soul, as an offspring of Frisian Viking itinerant trade, the transient camping place of people who disliked town life.

Beginning as depots, stopping places, marts, the Norse *vics* laid the foundations for medieval towns, but only as signposts on the way. Most of them remained aerial plants, touching base lightly, decaying after a brief efflorescence, or shrinking to a minimal existence. It was as though no families raised children here who became attached to the place, took pride in it, and needed it to last.

When Hedeby was destroyed in 1066 it was abandoned by the survivors, to be reclaimed by the heath, while on the other side of the Schlei a new town arose and took over Hedeby's Franconian name, Sliasvic. In Danish this became Slesvig; the Saxons called the new settlement by the name it still retains, Schleswig.

Viking Trade Goods

Stone, Pots, Rhenish Glass

The Viking dragon ships and the Frisian cogs were not built for bulk cargo. We know that Norway supplied England with dried fish in bulk, Ireland imported live cattle, and Greenland cereals, but the great mariner-merchants usually dealt in luxury goods from distant places, things that did not weigh down those graceful sea birds out of proportion to their value.

But there were exceptions. As in Roman times, the basalt bogs on Mayen on the Eifel in West Germany supplied the North with millstones, usually ready made but also half-finished. Digs at Hedeby brought to light such half-finished stones from Mayen. Hedeby seems to have been the center of the Norse stone trade. Rhenish Franconia also supplied pottery—thrown pots from the workshops in the Cologne foothills, Badorf pottery with its characteristic patterns of imprinted rectangles, Rhenish bas-relief amphoras and shiny black jugs with a thin layer of tinfoil. The more recent Pingsdorf pottery reached the Scandinavian countries chiefly in the form of those two-handled pots of yellowish clay with a pattern of irregular brown stripes and spots. Hedeby seems also to have been the terminus for Rhenish pottery, according to historian Herbert Jankuhn.

The glass trade extended far beyond Jutland, however. Swedish museums hold many examples of cone-shaped glass cups of Franconian make, dug up at Birka, as well as glass mirrors, glass gaming stones, even bits of window glass found at Birka and Helgö. One beautiful undamaged cone glass was found at Hedeby, but little glass otherwise; experts surmise that Hedeby had its own glass factory which melted down the broken glass, and sent its products to other markets.

Franconian jewelry was in great demand in northern Europe, especially the West Franconian, which introduced the antique acanthus motif of the Carolingian renaissance to the Viking world. There was also much Anglo-Saxon and Irish metalwork, chiefly church ornaments, probably stolen.

Weapons were another staple of Norse trade, beginning with the quantities of Rhenish sword blades already mentioned, which were smuggled northward after Charlemagne forbade their sale to his Viking attackers. These were half-finished goods, so we frequently find swords with a Frankish blade and a Norse handle. The best of these blades, which owed their quality to the process of damascening (clearly of Arab origin) and the excellent steel, as good as our high quality steel today, were made by a certain Ulfberth, the Stradivarius of the early medieval sword, whose workshop was probably in Cologne. Blades hallmarked with Ulfberth's name were found in England and Ireland, East Prussia and in Finnish-

Baltic Territory, even on the lower reaches of the Dnieper. We even have Arab testimony, from Ibn Fadlan, that Rus traders wore broad flat swords of Franconian make. Jankuhn believes that Ulfberth's blades were traded via Hedeby, even though only one such has been found there.

Rhine wine and Burgundian and Mediterranean vintages as well traveled northward via Dorestad and Hedeby, not for the benefit of Viking swordsmen and merchants alone, but for monks and missionaries as well. The many Frisian wine jugs dug up in Birka, that Swedish mission center, as well as the story of the widow Friedeburg, prove wine to have been a common article of consumption on the island in Lake Mälar.

Another witness strikes a wonderfully modern note on the subject. The monk Ermoldus Nigellus, living in Alsace, in 830 addressed an elegy of King Pippin of Aquitaine, in which he lamented the fact that wine is "sold dear to the seaman," while the vintner goes thirsty "in the very midst of his own vines." He was apparently relaying a local complaint to the king in a tactful fashion, by making it part of a dialogue in his poem. He even includes an answer to the complaint, which he puts in the mouth of "Father Rhine"—so abundant was the Alsatian grape harvest, replied Father Rhine, that the natives would long since have drowned in their own wine if they did not have to ship out so much of it to the Frisians.

Frisian Cloth for Wine

The same poem goes on to point out another connection: the fact that it was mostly for Frisian cloth that the Alsatian wine growers exchanged their product.

Frisian cloth was a highly prized article of trade; a best seller, in the popular term of our own era. Charlemagne sent his Arab friend, the Caliph Harun al-Rashid of Baghdad (and the *Arabian Nights*) Frisian coats in white, gray, red, and blue. Louis the Pious gave his court officials presents made of Frisian cloth several times a year, and when the Holy Father visited him in Rheims, in 816-17, the King made him a gift of woollen coats made in Franconia. The great Fulda monastery imported 835 coats a year from Frisia, Frisian woollens were bought by the monks of Essen-Werden, and Frisian goathair blankets were institutional necessities in many such places. There was a regular currency based on Frisian cloth, called a *Fries*, itself legal tender in Western Europe under the name of a "woollen robe" and in Northern Europe, a "cloth measure." In Sweden, twelve ells of Fries equalled a silver öre, ninety-six ells a silver mark.

The importance of the Frisian cloth trade is substantiated by the findings of archaeologists along the North Sea coasts, where the *wurts*—dwelling mounds or tumuli—have yielded up a profusion of spindles, fly wheels, weaver's beams and weights. Near Wilhelmshaven a seventh-century warehouse-dock was unearthed, with many remains of solid cloth in a large assortment of patterns, which makes Frisia a likely, well-developed center of high-grade woollen manufacture in Merovingian times.

Cloth is perishable stuff, so that the number of finds casting light on its importance as an article of consumption and trade in early times must be considered a special run of luck. Such lucky finds have been made in Birka, where beside the coarsely woven native cloth many bits of fine worsted of presumably Frisian origin turned up, as they did at Skiringssal, in East Gotland, and the famous Oseberg grave, and in one woman's grave of Hedeby.

In addition to the strong, warm, comfortable woollens, there were also luxury textiles such as linen, considered three times as valuable as wool. Theodulf of Orléans, a member of Charlemagne's Council at Aachen, reported that rich Franconians made gifts of linen to judges, as an antidote to the law's delays. Cloth shot through with gold thread, even more valuable than linen, was originally an oriental fashion that excited the covetous admiration of the Franconian lords, and in due course came to be prized by the luxury-loving Vikings as well. Louis the Pious presented the Danish King Harald with such Franconian gold cloth at the Dane's Ingelheim baptism in 826. And the Icelandic landowner Gunnar of Haldenende brought back from Hedeby "a prince's garment, gold-embroidered gloves, and a headband with gold knots" in the tenth century. Gold thread was found in Hedeby as well as Birka.

No fewer than forty-five Birka graves turned up bits of silk. Frisian traders participated in the silk trade only as middlemen, however, for products made in southern France and offered on European markets from the beginning of the ninth century. Most silk stuffs reached the European North by way of eastern caravan routes via Bulgar and Constantinople.

The Silver Age of the North

Not only silk came from the East but also ornaments and jewelry, toiletries and trinkets, and of these not only the best of their kind but a large assortment of trash made by the Arabs especially for the Northern barbarians—the equivalent of our modern-day tourist trinkets and souvenirs. Among these goods, as found in Birka graves among others, were leather belts with Sassanid decorations, Tartar bags, animal masks from Mongolia, Arab harness, Egyptian glass beads, Coptic vessels, Persian bronze flasks, Syrian silver dishes, Chazar pendants—all

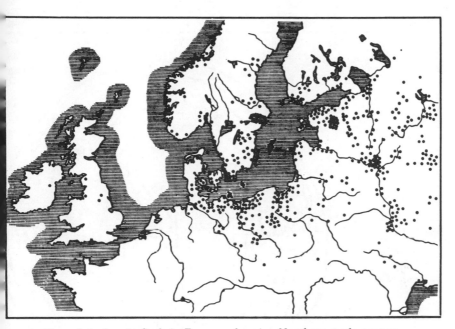

Map of Arab coin finds in Europe, showing Northern trade centers.

products of an inventive gift industry adapted to the vulgar tastes of the Viking nouveau riche.

The most important merchandise that reached Scandinavia via Russia from the Arab lands, however, was silver. Eric Oxenstierna calls the Viking Age, beginning about 900, the Silver Age of the North—its Golden Age having come to an end about 600. Sweden, for one, completely succumbed to the lure of silver. The raw material mostly came from the Caliph's eastern silver mines of Samarkand, Tashkent, and Afghanistan, which flourished between 913 and 943 under the reigning Samanid ruler Nasr ibn Ahmad, who exploited them without regard for his heirs.

According to Ibn Jaqub, the silver was mined ''on a mountain top that looked like a sieve from the Number of mineshafts with which it was pitted . . . here a single miner might make a profit of 300,000 dirhems.''

Prices were high, as is usual in profitable mining areas that have to import consumer goods; even a bunch of vegetables was worth its weight in silver, i.e., one dirhem, the three-gram coin introduced c. 700. The luck of mining camps being what it always is, capricious and highly selective, many a hopeful silver

Two Hedeby Half-Brakteats. The oldest coin

miner ended up poorer than he began. There was also the usual reign of violence, anger and malice, with murder a daily commonplace of life—the Klondike syndrome, "complete with ruffians, adventurers, prospectors and failures," as Oxenstierna remarks.

Viking Currency

Silver reached Scandinavia in pieces, ingots, finished jewelry, but chiefly in coins of various currencies.

After the reform of Franconian coinage under Pippin the Short and

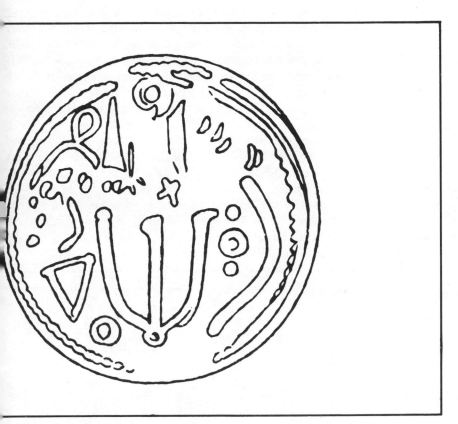

ern Europe (middle of the 10th century).

Charlemagne, the Domburg and Dorestad mints turned out the hard currency for the Frisian North Sea Trade. Scandinavia and the southern Baltic still used silver ingots around 800, as did Hedeby in its early years. A merchant who had concluded a deal commonly reached, not for his moneybag, but for a silver ingot in his pocket, and trimmed off the value of the goods from it, reckoned by weight. A mark, weighing 204 grams, corresponded to the value of eight öre or twenty-four ertogs. In addition to silver ingots there were also spirals, bangles, and cut jewelry, the so-called hacksilver; as such, the daintiest little works of the jeweler's art were brutally cut up for the mere value of their weight.

The first Carolingian coins came north at the beginning of the ninth century, beginning as a trickle. The coinage reached its height in the time of Ansgar, but its northward flow was arrested when the Frisian *vics* on the North Sea were destroyed. Instead, an endless stream of Arabic dirhems, beginning about 800, found its way by the eastern trade routes to the European Northwest, where they remained the Viking currency for 150 years. Hedeby is a curious exception, which speaks for its independence; when the West European coinage ceased to flow northward, the little *vic* on the Schlei took to minting its own coin, after the Carolingian model.

The first coins made in Hedeby were imitations of Dorestad coins, inscribed C A R O L U S. But they remain numismatic rarities to this day, since not many were turned out and on the whole, the use of silver by weight probably still predominated. Then for a while, the dirhem was current in Hedeby, until in 940 it became a fully independent and self-providing mint. So began the age of the "half-bracteate," the one-sided silver coins which quickly supplanted Arab money in Slesvig and Denmark and finally throughout the Baltic region, especially in the Oder area around Jumne-Wollin.

Coins which were probably minted in Hedeby. First three: Dorestad coins. Second four: Coins with Frisian cogs. Last three: Coins with Viking warships.

These were "silent" coins, undated, with no indication of origin or authority—unless their decorations are actually as yet undeciphered hieroglyphics—but they appeared in such numbers around Hedeby that this is where they must have originated. Payment in silver by weight, judging by the disappearance of hacksilver in grave goods, etc., went out of practice around 950. Buried treasure of that period consists entirely of minted hard currency. Since the source of the raw material for these one-sided coins is unknown, Jankuhn proposes a theory that Arab silver coins and raw silver was melted down and reminted Hedeby style, for the benefit of the authorities who could then collect a tax, the brassage, on the coinage changing hands.

The practice of minting coins happens to have come during the period of German dominance in Hedeby, but the absence of Saxon coinage eliminates the Ottonian emperors as those responsible for commissioning the work. Who did order that coinage is still a question. Between 980 and 990 the Hedeby mint closed down; nor does it appear in the list of royal mints installed under Sven Forkbeard, even though Hedeby was Danish again after 983-84. The wave of Anglo-Saxon coins that swept all Denmark passed Hedeby over, as did the flood of German silverlings from the Harz region around the millennium. So far, only one Saxon penny has been found within the Hedeby semi-circle.

Birka, too, tried its hand at minting money. Her ninth-century graves contain many imitations of Anglo-Saxon silverlings known since the seventh century. Among the Birka imitations the most frequent is the Wotan type, a coin whose obverse shows the head of a bearded man, modeled on a coin a century old by that time. But they constituted an even briefer intermezzo than the Hedeby coinage. German coinage and Anglo-Saxon took over until, in the day of the Hanseatic League, they dominated the market entirely.

The value of money in terms of goods has been looked into, with meager results so far, but Herbert Jankuhn has established that around 1000 a man could buy a pregnant cow for fifteen silver öre. A strong slave could be bought for about eleven öre, an average slave, female, for about eight öre. Since we know from Rimbert that he bought a female slave's freedom for a horse, the value of the horse may be estimated at about two to three hundred grams of silver. Tangential clues at best—the law of supply and demand caused prices to fluctuate then as now, as dependent on time, place, the weather, as always.

Furs—"Venom of Ostentation"

In what coin did the Vikings basically pay for their jewelry from the East, their wine from the South, their Frisian cloth, Rhenish glass and swords, their Arab silver and the rest?

Skins and furs must certainly have been the most important Norse asset. Scandinavian pelts, on the continental market since Roman times, highly esteemed and well paid for even in the warm Mediterranean countries, did not fall in value with the fall of the Roman Empire. The sixth-century history of the Goths by Jordanes refers to the valuable Swedish furs that came to Rome by way of trade among many and various peoples. Five centuries later Master Adam of Bremen credits the Prussians and Samlanders with possession of "vast stores of exotic furs, the fragrance whereof has brought the venom of ostentation into the world" and notes that there are people who "lust after a mink cloak as though it were Bliss Eternal!" (The little French saying seems appropriate: the more things change, the more they remain the same.)

Sweden was the leading source of furs, but a large percentage also came from the polar regions of Norway. Up in the Far North was so much game, wrote Adam, that the whole country could live on the beasts of the forests, the bison, buffalo, elks, white mink and polar bears. (Adam marveled most at the polar bears, who reportedly thrived like young dolphins in the icy waters of the polar seas.)

Archaeologists have found many hunters' graves on the well-traveled routes between the polar hunting grounds and the Birch Island in Lake Mälar (not to be confused with Birch Island on the Dnieper). These graves contained arrowheads and spears, hatchets and hunting knives and whatever else a trapper up North might need by way of equipment.

Little trace of the fur hunters' perishable wares has been found in graves anywhere, but at Birka, a noted fur-trading center according to written sources, a great many skates were found, made in those days not of iron but of pigs' trotters and the hooves of horses and cows. "Flattened somewhat, with two holes for laces," according to Oxenstierna, these skates enabled a man to race along the express highways of lakes and rivers in late winter." The annual fur fairs always took place after the end of the winter hunting season, including the one on Gotland which supplied central Germany, so the itinerant traders could stock up in time for their annual spring voyages.

In Russia the Perm area was the great hunting ground, and Bulgar was the hunters' and trappers' most important market, since it was one of the great fur trading centers in the world at the time. The Arab travelers in particular have left behind many zestful descriptions of it at the height of its season. Al-Masudi described many ships bringing their cargo of black fox furs, and whoever had enough dirhems could buy all the sables, miniver, ermine, marten, beaver, and varicolored rabbit he desired. The leaders of expeditions, barbarians to the Arabs, paraded their fur hats and flowing fur cloaks for good measure. The scene was probably similar to that at Hedeby, which was the most important fur mart in its own area according both to Adam and to Ottar before him.

Soapstone, Iron, and Sea Produce

Norwegian soapstone goods have left clearer traces for archaeologists than the furs. Soapstone was an easily carved, malleable but fireproof mineral, quarried chiefly in the Oslo Fjord, and popular as material for cooking pots, bowls, and dishes distributed in Norway, Jutland, Skiringssal, Hedeby, and Birka. North of central Sweden, however, iron and ironware probably took over. Sweden was called the land of iron even in Viking times, and iron goods were probably a staple of the Viking trade.

Produce of various kinds from the sea was another important mainstay of trade: dried, smoked, and salted herring, sent chiefly to England; sealskins, seal oil, and seal meat; whale meat; and walrus tusks. These latter were sold on continental markets by self-styled miracle healers as wonder-working relics of the mythical unicorn, and brought enormous sums. One walrus tusk made history when Ottar presented it to King Alfred the Great. Ottar also sold wild bird eggs, feathers, and tallow, from the bird colonies of the rocky northern coastline. Live birds were traded by the sea merchants from Iceland and Greenland, including the best hunting hawks known to the Middle Ages, especially the white, black-spotted Greenland falcon, the king of all birds of prey.

But more important than any of these goods, highly valued as they were, was a special kind of live merchandise. The Vikings were the leading slave traders of their time.

The Bishop Buys a Nun

The right to own slaves was not questioned anywhere in the year 1000, not even by the Church, though Christians stood under its protection, so that the chief source of the slave trade were the heathen peoples of the East European flatlands. The Caliph of Cordoba's bodyguards in the tenth century were composed of Slavic chattels. The term slave, in fact, was derived from Slav, precisely because the terms were synonymous in western Europe after the expansion of the Germanic tribes brought about the enslavement of so many eastern Europeans.

The acquisition of slaves was one of the monopolies of the Rus-Varangian traders, who organized manhunts to collect them. The Slavs themselves pursued the Muslims along the Black Sea coast and the shores of the Near East, and sold them in Greece and Constantinople. The Italian slave trade drew on North Africa, even as Muslim manhunters menaced the freedom of the Mediterranean sea coasts' Christian inhabitants, and the Vikings enslaved Christian prisoners they brought back from their raids on Western Europe.

These slave goods were taken to market over a vast network of routes: via the Volga and Don rivers and Caspian Sea to the Caliphate, via the Dnieper to Constantinople and the Near East, cross-country from Kiev to Cracow, through Central and Western Europe to Spain. Or else they'd be taken along the "wet route," via the Baltic and North Sea, then southward along the Atlantic coast. The most important slave marts of Central Europe were Prague, Regensburg, and Magdeburg, which maintained contact with the marts of northern Italy to the south, and with Verdun and Lyons to the west. Regensburg and Magdeburg were so successful that they minted their own coins in the tenth and eleventh centuries; coins which, with Saxon pennies and the Otto-Adelheid pennies from Goslar in Saxony, made their way in large numbers far into the continental East. This is an infallible sign of flourishing business activity, based mainly on the slave trade, according to present-day analysts.

Hedeby was the center of the slave trade on the Baltic-North Sea route, and here again the wide distribution of its coins, particularly the characteristic Hedeby half-bracteates, signifies a constant exchange of goods with the Slav settlements. The missionaries' writings confirm this repeatedly. Rimbert mentions that Ansgar, his predecessor, "brought home, from among many prisoners carried off to distant Sweden, the son of a widow, whom he had bought off . . . and . . . had also bought young Norsemen and Slavs" in order to prepare them for holy struggle. Ansgar concerned himself with improving the lot of slaves and took much trouble upon himself for their sake. According to Adam, Rimbert also did what he could to mitigate the slave trade in his own diocese. "He gave nearly all he had to buy off prisoners" and in heathen countries he "even sacrificed altar vessels" for their sake. To this concern we owe an exceptionally vivid account of an incident at Hedeby:

Once when Rimbert came to the land of the Danes, he saw in Sliasvic [Hedeby]—where he had recently built a new church for a young Christian congregation—a large Number of Christian prisoners dragging themselves along in chains. Among them was a nun who genuflected, bowed her head to him repeatedly, doing him honor; at the same time she seemed to be pleading for mercy, that he might release her. Then, too, she began . . . to sing psalms aloud.

The Bishop, deeply moved to pity, wept and prayed God to help her. As he prayed, the chain with which she was fettered broke at her neck. However, the heathens held her fast and easily kept her from escaping. The holy Bishop, moved by fear and love, began to offer her heathen captors various valuables in exchange for her; but they would agree to nothing unless he gave them the horse on which he was riding.

He did not refuse but leapt out of the saddle at once and gave them the horse, fully harnessed as it was, in exchange for the captive nun. He then gave her back her freedom, to go whither she would.

The Story of Höskuld and Melkorka

The story of the liberated nun, accurately detailed as it is, nevertheless deals with an exceptional case. But we also have descriptions of more commonplace transactions as they might occur in the day to day slave trade, especially from Arab chroniclers.

According to these, the professional slave traders did not scruple to employ every kind of trick to make their wares look better than they were. They "brushed, made up, and filed away" at both men and women to make them look young and attractive. They could dye black hair blonde, and paint the women's faces for effect; they had juices that could make tired eyes sparkle. They padded men's shoulders and women's curves. They would even sell a pretty boy as a girl or vice versa, if the client happened to want something they did not have in stock. The buyers had learned to be suspicious; some, according to Ali Mazaheri, brought doctors with them to the slave market, to give the slaves of their choice a thorough health check.

One of the Norse sagas tells the story of one such sale: Höskuld, a rich Norwegian farmer, on his way to a royal council meeting in about 950, approached a trader known as Gilli the Russian and said that he wanted to buy a slave girl if there was one to be had.

Gilli raised a curtain that was drawn right across his tent, and Höskuld saw twelve women sitting there, all in a row. One woman at the end of the row, near the wall, poorly dressed but beautiful, caught his eye. Höskuld said, ''What price will you ask for this woman?'' Gilli answered: ''You must pay three marks in silver for her.'' Höskuld said: ''Aren't you asking a great deal for this girl, the price of three slaves, in fact?'' Gilli replied: ''You are right, I am asking more for her than for the others. You can have any of the other eleven for one mark in silver, and I will keep this one.'' Höskuld then asked Gilli to bring the scales and reached for his moneybag. Then Gilli said: ''I wish to deal honestly with you. This woman has something wrong with her. She is a mute. I have tried to make her speak, every way I could, but I have never gotten a word out of her.''

Then Höskuld said: ''Bring your scales and let us see how much this bag weighs.'' Gilli brought the scales and they weighed the silver; it came to three marks in weight. Then Höskuld said: ''This then is our deal. You take the silver, I shall take the woman. And I grant you that you have dealt honestly with me in this matter.'' Then Höskuld returned to his own tent.

The story has a romantic epilogue. Gilli's mute slave bore her new owner a son in due course. One day when she thought herself unobserved she bent over the infant's cradle and began to speak to him. Höskuld, who had been eavesdropping, then came forward, and the young mother ceased pretending that she could not speak. She told him her name, Melkorka, and that she had been kidnapped at the age of fifteen from her father, King Myrkjarten of Ireland.

This melodramatic finish may be more poetry than truth, but there is no reason to doubt that the transaction itself was realistically described by the saga's author. A coastal market place, an assembly of the Thing nearby to stimulate business, the stalls and tents of the merchants, a trader known as ''the Russian,'' the process of bargaining, slow, cautious, ritualized, the weighing of words and of silver—it all has the necessary verisimilitude.

The slave trade was big, profitable business everywhere. It served not only as the world labor market—slaves were needed everywhere, in the household, the fields, the fishing industry, enterprises of state and war—but also certain religious requirements. Slaves might be brought fresh from the market to be sacrificed to the gods in the temples.

Part Six

The Mirror of Myth

*Statuette of the
fertility god Freyr,
found in Rallinge
in Sweden.*

The Gods of Asgard

Ritual Feasts in Uppsala
A Giant Born of Ice and Fire
Genghis Khan in the Clouds
Thor's Hammer
Loki the Cunning and Balder the Fair
No Heaven Without Love
Ragnarok—the Doom of the Gods
Religion: Mirror of a People
Nordic Saturnalia

Ritual Feasts in Uppsala

The old pagan temple of Old Uppsala is described by Adam of Bremen:

> The Swedes have a famous temple called Uppsala. . . . It is built all of gold.
> . . . The temple is encircled by a gold chain which is suspended from the
> gable of the building and glitters as a person approaches it, because the sacred
> place itself lies in a valley and is surrounded on all sides by hills, like a
> theater.

A sacrificial tree with hanged men as represented by the Oseberg tapestry.

These hills might have been the three huge royal barrows, but in any case the effect was that of a stage setting in a natural amphitheater.

Near the shrine stood an ancient, huge evergreen, spreading its branches wide above a sacred well-spring. During the spring sacrifice of the Svea, a ritual so sacred it could be performed only once in nine years, men were submerged alive in this well. If they did not surface again, it was considered a sign that the people's prayers had been favorably received. These rites were attended by all the Swedish clans, who arrived laden with gifts, from each individual as well as each clan. Nine males of every living species—dogs, horses, men—had to be offered in sacrifice, then hung from the trees near the shrine. One Christian traveler reported to Adam that he had seen 72 such corpses hanging pell-mell from the branches.

Similar ritual observances are reported from Lejre in Denmark and Skirings-sal in Norway. The preference was for hangings, but victims might also be speared. In each case the carnage was accompanied by obscene song and mime, with much stress on the comic value of effeminate body movements, and much ringing of bells. Victims of high rank were burnt to death inside their houses, or drowned in a butt of mead—a luxurious death for the luxury class, echoed centuries later in *Richard III*, when the Duke of Clarence is drowned in a butt of Malmsey in the Tower. When the victim was a prisoner of war, priests slit open his rib-cage and tore out his lungs, rather like the Aztec priests half a world away who tore the living heart from their sacrificial victims.

From the Arab Ibn Rustah comes another description of such sacrifices among the Rus. He wrote that the Rus medicine men or shamans decided who was to be the victim—man, woman, or beast—then hanged the unfortunate one by a leather thong around the neck from a wooden post until death set in, as ''a gift for our gods.'' Such power in the hands of the priests could account very well for much judicious generosity to them throughout the year.

Who were the gods whose favors had to be bought with such blood offerings?

A Giant Born of Ice and Fire

The mythological poem *Voluspa* (The Prophecy of the Sibyl) begins, like the Hebrew account of Genesis, with the statement: In the beginning there was Chaos. Northward lay Niflheim, a misty region of towering mountains capped with perpetual ice. Muspell, to the South, was lit with red flames of eternal fires. From the encounter between fire and ice sprang the first living being that drew breath in the world: the giant Ymir, who lived alone in the fearful void between North and South.

> There was no land, nor salt waves of the sea,
> Neither earth below nor sky above,
> Nothing, no blade of grass, only the yawning void.

Ymir's first companion was the cow Audumbla, who like himself was born of the melting ice. They both reproduced themselves: out of Ymir's armpit two titans were born, a man and a woman. Audumbla's warm red tongue licked from the frost-covered rocks a creature of human shape, named Buri, who in turn had a son named Bor. From the marriage of Bor and Bestla, the titaness, came three gods: Odin, Vili, and Ve.

The sons of Bor killed Ymir. From his body sprang the forests, from his skull the sky, from his brain the clouds, from his flesh all lands and islands, from his blood, the seas. From his bushy eyebrows the gods made ramparts for the realm between the Underworld and the Heavens, and called that realm Midgard: the World Between, the Midworld. The giants were then banished to Utgard, the Outerworld, the periphery—a stony wasteland where the world ends. But not before they had built the gods a permanent residence called Asgard.

Asgard, the home of the gods, had an enormous central hall. Here grew the world tree Yggdrasill, an ash tree, with evergreen branches reaching to the sky, dripping down mead as sweet as honey, and roots reaching down to the depths of the Underworld. These roots were nourished by three springs, and beside these springs sat the three Nordic Fates, the Norns—Urd, Verdandi, and Skuld—spinning the web of destiny in which all life was caught, not excepting that of the gods themselves.

The names of the Norns, Urd, Verdandi, and Skuld can be roughly translated as Past, Present, and Future, but the words themselves are more interesting than that. Urd means that-which-has-become, is done growing. Verdandi (in German, das *Werdende*), that-which-is-still-becoming, is continuing to grow. And as for Skuld, it must be related to the German *Schuld* and the English *should*: that which we owe, our debts to be paid, our "oughts" or moral obligations. So while the first two Norns, mistresses of man's fate, are fairly obvious spirits of realities, complete and in the making, the concept of the future represented by Skuld is a highly specialized, socialized emphasis, not on what we want and hope for, but on what we owe.

A rainbow bridge made by the gods themselves led from Asgard to the nearby field of Ida on Midgard, where they erected shrines and smithies. Then they breathed life into two tree trunks that came drifting in from the sea, and so created the first man, Askr, and the first woman, Embla. To their descendants the gods gave all the lands of the world, embraced by the sea and securely held in the engirdling coils of the great Midgard Serpent.

Their work of creation done, the gods withdrew to their own high domain of Asgard, where they lived as gods 'should: banqueting, drinking, making love, fighting among themselves, and absorbed in their board games. It was not a peaceful life. Rivalries, clashes, conflicts, competitions among themselves, quite apart from threats of insurrection from the mutinous exiled titans, kept them from growing bored. Also the fact that the gods were not just one happy family but two: the Aesir, who claimed precedence and stubbornly defended their priority on the scene, and the Vanir, a clan of gods who had been accepted into Asgard only after long bitter struggles, and formed a kind of opposition party in the government. A House of Lords and a House of Commons, perhaps?

Genghis Khan in the Clouds

Odin, the eldest son of Bor and Bestla, Chief of the Aesir, presided over the gods in council. He was Lord of Heaven, the All-knowing and All-powerful, possessed of all the Mysteries, poet and philosopher; like Jupiter, he was a great womanizer; a perpetual wanderer and seeker, he also was lord of battles and of the dead.

As Lord of Heaven he resided at Asgard, seated on a richly carved throne, with two wolves, Geri and Freki, at his feet, devouring tidbits of meat he tossed them. Odin himself drank only mead for sustenance. On his shoulders crouched two ravens, Hugin and Mugin, i.e., thought and memory, whispering in his ear all they had learned in their flights round the world.

But Odin knew far more than the ravens could tell him. Indefatigable in his quest for perfect knowledge, he wandered the earth to talk with giants and elves, wood goblins and water sprites; for his encounters with men he took on human form. He often visited Mimir, an uncle, who guarded the spring of wisdom at the roots of the world ash. To look deep into the well of knowledge, Odin had "paid" Mimir one of his eyes; since then he wandered the world in his flowing cloak, his wide-brimmed hat pulled well down to hide his face, as lonely as he was wise.

The one-eyed god of gods saw more than anyone, however, the future included, according to the *Ynglinga Saga*. Odin could prophesy a man's fate and "foretell death, misfortune, and disease." He knew where treasure was buried, and how to make the earth open by using song or magic spells that made everything on earth subject to his will. Like Proteus, he could change shape at will. While "his body lay as if dead" Odin might be leading the life of a bird, a wild beast, a fish or serpent, somewhere far away.

Odin is also credited with discovering the runes, the Nordic alphabet used more for magic than communication, hence found mostly on grave and memorial stones. To win this knowledge, Odin again had to pay with self-sacrifice: he hung for nine days in the branches of the world ash Yggdrasill, suffering from a spear wound, waiting in vain for rescue. Then, far down on the ground, he saw the magic signs, and reached for them, though the effort was torturous. When at last he touched them he fell free, to rise from the ground renewed and rejuvenated, by virtue of possessing the magic key to knowledge and the transmission of knowledge: the potency of an alphabet.

As master of the alphabet, Odin was the protector of the bards—thus playing in the Nordic heaven the role of Apollo, patron of poets, as well as that of Jupiter, Mars, and Pluto. From a giant whose daughter he had seduced, Odin won the mead of the bards; when he spoke after drinking it, he spoke in verse and rhyme. Men whom he befriended might be given a sip of this inspiring drink. The bards, "oral historians" and charmers of the North, naturally saw their patron in this god of wisdom, seer of things to come, and foremost beguiler and seducer of young maidens.

But even more than a culture god, Odin was a war god. A god of wrath, he rode his eight-legged steed Sleipnir, the fastest and most tireless of horses, commanding the winds and tempests, leading a horde of berserk warriors galloping through the clouds on foaming steeds. And yet, even in his golden helmet and shining armor, armed with his lance Gungnir, which like our self-guided missiles sought and found its own target, Odin (or Wotan as he was called in the south) was envisioned as a conqueror. Yet he might be called the Hamlet of war gods, for he was always shadowed with the pale cast of thought, too knowing to be optimistic. He saw the future, and knew that there was no eternal security even for the gods; one day the titans, terrifying as the elemental forces of nature they represented, would come to revenge themselves on Asgard. To prepare for that ultimate attack, he gathered heroes fallen in battle to make up his armies. The Valkyries, Odin's adopted daughters, rode down to every Midgard battlefield to bring back to Asgard the dead warriors.

Thus recruited, the heroes, who had passed through death to immortality, had to earn each evening's banquet with the gods by marching forth each day to do battle, to keep in practice and develop their martial skills against the great final conflict in heaven. At sundown they returned to Valhalla, Asgard's most splendid hall with its ceiling of golden shields, to feast opulently on the flesh of the divine boar and streams of honey-mead served by the Valkyries. Odin himself presided over these state banquets, enthroned in somber majesty at the head of the table.

In Odin the Wanderer—seer and sage, patron of singers and poets, Genghis Khan of the clouds, god of death's kingdom, seeker of truth—Norse mythology has a figure of extraordinary magnitude, complexity, and poetic suggestiveness. As a ruler, he was ruthless in the pursuit of power and glory, even to cheating his

Roast pork in Valhalla: detail of a Gotland picture stone.

architect of the promised fee for work done; as a thinker, he kept his one eye fixed on the inescapable place of death in life; as a god he was, like Zeus, a great seducer of women and progenitor of heroes, a sex god, in short. To this day, long after the worship of Odin was replaced by Christianity, the European Northwest is noted for its great, death-obsessed melancholics from Strindberg to Ingmar Bergman, its high suicide rate, its sexual freedom and highly rational statesmanship.

Thor's Hammer

Thor, the most popular of the Norse gods, is a common clodhopper by comparison with the noble Odin; but he is likable, cheerful, comparatively unassuming. Big, heavy, muscular, red-bearded, he occupied a palace that had 540 rooms. He could eat an ox at one sitting and polish it off with eight large salmon and any number of side dishes, washing it all down with three barrels of mead. In his goat-drawn chariot he thundered through the clouds, roaring and bawling, looking for a fight and finding it every time, with the giants who resembled him in appearance but were, unlike him, guileful, treacherous, and incessantly scheming.

Thor was free from malice, though he had a volcanic temperament that was easily aroused; but basically he was good-natured and well-disposed toward men, particularly the hard-working peasants who were his special protegés. Thor looked after the grain in the fields, the hay in the meadows, the cattle in the stables; he sent rain and dew, sun and wind; men prayed to him for strength, for their brides to be made fruitful. He was the guardian of tradition, clan, and family, patron of blacksmiths, ship captains, and fishermen; he watched over the peace of the dead. He was rough and noisy, but honest and kind. Being guileless and not overly sharp, he guarded against falling prey to his enemies' stratagems by keeping the cunning Loki with him on long voyages or special enterprises.

The red-bearded god of thunder had three talismans to make him invincible in battle: a belt which doubled his immense strength; iron gloves with which to grip his hammer; and the hammer itself, Mjollnir, which he could throw like an axe, and which sent off streaks of lightning as it sped faster than an arrow to its target, crushed whatever it encountered, and then like a boomerang returned to its master.

Thor was a special favorite of the Icelandic bards, and the sagas keep his memory green with many lusty stories about him. He was the chief deity in the temple at Uppsala; the Trondheim temple, too, was dominated by the image of Thor driving his goat-drawn chariot. On house-posts, ships' sterns, bedposts, wood carvers perpetuated his image everywhere, as did sculptors in stone, jewelers in precious metals. Every household had its replica of Thor's flying hammer. The Viking male saw his idealized self-image in Thor; from him the Norse nobles in Ireland traced their descent. No fewer than 984 of the over 4,000 names in the Icelandic *Landnamabok* are variants on his name, or linked with it. The Normans worshiped him under the name of Tur. He was the Vikings' household god, and they were proud to call themselves Thor's people.

Loki the Cunning and Balder the Fair

Compared with Odin and Thor, the rest of the Norse gods played only minor roles. There was Tyr, god of war, one of the oldest of the Indo-Germanic deities and honored above all in Denmark, but also in Norway and Sweden. Tyr was the legendary tamer of the gigantic Fenrir wolf, whom he succeeded in chaining up till the end of the world, but not until he'd lost a hand in the struggle. (The presence of two maimed gods in the Norse pantheon suggests that maimed heroes were not uncommon in the Viking population.)

Tyr's reputation for keeping his word—unlike some other gods—led to his becoming the leader of the Asgard council of the gods, and therefore protector of all Things on earth; his name was invoked as a witness to weddings, and by the magicians of the runes. When sacrifice was made to Tyr, who was as skilled with the sword as he was in interpreting the law, the victims were most likely to be criminals or prisoners of war.

In contrast to the honorable Tyr, the sly, treacherous Loki, "half god, half devil" like Lucifer, is the most ambiguous and elusive character among Norse gods. This "psychopath among gods" counts as an Aesir, though not really a member of the ruling clan. As Odin's blood brother he lived at Asgard, but he hated the gods and plotted their downfall. Loki is a species of fire spirit; to this day, Norwegians say that Loki is beating his children when the hearth fire spits and crackles. These children, begotten upon the giant lady Angerboda (Bringer of Sorrows), were not improved by his beatings, but grew up into monsters: the Midgard serpent that holds the world in its grip, not to be tamed even by the powerful Thor; the fierce Fenrir wolf, and somber Hel, goddess of the underworld. Loki was also capable of producing offspring by parthenogenesis: Odin's eight-legged steed Sleipnir was a son of Loki's.

Loki was a god of many talents. Like Odin, he could change shape at will (and Odin at times could be just as underhanded as Loki). He had a pair of shoes that could whisk him out of sight instantly. And he had set up an observatory that enabled him to keep an eye on everything that went on in Asgard, Midgard, and Utgard. Needless to say, he made such knowledge serve his own purposes, unscrupulously and ruthlessly. A born schemer, he played Iago to every Othello among the gods, pursued all the goddesses, and later boasted loudly of favors won. He slandered everyone, rubbed salt into every wound, poisoned all the wells, stirred up trouble and delighted in seeing his spiteful lies bear fruit. An Odysseus and Mephistopheles rolled into one, he gave shady advice to those who were troubled enough to ask for his counsel, and in this way had acquired a privileged position in Asgard, which he held for a long time, even after he began to collaborate with the titans quite openly.

It was only when his part in the murder of Balder the Fair came to light that the patience of the gods wore out. He was then chained to a rock, and subjected to the constantly dripping venom of a poisonous snake above him.

Balder the Fair is the figure of light in Norse mythology: wholly pure, good, virtuous, beautiful to behold, radiant, he was not only the most intelligent but also the gentlest of the Aesir, a peacemaker who looks strangely isolated among the warlike and shifty Norse gods, like a saint surrounded on all sides by sinners. The lines of the *Edda* lamenting Balder's murder suggest an unuttered judgment that peace, gentleness, harmony, are not of this world nor indeed of any world.

All nature had sworn to do no harm to Balder: fire and water, rocks and trees, beasts of field and wood, poisons and diseases. Only "a little sapling west of Valhalla"—a slip of mistletoe—was overlooked when the oath was taken. Out of this Loki carved an arrow which he gave to blind Hödr, a son of Odin and Frigga, like Balder. The blind brother, not knowing what he was doing, his aim guided by Loki, shot Balder, and pierced by Loki's arrow, the beautiful "best of the gods" fell dead. At his funeral all the gods wept and mourned; even the hostile titans sent delegates to bid farewell to Balder. With Balder dead, pure, unadulterated feeling had no place left on earth; goodness and malice became inextricably intermingled; man lived henceforth in a state of guilt or sin.

No Heaven Without Love

The family chronicle of the peace-loving Vanir contains no such tragedies. They taught men to love life, the warmth of the sun, the fruits of the soil, the breath of the sea and the laughter of children, the pleasures of the table and the bed, trade and riches and getting enough of everything—all the simple joys of daily living.

Njord, their clan elder, was lord of the sea and the wind; hence the patron of hunters, fishermen, merchants. He loved his home by the sea, the roaring of waves, rushing of wind, screaming of gulls. His wife Skadi, a Norse Diana, was at home in the mountains and forests where she wandered in snowshoes even in the coldest winter, with spear and bow; when she came home she brought a good bag of game with her. Every nine days Njord accompanied the huntress to the mountains, and every other nine days she visited him by the sea, though the screeching of the birds robbed her of sleep.

But the chief god of the Vanir was Frey, a generous and kind ruler, who drove a chariot drawn by a golden boar as light-footed and swift as a horse. Frey also had a magic sword that attacked the enemy of its own accord and a miraculous ship large enough to hold all the gods, though, when not in use, Frey could fold it and put it in his pocket.

Frey understood the needs of men, and was himself occasionally prey to human desires. Seated on Odin's throne one day, he could see into the chambers of the beautiful young giantess Gerd—and instantly fell in love. He sent his servant Skirnir at once to woo her, though she was guarded by fierce dogs and leaping flames. The report breaks off at this point, but we do know that in the temple of Old Uppsala there was an image of Frey sporting an "immense erection" and that the royal line of the Swedish Ynglings regards itself as sprung from his seed.

Like Frey the Fruitful, his slender sister Freyja enjoyed high honors in northern Europe. As leader of the Valkyries, she was in charge of the household and of protocol at Valhalla. It was she who received the fallen heroes on arrival and showed them to their places at the great banqueting table, depending on rank and family. She could also choose to welcome every other hero to her own hall, Folkvangar, as her guest. As the goddess of love and beauty, she was an adept at all

A valkyrie serving maid greets a dead warrior in Valhalla. His dog is hurrying out before him.

the secret arts of pleasing. She had a dress of falcon feathers by means of which she could change and beautify her figure, for example. Like Odin's beautiful, flirtatious wife Frigga, her sister with whom she is often confused—Freyja was not married, however—she loved jewelry and trinkets, particularly her golden necklace bought with four nights given to four dwarves, skilled jewelers of the underworld.

Viking goddesses were dedicated to taking pleasure in life, and even Odin's wife was not above suspicion—during her husband's frequent absences she bestowed herself on other gods. She was deeply venerated, perhaps wistfully, by the Norse women, voyagers' grass widows so much of the time. The gods of Asgard eliminated temptation by yielding to it.

Ragnarok—the Doom of the Gods

The Norse peoples were realists about the impermanence of things, of the world, even the gods. Their prophets foretold the end of the world through the coming of a severe ice age that would destroy all civilization. Then the titans—the forces of nature and of chaos, long held under subjection by the gods—would make war on the gods under Loki's leadership, and all would go down in flames together. They named it Ragnarok, the doom of the gods, inescapable because the gods had richly earned it.

From the beginning, trickery, deceit, double-dealing had been their way to get what they wanted. Asgard, for example, was built by one of the titans who was promised the sun, the moon, and Freya, the Norse Venus, for his own, if he would get the immense palace ready by a specified date. The builder set to work, fired with zeal, and with the help of his horse that could haul enormous loads of rock with ease, he managed to keep on schedule. The gods, who never intended to pay, asked Loki for advice on how to get around keeping their promises. This being the sort of thing Loki did best, he turned himself into a mare in heat and lured the titan's work horse away from the building site, so that Asgard was not completed in time. When the tricked titan raged and threatened the gods with vengeance, Thor killed him with his flying hammer.

Another case in point is that of the sorceress Gullveig, who would not give the gods her secret for making gold; when she resisted torture, they burnt her to death three times. The misdeeds and faithlessness of the gods were the reason the earth was plagued with war, and the reason Odin knew that the gods themselves would have to fight for their lives in the end.

And so he had converted Asgard into an immense military encampment by collecting all the best men fallen in battle. Heimdall, one of the many petty princes among the Norse gods, he to whose journeys on the earth so many slaves, peasants, and jarls owed their being, was set to spy out all enemy activity, and blow his great horn at any sign of danger. He had the assistance of a gold-crested rooster, posted high in the branches of the world ash Yggdrasill, who never took his eyes off the world, and never shut them in sleep.

Under such gods, life on earth was necessarily plagued by every kind of evil. The *Voluspa*, the poem with which the *Poetic Edda* begins, somberly drums out its prophecy of doom:

> Brothers fight and deal out death to each other.
> Brothers' sons break the bonds of the clan.
> The world is evil, foul with adultery.
> Sword age, axe age, shields shattering,
> Storm age, age of the wolf, till the world ends.

After this overture comes an outline of the catastrophe to come: Heimdall gives a bloodcurdling blast on his horn; Goldcrest the Rooster crows, the branches of the world ash tremble, Bifrost the Rainbow Bridge cracks, the earth quakes, Gorm, the hellhound, howls, the Fenrir wolf breaks his chain and opens his dread jaws wide to the heavens, and the Midgard Serpent lashes the oceans in preparation for the grand finale.

On a battlefield a hundred square miles in extent, gods and men line up for battle. Odin, flanked by his Valkyries on their winged horses, is the first to attack. The Fenrir wolf swallows Odin, but is killed on the spot by Vidar, son of Odin, who drives his sword into the monster's heart. Thor slays the Midgard Serpent, but dies from the effects of the venom she sprays around in dying. Loki and Heimdall kill each other, as do Tyr and Gorm. The gods all die in a climax of destruction from which none escapes. The world of men perishes by fire, earthquakes, and tidal floods.

Now there is only chaos, naked rock and yawning abysses, a sky without sun or stars, a gray chill void shrouded in dense mists.

But out of this void a new world is born. Virgin land rises from the floods, the earth grows green once more, the waters fill with fish, fields replenish house and cellar though there is no one to plow and sow them.

A new generation of gods, led by Balder returning from the underworld and the sons of Odin—Hodr, Vidar, and Vali, who, like Balder, had no part in the guilt of Asgard—comes to rule over a new world without strife: a world of love, goodness, purity, and happiness.

Religion: Mirror of a People

Norse mythology is full of mysteries, contradictions, obscurities. The same stories recur with a different cast of characters, outlines remain sketchy and vague, the goddesses in particular are hard to tell apart. And yet, despite these and related flaws, perhaps owing to the purely oral transmission of the stories for many centuries before there was anyone to set them down in writing, it forms a grandiose whole, a vast composition in which each episode has a dramatic importance of its own while interacting with the rest. Artists again and again find rewarding themes here for their work, though the best known example worldwide must be Richard Wagner's *Ring of the Nibelungen*.

The rich scenario of Norse mythology found in the songs of the *Poetic Edda*, almost as popular as that of classical mythology, has provided many a scholar and historian with his life's work. Its origins are to be found in Indo-European as well as Oriental cultures. The Aesir reflect the outlook of an Indo-Germanic lordly class of nomad hunters and conquerors, just as the cult of the Vanir probably arose from a megalithic peasant world, comparative late-comers on the prehistoric scene compared with the Battle-axe People; hence the aristocratic status of the Aesir in Valhalla, compared with the peaceable, productive Vanir, gods of a people who acquired their riches by vulgarly working for them in field or marketplace.

Students of comparative mythology are bound to see many of the Norse gods as relatives, if not mere translations, of the gods of classical and other mythologies. Great Tyr, for example, is related to the Indian god Dyaub; his south Germanic name Ziu is reminiscent of Greek Zeus and Latin Jupiter (Dziu-pater). Thor and Hercules might be cousins. And Odin/Wotan has the blood of Dionysus in his veins. Near Eastern fertility and resurrection myths certainly influenced the Norse imagination, but so did Judaeo-Christian elements, picked up by Viking traders who had to embrace Christianity in order to have access to the trading centers of Western Europe. It's too much to be coincidence, for example, that the original human couple have the same initials in the Hebraic Genesis as in the Norse version: Adam and Eve, Askr and Embla. While the Jews in heaven feast endlessly on Leviathan, a whale of a fish, the Norse gods and heroes have their inexhaustible roast boar. Odin hanging in a tree for days, wounded by a spear, seems to echo the crucifixion of Jesus; both are resurrected in their different ways. Comparisons are endlessly fascinating in this area, but this is not the place to exhaust them.

Nevertheless, the Norse gods have uniquely Viking personalities of their own. Odin, complex, self-contradictory, full of inner tensions, a character both benign and sinister, a god of triumph and despair, is unique, but Balder is also distinctively Nordic, for all that he resembles certain Persian and Syrian myths of divine youthful beauty sacrificed and resurrected, of the Egyptian Osiris, of Orpheus and others.

Whatever their indebtedness to older mythologies, the Vikings made their religion into a faithful reflection of their own worldly and otherworldly ideals, fears, and hopes. Norse religion is a mirror image of a loosely bound society of peasant princes; gods, like men, live in their halls lit by the fire in the hearth, eating, drinking, loving, attending their council meetings. They have their swords and horses, take pride in their burnished armor, forge their own weapons, fight their battles, play their board games, as the historian Jan de Vries puts it. These gods "are wounded and die, they suffer the malice of giants and demons, they age unless they can have access to the golden apples of the Youth goddess, Idun." They know pain, grief, and sorrow, and foresee the tragic end of everything. "They fight not because princes must fight, but as a way to counteract the threat of a hostile fate." Their elixir of life is a blend of defiance and obstinacy which enables them to look their fate in the eye and go on resisting the irresistible.

Nordic Saturnalia

The Norse peoples lived familiarly with their gods who were in many ways huge blow-ups of themselves, but they also feared and revered the incomprehensible, indomitable, and ultimately death-dealing forces of nature, personified as spirits, titans, monsters, demons surrounding men on all sides. The world was a magical setting full of mysterious beings to be placated, won over, or tricked if possible into benignity; and full of evil powers to guard against. Blood, spittle, hair, nails were magic substances. People could do you in by giving you the evil eye. The male genital organ was revered, even deified, as on Frey's statue in the shrine at Uppsala, and hands could heal the sick or wounded. (Such superstitions, incidentally, have never quite died out, as anyone who has watched a talk show on television in New York City in 1974, with psychics healing members of the audience by kneading the air around their bodies with fluttering, massaging hands, can testify.)

According to the sagas, "women laid hands on a warrior's body to learn what his fate was to be." Evil spells could be warded off by touching the bare earth. Grass held mysterious earth powers. Kind spirits blessed the tilled fields. Mistletoe and flax had healing powers. Oak trees, lilac and hazelbushes were sacred. Every spring, brook, pond, meadow, wood, grove, and tree had a spirit of its own, for good or bad. Mysterious apparitions, the Disen, foretold the coming of disease and death. Elves danced at night on the mist-shrouded meadows, industrious dwarves forged weapons and made precious ornaments in their mountain cave smithies, giant enemies of gods and men lay in ambush, plotting mischief and catastrophe, or sending hail and snow, hurricanes and floods, earthquakes and forest fires.

The sagas and artifacts reveal much about religious practices, rites and ceremonials to please the gods and appease the threatening forces of nature, or to fight them off by exerting allied forces against them. Many such customs continued far into Christian times, some to this day. Ritual processions to bless the fields at seed and harvest times, and for other purposes, are the ancestors of our processions in lent and seasonal parades. The feasts of the winter and summer solstice were the most important celebrations of the year. The Yuletide feast of Midwinter, fertility rite and ancestor worship in one, lasting twelve days, is a recognizable forerunner of our Christmas. Everyone was invited, including the dead, for whom a special table was set. The cattle were given the last of the harvest sheaves as feast-fodder. Men masked as horses and rams went around playing tricks on each other, clowning, and making an endless uproar.

The Byzantine Emperor Constantine Porphyrogenetos noted down that even the Varangian palace guards celebrated the winter solstice according to their own native custom. Wearing skins and masks, "the Goths," as he calls them, rushed into the banqueting hall, struck their wooden shields with their spears, shouted "Yule, Yule" and walked three times around the sacred banqueting table, before sitting down to the traditional feast, its centerpiece an enormous cauldron full of foaming mead. Odin, "the one-eyed graybeard" himself was the omnipresent patron of these Viking Saturnalia.

At all the festivals sacrifice to the gods took its toll of sheep, and goats; even horses, the nobleman's proudest possession, were offered and eaten on special occasions. The chieftain-priests on Iceland caught the spurting blood of the animal in a vessel and sprinkled it on the congregation. The meat was dedicated to the gods, then eaten in ritual order, and washed down with floods of mead. Sacrifices had their practical uses as well. Men gave to the gods in order to receive favors in return. There was a certain pride, even arrogance, to their giving, as if it set them on an equal level with the higher-ups.

In the early days, sacrifice was made in the woods or sacred groves mentioned by Tacitus. Temples did not exist until late Viking times, perhaps forced into being by the rise of the competing Christian churches.

At Jelling, the ancient royal seat of the Danes on central Jutland, archaeologists have found the most informative of Viking temple sites. Its dis-

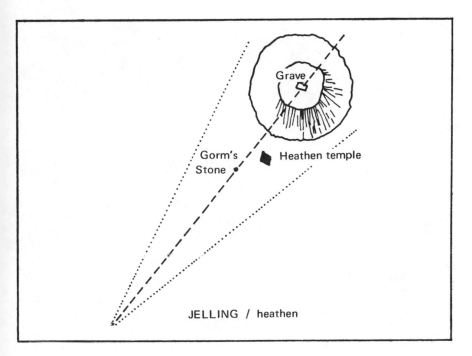

Grave

Gorm's Stone

Heathen temple

JELLING / heathen

covery is credited to Ejnar Dyggve. A circular sacred area held a grave mound 35 feet high and 250 feet in diameter. The sides of the V forming the groundplan, at an angle of 25°, were formed by 200 unworked stones the height of a man. The sacred shrine stood a few meters from the mound, a little distance from the center axis, so that "the most sacred point . . . was reserved for sacrifices in the open air." The remains of the shrine reveal only that it was a small rectangular wooden structure with a floor of stamped clay.

The remains of the temple at Old Uppsala so vividly described by Adam were not found before 1926. Here the traces of the pillars formed two concentric wall-squares, rather similar to the medieval Norse stave churches in structure. The central section was probably taller than the outer quadrangle with its "weaker wooden outside walls," and probably was the Inner Sanctum, containing the images of Odin, Thor, and Tyr as described by Adam. To these gods human sacrifice was made even in late pagan times, even though they had been made into a trinity in imitation of, and in competition with, the Christian concept.

Better a Dead Lion: Viking Burials

A Man Must Die Fighting
Ashes, Nails, Rivets
A Varangian Chieftain's Funeral
Arsenals of Death
King Ships on Their Final Voyage

A Man Must Die Fighting

The fallen warriors went on to Valhalla, to fight and feast forever. Men lost at sea, if not in combat, were gathered into a huge net by Ran, wife of the sea god Aegir. Those who had died ingloriously at home descended to Niflheim, the subterranean realm of shades.

The earliest conceptions of Niflheim placed it in the far North, a place of eternal night, of icy fogs and frost. In time it became the underworld of the dead, a vast dark limbo similar to that of classical antiquity, where wild torrents rushed endlessly downward. A broad bridge paved with glittering gold spanned one of those cataracts; it led to Hel, abode of the dead, somber, penitential. Hel was also the name of its presiding goddess, one of Loki's fearsome offspring according to the *Edda*, and the dread queen of nine underworlds. Her palace, comparable to that of the Aesir and Vanir, had a great hall of gold where she spent eternity feasting, like the high gods of Valhalla, though the hosts of grey, formless, lifeless nonbeings she ruled could not have made the best of company at table, to judge by how little is ever said about them. The fate of the dead in Niflheim appears to have been endless boredom, perhaps both the simplest and most sophisticated conception of hell anywhere in the world.

Hel seems to be an afterthought, relatively, in Norse mythology, as though the early settlers and voyagers had given little if any thought to it until, in the late Middle Ages, the imagination of the Icelandic poets may have been fired by the Christian belief in punishment after death. Like the Greek Hades, the Viking hell was a place of degraded, dreary, pseudo-existence.

Such literary borrowings have little to do with the traditional funerary customs of the Viking North, which reflect a view of death not as an end but "a crisis of life"—a new direction, which did not actually destroy life. The time and manner of death were therefore supremely significant. It was better to die, "to pass on to Odin" in the prime of one's powers rather than weakened and worn out by long illness, unfit for eternity. Jan de Vries suspects, therefore, that the killing of old men was religious in origin, and was regarded by the victims themselves as necessary and desirable. The belief in an active life after death would account for ancestor worship and rites of appeasement toward the dead who remained part of the community of the living though residing elsewhere, whether in the shadows of Hel, the net of Ran, or the glow of Valhalla.

Those whom they left behind on earth had to fit them out for their new circumstances, bury them in proper style, sing their praises, and continue to include them in the life of the clan by offering up sacrifices to them, inviting them to holiday feasts and family occasions. To forget and neglect the dead was to risk angering them; they might then come back and make trouble in the form of feuds, sickness, misfortune. In such cases the clan had to kill the dead person all over again. It is possible that many of the graves archaeologists found to have been tampered with were opened not by grave robbers but under religious sanctions.

Ashes, Nails, Rivets

Norse burial customs were complex and various even in the pre-Viking Vendel era, beginning c. 600, according to documents and archaeologists. It was still customary under the Roman emperors to cremate the dead and bury the urns with their ashes in shallow grave mounds. But the early Christians brought their burial customs to Denmark during late antiquity, whence they spread to the rest of Northern Europe. Cremated or not, the mortal remains were buried in a mound, because of the widespread belief in a mound as a center of energy. Mounds varied in position and form, depending on the locality. Rocky promontories overlooking the sea, or small mounds inland overlooking the deceased's property were preferred sites. The height of a burial mound varied, rising with the rank and wealth of its tenant; the larger of the two royal mounds at Jelling in Denmark, for example, is four stories tall.

The Vikings often buried their dead in wooden burial chambers, and also in ships, favored especially by the Swedes and Norwegians. Sometimes the ship burial was completed by setting the whole ship on fire; in such a case archaeologists centuries afterward find ship's nails and iron rivets mingled with human ashes. Or else cremated remains might be buried inside an unburnt ship, or the ship buried with its dead passengers intact. A ship burial was, in any case, a luxury reserved for royalty. The seafaring commoner had to be content with a stone memorial in the form of a ship; such memorials are to this day a distinguishing feature of Northern Europe's landscapes.

The dead were not sent on their way empty-handed; rich gifts and elaborate equipment and supplies went into the grave with them as a rule. Adam notes that the Norwegians buried the dead man's possessions, his weapons, his favorite and most valued things with him, as well as the essentials of everyday life: basic utensils, clothing, bread and meat, wine or mead. Kings, chieftains, and the rich were also given horses, dogs, and slave girls. Between the wildly extravagant and the simplest conceivable form of burial, researchers have found a vast range of variations.

According to the sagas, it was a Viking's duty to bury the dead, including a slain enemy. A dying man's lips and nostrils were closed, to enable his soul to escape the more easily. The entire clan was invited to the funeral, and treated to a

wake that might last for days of feasting and song recitals glorifying the deceased's
career. In Iceland such funeral rites were known to have been attended by up to a
thousand participants.

A Varangian Chieftain's Funeral

The Arab diplomat Ibn Fadlan, who happened to witness the funeral of a
Varangian chief somewhere along the Volga in 921-22, has left us the most
detailed, revealing, and lively account of such an occasion.

> I had heard so many times that the actual cremation is the least of all the
> things they do at the death of one of their leaders. I was interested in learning
> more, and one day I heard that one of their most esteemed generals had died.
> They laid him in his grave and covered it over for ten days until they had
> finished cutting out and sewing his clothes.
>
> For the poor they make a small replica of a ship, place the body inside,
> and set fire to it. But when a rich man dies they gather together everything he
> owns and divide it into three parts: one third for his family, one third to pay
> for his grave clothes, one third for brewing nabid [probably mead]. They are
> mad for this liquor and drink it night and day. Often enough one of them dies,
> cup in hand.
>
> At the death of a chieftain, the family ask the slave women and servants,
> "Who wants to go with him?" Those who say they do may not go back on
> their word. The ones who do are usually female slaves.
>
> In the case of this particular chieftain, the slave who chose to accompany
> him in death was immediately given a guard of two other slave women who
> went with her everywhere she went. While the prince's clothes and grave
> gifts were prepared, this slave drank and sang every day, full of joy, as though
> anticipating great good fortune.
>
> When the day dawned on which the prince and his servant were to be
> cremated, I went to the river where the ship was now moored on land. Four
> corner posts of birch and other woods were set up, and many large wooden
> statues stood roundabout. The ship was drawn up and placed between these
> supports. The men walked about, saying things I did not understand, while
> the dead man still lay in his grave. Then they placed a bench on the deck and
> covered it with soft cushions, Greek silk brocade, and pillows of the same
> stuff.
>
> After that, an old woman arrived, huge, fat, and grim to look at. They

called her the angel of death, and it was her task to provide for the dead man's grave clothes and to kill the slave. . . . [They] took off the clothes in which he had died. I noticed that he had turned black with frost, but there was no stench, strange to say, and he was unchanged except for the color of his skin. They dressed him in leggings and trousers, boots, a tunic and cloak of gold embroidered stuff with gold buttons, a cap of silk trimmed with marten, and carried him into the tent on board the ship, where they laid him on the richly draped bench and supported the body with pillows.

Then they brought nabid, fruit, and aromatic herbs, to set beside the bier. They also set bread, meat, and onions before him. After that they fetched a dog, cut him in two, and carried him on board. After they placed the dead man's weapons beside him they led two horses hither, chased them until the sweat poured from them, then hacked them to pieces with their swords and flung the pieces of flesh on board. They also chopped up two oxen and threw the pieces on board, and did the same with a cock and a hen.

The slave who wished to be killed meanwhile went from one tent to another, to be bedded by the man inside who then said: "Tell your master that I did this for love of you."

That afternoon they took the slave to a framework shaped like a doorway, lifted her high above the top of the frame, and spoke to her in her own language. This they did three times. Then they gave her a hen. The woman cut off the hen's head and then tossed the hen on board the ship. I asked the interpreter what this meant. He replied: "When they lifted up the servant the first time, she said: Oh look, I see my father and mother. The second time, she said, I see all my dead relatives. The third time she said, I see my master seated in the Hereafter, it is a lovely green place, and he has men and young servants around him. He is calling to me. Let me go to him."

Then they took her aboard. But first she took off both her armbands and gave them to the old woman, the one called the Angel of Death, who was to kill her. She took off both her anklets and gave them to the woman's daughters. She was lifted on deck, but was not yet allowed to enter the tent. Some men came with shields and wooden staves, who handed her a cup of nabid. She took it, sang something, and emptied the cup.

"With this cup," the interpreter said, "she is taking leave of her women friends."

Then they gave her another cup. She took it and sang a long time. But the old woman made her hurry it up, finish her drink, and go inside her dead master's tent. I looked at her and saw that she was full of fear. She wanted to

go inside the tent, but managed only to stick her head inside. Then the old
woman took hold of her, pushed her all the way in, and went in after her. Then
the men began beating their shields with their wooden staves to drown out her
screams, so that other women would not hear them and become frightened
and unwilling to die with their masters.

Now six men entered the tent, and all had intercourse with the slave.
Afterward, they laid her beside the corpse. Two men held her feet, two men
held her hands down, and the old woman called the Angel of Death put a
noose around her neck and gave the knotted ends of rope to the last two men,
to draw it tight. She herself stepped forward with a big broad knife, stabbed
the slave between the ribs with it, then pulled the knife out again. The two
men tightened the noose around the girl's neck until she died.

Thereupon her closest of kin came forward, took a stick of wood, and set
it alight. He then walked backwards to the ship, his face to the onlookers, the
firebrand in one hand while the other hand lay on his buttocks; he was naked
and had to light the firewood they had piled up under the ship. Then other men
came with their firebrands which they threw on the pyre. Soon it went up in
flames, with the ship, the tent, the master and his maid and everything that
was on the ship.

A strong wind blew up so that the flames burned more fiercely and the
fire raged with greater force . . . so that in less than an hour the wood, the
ship, the maid and the dead man were turned to ashes. Now they built a
mound where the ship had stood. On top they planted a large stake of birch
wood. On this they inscribed the dead man's name, and the name of the Rus
king. Then they went their several ways.

Ibn Fadlan's graphic description is confirmed by other Arab witnesses.
Al-Masudi reported that a man's widow was burnt alive with his corpse, and that
many widows were eager to follow their husbands to paradise in this manner.
According to Ibn Rustah, the Varangians built spacious houses for their chieftains'
corpses to be cremated in, together with their clothes, weapons, gold armbands,
food, coins, and their favorite concubines, locked inside alive with the corpse.
''Then the door was sealed and so they died there.''

The archaeologists have dug up many graves that bear out the reports of these
contemporary witnesses.

Arsenals of Death

Many cremation sites, particularly in Sweden, have been found with remains of weapons as well as traces of women's jewelry in the ashes—a sure sign that a woman was cremated with her husband (or owner).

Many earth burials, too, contain the remains of couples buried together. The rich merchants of Birka, on the evidence found in their burial chambers, took along their wives or young slave girls on that final voyage; and their wives did not go without a servant into the hereafter. In one large burial chamber, archaeologists found the skeletons of two women, one of whom had come to rest in an oddly contorted position. This could be accounted for by her having been sealed into the grave Chamber alive, to die of suffocation. The queen buried in the famous Norwegian Oseberg ship had as a companion in death an old woman of between sixty and seventy, with a stiff back and other indications of gout and rheumatism—clearly a servant.

Viking graves, through 150 years of excavation, have by now yielded vast quantities of grave goods that fill the showcases and storerooms of museums, enough to give us a comprehensive view of Viking life. These include five large sites excavated at Hedeby by German expeditions, though only 2,000 burials of a total 10,000 have so far been explored. These finds confirm the great variety of burial customs, cults, and rites. Chamber burials, for example, tended to be richly filled with gifts, vault burials only rarely. In the coffin cemetery on the southern slope of the Hochburg only women's graves contained jewelry and utensils; the men's graves, with a few exceptions, were empty. But the cemetery of the Hochburg itself contained cremations only. A graveyard at the south gate, not identified as such until 1957, has been identified as an urn burial field laid out by Frisians around 800.

The great Danish cemetery of Lindholm Høje, near Aalborg in northern Jutland, has achieved international renown, although unremarkable as to actual findings, because the grave goods had all been reduced to slag and ashes. This made it all the easier, however, to reconstruct the process of cremation. The following description was given by Thorkild Ramskov, director of the six years' excavation concluded in 1958:

> Cremation did not take place at the grave sites but in places unknown. Grave goods were incinerated with the corpse. They might be jewelry, glass beads, knives, distaffs, whetstones, stones used in board games, a dog, a sheep, more rarely a horse or cow. The remains of the pyre were then taken to

the graveyard and scattered on a spot about one yard in diameter, then covered with a thin layer of earth. A sacrificial vessel might then be placed over it.

In this cemetery the technique of stone-setting can be studied better than anywhere else, especially because some of the more ancient forms—triangular, square, round or oval—are preserved in it, though the majority of grave markers are certainly made in the form of a ship, so typical for the Viking era. Ramskov found that these grave enclosures had not been looked after, and concluded that the burial itself was all that counted. The point was to supply the soul of the dead with a ship, or a reasonable facsimile thereof, for transportation; once they had embarked on it, the grave itself was of no interest.

The large cemetery of Birka, the island in Lake Mälar near present-day Stockholm also shows the great variety of burials characteristic of Viking times. The most prominent men tended to be buried in chamber graves, with horses and dogs, weapons and armor. Women were normally buried in simple wooden coffins—possibly a sign of early Christianization, which took strong root on this island of merchant mariners. Yet there are still many cremations among the 2,500 grave mounds in the Birka cemetery. It was clearly a form of interment slow to be relinquished, especially in Sweden.

Hedeby, Lindholm Høje, and Birka are the three great arsenals of the Viking dead. But the best known sites are individual tombs, the renowned mausoleums of certain Norse captains and kings, foremost among them being: the ship-burial of Hedeby, the royal grave mound of Jelling, the chieftain's grave at Mammen, and the ship-burial of the Master of Ladby, as well as the three ship-burials of Tune, Gokstad and Oseberg, near the Oslo Fjord.

King Ships on Their Final Voyage

The ship-burial chamber of Hedeby near Slesvig lay to the south of the walled-in settlement area and one-time great Viking trading center. Before it was excavated in 1908 it appeared as a "shallow oval rising" in the landscape.

The wooden chamber measured about ten by seven feet, and was partitioned by a low plank into two sections containing, "in part grave goods of great value, for two or three men" such as three valuable swords, fragments of several shields, arrows, harness and spurs, a glass cup, a bronze dish, and a wooden pail with iron hoops. At one end of the chamber three horses were buried in a shallow grave.

On top of the grave mound a ship had been set up, supported by stones. It was

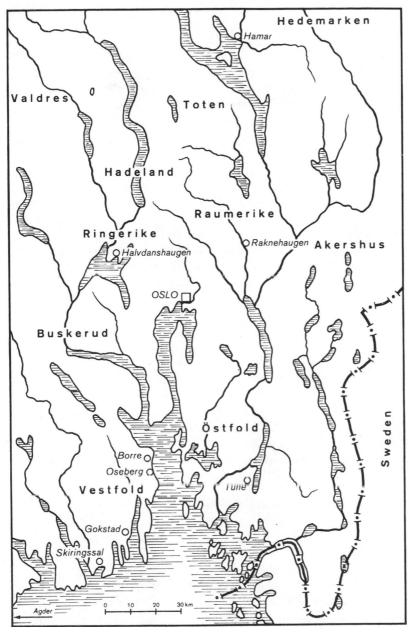

The most important archaeological sites on the Oslo Fjord indicate that this part of Norway was thickly populated in Viking times.

a small, seaworthy freighter about forty-nine to fifty-eight feet long, though only rotten boards and rusted rivets remained of its bottom. Dating from the late ninth century, this mound most probably had held a king or other highly placed person. But in this instance, analysis of the grave goods yielded no clue to the identity of the grave's tenants, or their origins. No conclusions could be drawn, either, from the construction of the burial chamber. But since there was no other known case of a burial in which the chamber was underneath the ship, the ship-chamber burial of Hedeby is as unique as it is mysterious.

Also unique, at least for Denmark, are the two royal mounds at Jelling near Vejle on the Jutland peninsula, within the V-shaped temple area discovered by Ejnar Dyggve. Both have been excavated, the northern mound twice in the nineteenth century. In 1820 the thirty-six-foot-high mound was found to contain a wooden grave chamber about four and a half feet high by twenty-one feet long and nine feet wide, obviously intended for two bodies—but with no skeletal remains or furnishings inside. When King Frederick VII had it reopened in 1861, even the second, more thorough dig produced no more than a silver cup and a few pieces of carved wood.

Exactly eighty years later, Danish archaeologists tackled the second mound with all the most up-to-date tools and resources of their discipline. For a whole year they peeled away at the enormous earthworks layer by layer. They found a wooden post pointing from the summit to the base, a few wooden implements, fragments of chariots, some spades, but no grave chamber or indeed any signs of a burial. The mound was a memorial—no more. And a great disappointment. They had hoped to find the graves of Gorm the Elder and his wife, Tyra; indeed, they had good reason to be confident in the expectation of this, for one of the two famous rune stones of Jelling bears the inscription: "Gorm, the King, raised these memorials for Tyra, his wife—Denmark's benefactor."

The grave in Mammen, central Jutland, was another story. Though the Danish chieftain buried there under a large mound in an oaken coffin remained unidentified, his grave and its contents were undisturbed and unharmed. Wearing fine woollens with woven ornaments, a fine silk ribbon, and gold-embroidered silk cuffs, he reposed on pillows of eiderdown. Among the grave goods were a beautiful bronze cauldron, a large wooden pail, and a wax candle. At the foot of the bier lay two battle-axes, one richly inlaid with silver; their ornamentation, together with the lion-headed horse-collar, has given the Mammen style its name.

Though the grave goods of Ladby were not as noteworthy, that excavation nevertheless counts as one of the highlights of Scandinavian archaeology, being the only ship burial so far discovered in Denmark. The death ship itself stood upright in a trench dug for it, to prevent its keeling over or collapsing under the weight of the grave goods. The front-and-starboard side had nevertheless given way beneath the weight of its macabre cargo: no fewer than eleven horses, to accompany the master of Ladby in the next life. One of them, which lay to larboard, amidships, was still wearing its bejeweled harness—a favorite mount, most likely. There was also a large quantity of dog bones and a dog's harness for keeping four animals on the leash at a time. The Ladby chief's high rank is also confirmed by a belt buckle of solid silver ornamented with gilt foliage, a gilded plate, a bronze dish, a wooden bucket almost two feet in diameter, a gaming board. Remains of twenty-five other objects, unidentifiable, were also found. The grave clothes at Ladby were also interwoven with gold, like those of Mammen, and the body had also been laid on pillows of eiderdown. Weapons were less in evidence. But their absence, apart from an iron shield and 45 arrowheads, can probably be explained on the grounds that the chief of Ladby's grave had been looted in ancient times. Grave desecrators had opened the mound and had removed its tenant himself, in fact. It was done so thoroughly and methodically, in fact, that there could be no question of stealthy doings by night. Internal evidence suggested that the "caper" must have taken at least two weeks.

So it had to have been a planned "excavation." The reason can only be surmised. Possibly the lord of Ladby was thought to rest uneasily in his grave, rumored to "walk at night," so that his relatives decided to move him and render him harmless. More likely, it was done to discourage the continuance of sacrificial rites at the pagan grave site, after Christianization. Perhaps the weapons of the Danish prince, buried with him c. 950, were found to be still in good condition, so when the corpse changed quarters, they changed ownership.

A number of such ship graves are known in Sweden as well. Uppsala boasts cemeteries in which every grave mound once covered a boat, as attested by the iron rivets found in it. But the most elaborate ship graves of all were found in Norway.

The grave mound of Tune, on the eastern shore of the Oslo Fjord, opened in 1867, held the mortal remains of a man buried with his horse on the quarterdeck of his ship packed with moss and juniper, which had not contributed much to the preservation of the grave goods. Most objects had become unidentifiable, except for a sword, a shield buckler, the tip of a lance, some glass beads, bits of cloth and carved wood. The Tune grave had also been looted. But the ship and the earth mound, nearly ninety feet wide, bore witness to the wealth and high standing of the man buried in it.

A rich Viking prince of good physique, buried in a rough-hewn tent-shaped wooden chamber on the quarterdeck with twelve horses, six dogs, and much

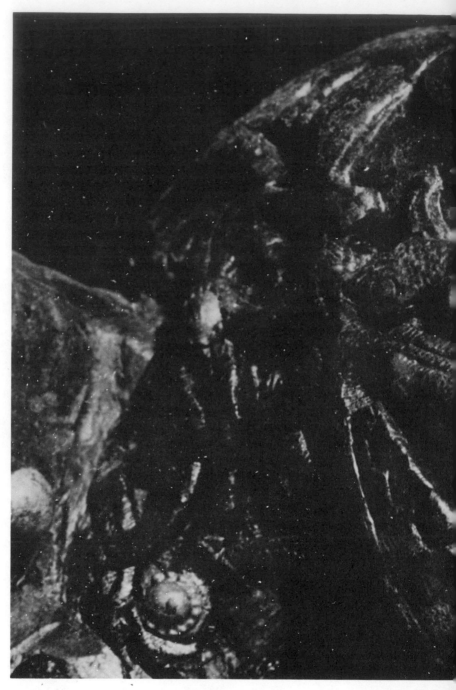

Wild-beast head from the Gustafsson sledge of the Osebe...

decorates one of the four corner posts of the sledge.

equipment, was found inside the famed Gokstad ship, discovered in 1880 on the western shore of the Oslo Fjord. From bronze cauldron to candlestick, wooden spade to hunting spear, kitchen utensils, drinking jug, gaming board, carved sled, he had everything a gentleman might need on a long voyage—plus three oakwood rowboats and six spacious beds.

But the Gokstad man's lordly dower pales beside the wealth of the lady who took her last voyage on the Oseberg ship, excavated in 1904. The ship itself is not quite as long or as light as the Gokstad ship, perhaps not quite as elegant, but the carving from stem to stern is magnificent. Ship and contents were exceptionally well preserved by the sod of the grave mound. A selective enumeration of those contents might begin with three royal sledges and a luxurious wagon, three beds, three chests, two tents, a chair, an iron standing lamp, a wooden bucket large enough to hold over 130 quarts of liquid. There were fifteen horses, an ox, four dogs, field implements, a sturdy manure sled for stable and pasture; a complete kitchen inventory; wheat and oats, apples and nuts, and of course a generous supply of meat.

For domestic tasks, there were four looms with reels and spindles, scissors and awls, whetstones, irons, everything needed to make fine clothes. The chamber was hung with tapestries and wall hangings of the finest workmanship; rugs and clothing, cushions and bolsters, all testified to the occupant's love of comfort and luxury, her good taste, her lively sense of the good things in life.

In addition to being the most richly made and furnished of the ship graves, full of objects of high aesthetic significance and worth, the Oseberg ship also is believed to have an identifiable personage as its tenant: none other than Queen Asa, daughter of Harald Redbeard; she who became the founder of the Scandinavian monarchy.

The *Ynglinga Saga* tells her story: King Harald Redbeard refused his beautiful daughter's hand in marriage to King Gudröd of Vestfold, who promptly brought an army to King Harald's door and killed Asa's father, whose defense forces were no match for the enemy. Gudröd then abducted the princess and forced her into his bridal bed; she had no choice but to submit. Soon afterward she found herself with child. But cunning Asa never forgave, and planned her revenge from the first. Her opportunity came a year after the birth of her son Halfdan. In the words of the saga,

> Gudröd set out on a pleasure jaunt and made a stop . . . in Stiflusund. There the mead was passed around lustily on board, and the King came to be very drunk himself. That evening after dark he set out to leave the ship, and as he

reached the end of the gangplank, a man pounced on him, thrust a spear through his body, and so he died. The man was instantly killed in turn, and the following morning, as the light broke, they saw that he was the servant of Queen Asa.

The resolute, proud Queen openly admitted her part in the assassination, whereupon King Gudröd's men knelt to her in homage. Asa reigned alone for many years, with a strong hand, until her son Halfdan, called the Black, was ready to take power jointly with his half-brother Olaf.

When Asa died at the age of about fifty, she was buried like a king. When they found what was left of her in the Oseberg ship, the evidence showed that she had been a graceful, slender, delicately made woman.

Lion-headed Serpents: Viking Art

Fantastic Fauna
Klee and Picasso in the Teutonic North
Lion into Norse Gargoyle
Baroque Opulence in Miniature
Borre Style to Urnes Style
Microcosms of Movement
The Fifty Years of Oseberg

Detail of a carving on the Oseberg carriage.

Fantastic Fauna

The slender, deerlike woman who restored the honor of her family by arranging to have her royal husband assassinated was not only a forceful ruler. She was also a connoisseur and generous sponsor of art, an arbiter of taste who employed many fine artists and craftsmen; especially wood carvers, at her court. Their imagination and style can be admired today on the ship, the wagon, and the sleds found with her at Oseberg.

Haakon Shetelig, the chronicler and interpreter of Oseberg art, found that the abundant wood-carvings on all these royal vehicles were the work of six different masters and at least three artisans. Their work, packed in sod, exceptionally well

preserved for over 1,000 years, illuminates one of the most exciting events in the dramatic life of North European art.

Both the ship's bows end in a spiral, a stylized snake's head on the prow, and a curled snake's tail aft. On both sides, the stem and stern posts are decorated with friezes of magnificently carved, stylized animals interlaced in rhythmic loops, with ribbon bodies, human hands, and gnome's beards. Each beast differs from the others while forming a harmonious part of the overall composition. The three-edged planks on the inside of the prow are decorated with lively reliefs, again a quasi-infinite series of intertwined gargoyles with huge protruding eyeballs that exert a strangely hypnotic effect.

Occasionally these carvings seem to illustrate a story. The gable end of the

Oseberg cart shows a Man in a snake pit: it is the hero Gunnar, the Gunther of the Nibelung-, or as the *Edda* has it, the *Niflungs Saga*, whose ordeal in the snake pit is related in many of the sagas and was a favorite theme of Norse artists, their version of the Hero's Harrowing of Hell, perhaps.

On the topmost plank to the right is another story illustration: A knight on horseback under attack from a warrior on foot who has grasped the horse's reins with one hand, while swinging his sword high with the other. A well-dressed lady with many armbands tries to stop him from striking the man on horseback. The supports on which the cart rests end in carved animal heads with bulging eyes and bearded jaws. These sculptures incidentally served a practical purpose; the ropes that secured the mobile wagon were tied to them.

The unknown master who decorated the sleds covered the skids, shafts and supports, as well as the main body of each, with ornamentation, leaving hardly a square inch bare. The most famous of them, called the Shetelig sled after its describer, has four terrifying gargoyles baring their teeth from its corner posts; their wide-open jaws are clearly intended to frighten off anyone who looked at them. The framework is ornamented with mysterious interlacing geometrical patterns. These four gargoyles are the most admired sculptures of the Oseberg find, despite the 16 square yards of carvings on the ship itself.

Fantastic, ferocious-looking beasts dominate the designs everywhere. The artists who made them were not interested in copying from nature—though they had keen powers of observation and an eye for the individual trait, as their human portraits prove. The world of their imagination swarmed with mythological fauna, dragons, reptiles, monsters of all kinds, ornamentally intertwined, in curving lines suggestive of plant life, or within geometric patterns. It was a highly stylized art, full of fierce energy rigidly controlled.

Within this pattern, however, was room for great individuality, for differences in temperament, and stylistic development. Shetelig has dated the oldest carvings of the Oseberg find around the turn of the eighth to the ninth century. The most recent date from about fifty years later. A dramatic development in Viking art is illustrated by the Oseberg works: the influence of Carolingian art forms, and the beginnings of the intricate gripping beast style that became prevalent in Scandinavian lands during the ninth century.

Klee and Picasso in the Teutonic North

There was no fine art in our sense of the term in northwestern, Germanic Europe. What there was served almost entirely purposes of decoration—on brooches and buckles, swords and shields, wagon shafts and ship's prows, wherever a bare surface presented itself. Like nature itself, Norse craftsmen and artisans seem to have abhorred a vacuum. They were chiefly carvers and metalworkers, but we also have their rune stones and those picture stones, about man-size, which are a specialty of the island of Gotland, in mid-Baltic.

With a very few exceptions, early Germanic art, from roughly the fifth to the twelfth centuries, is ornamental and dominated by animal motifs, as in the Oseberg carvings. The chief influence is the art of late antiquity, to which Germanic goldsmiths owed not only their animal motifs, but also their encounters with the chip carvings of the Roman Rhine and Danube territories, whose highly sophisticated, technically brilliant ornamental style owed its effectiveness to the sensual charm of surfaces in ceaseless motion.

However, late Roman art was not alone in inspiring Germanic gold- and silversmiths. In their jewelry and weapons one can discern Celtic influences, as well as Scythian-Sarmatian traditions transmitted by Gothic workshops. Holm-qvist lists three main components in Nordic art: an oriental element chiefly from the Asiatic culture of the steppes; the Celtic; and the Roman. But it is not a matter of three clearly differentiated aspects, but rather a multiplicity of mixtures: the Scythian-Celtic, the Romano-Celtic, etc., in the East, and the Romano-Teutonic, Romano-Celtic blends in the West. A wealth of forms and influences were assimilated in the work of Teutonic artists, as one would expect in a culture of world travelers.

On the North Sea coastal areas of Germany, Denmark, and Norway, the so-called Animal Style I originated in the second half of the fifth century. It is characterized by stylization of animal figures, the first step toward subordinating naturalistic shapes to abstract ornamentation. By the end of the century Nordic artists, led by the Swedes, had advanced far toward abstract patterning. "They ruthlessly cut up animal forms." Head and body, legs and arms were detached from their anatomical context and freely used in the decorative play of lines, subordinated to the powerful effect of energy in motion.

Typical of Style I is a dress clasp found at Ekby in Sweden, made of gilded silver. Heads with bulging eyes and human limbs are worked into the composition "like the thrown-out remains of a meal," all framed in a frieze of fantastic crawling beasts about to leap. (Looking at it, one is reminded of Picasso's fragmented human figures. Curvilinear compositions in the style of an early Paul Klee were also favored in this period.)

Animal Style II, which developed in the sixth century through the absorption of eastern Mediterranean plaited-ribbon patterns, came northward from Langobard Italy, entered the Frankish Rhineland and swept the Anglo-Saxon island world before it reached the Scandinavian countries. In Sweden, where it

Weathervane of a Viking ship, which survived a thousand years on the church of Söderala in Northern Sweden—it is today one of the treasures of the State Historical Museum in Stockholm.

was taken up by the jewelers of the Svea, it became completely naturalized as the Vendel style, so named after the boat-burial site of Vendel in Uppland. Laws of anatomy went completely by the board, and the thin ribbon-like animal bodies of the sixth century were stretched and twisted into intricate interlaced linear ornamentation; spidery legs were made into strange loops and bows. Then bodies disappeared altogether, and even the heads with their gaping jaws, flickering tongues, and threadlike necks, vanished in the jungle of ornamental lines.

Along with the Mediterranean trellis-work style, the classical vine and acanthus leaves also made their way northward. But Viking woodcarvers would not be turned into "vegetarians" and tended to substitute garlands of snarling, glaring animal heads for the acanthus and vine wreaths of Greco-Roman inspiration, so creating the characteristically North German variation of Animal Style II.

The late flowering of the Vendel style—labeled Vendel-E by the specialists, with Vendel-A referring to Animal Style I—falls into the period of Style III, purely Scandinavian in origin. This final form of pre-Viking art began about 700, under Irish and Anglo-Saxon formal impulses that were never fully naturalized. Complicated animal figures from Ireland and botanical and zoological garlands from England, were added onto the traditional forms, creating S- and Figure 8-shaped loop patterns with an ever more intricate and capricious movement that was increasingly hard to follow. Handworking techniques attained a new degree of perfection with this extremely fine-edged puzzle-style ornamentation.

But perfection as an end in itself signalled a dead end for art. Graceful, willfull, ecstatic, but impoverished of substance, the art of the late eighth century showed every symptom of incipient anemia. At this point the encounter with the art of the Carolingian renaissance at the beginning of the Viking era had the effect of a blood transfusion.

Lion into Norse Gargoyle

The motif that captivated the Nordic imagination at this time was the favored image of Frankish manuscript illuminators and fresco painters: the lion. But in their hands the desert king was transformed almost beyond recognition, and in time entered art history as the Viking gripping beast, so named because its innumerable pairs of grasping paws were taking hold of something all over the design.

The gripping beast became the most versatile beast in all iconography—boar, dog, ram all at once, supple as a cat or a snake, cuddly as a toy panda. As Brøndsted says, "The creature is capable of endless variations, with its round staring eyes like spectacles, its bald head and long tuft of hair. Its body is

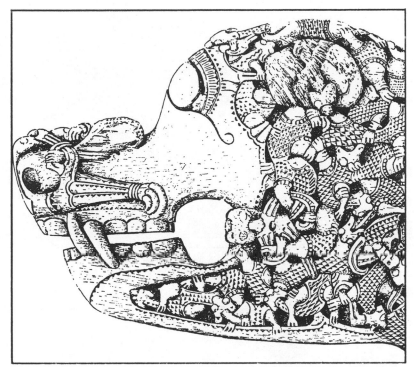

The dance of the gripping beasts on the dragon head of "the Carolingian."

sometimes elongated like a thin wire. A tiny savage troll, a fool with a gnome's pointed hat . . . rounded limbs, paws always ready to scratch and seize something . . . a fantastic beast surely designed to amuse."

Scurrilous but dynamic, grotesque but menacing, charming though aggressive, the beast is ever ready to leap; it rears up, stretches, ties itself into knots and unravels again, always full of movement, full of "vital, venomous energy on the offensive." It is the key motif in a resurgence of vitality, a great renewal of the old Teutonic decorative art, giving it its unmistakable flavor for the next two hundred years.

Baroque Opulence in Miniature

The stages of this renewal are clearly reflected in the Oseberg carvings, particularly of the various animal heads. Following Haakon Shetelig's classification of the

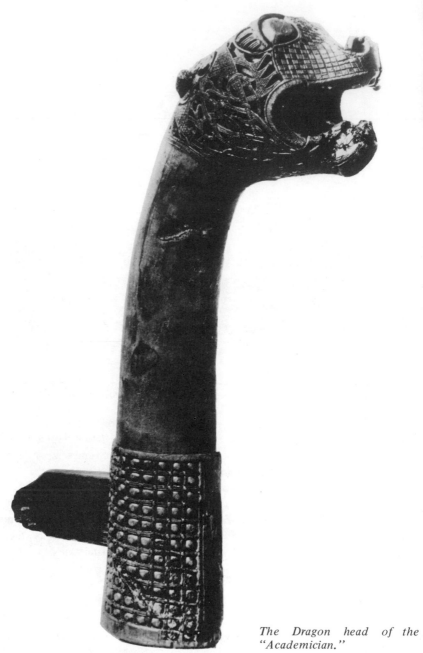

The Dragon head of the "Academician."

One of the "baroque" animal heads of the Oseberg find.

Oseberg masters, the earliest of them, the so-called Academician, who carved the shaft of the ceremonial sled with intertwined birds and a viciously grinning dragon's head, is considered the most painstakingly accurate of all. The filigree on his dragon's head on the brownish sycamore wood is done with uncanny precision. The distinguishing mark of this elegant, majestic sculpture is the smooth neck between the elaborately carved head and the neckruff below. But the overall impression is a touch too suave, too polished, too finished. It is the product of a perfectionism characterizing this kind of work around 800.

In striking contrast is "the Carolingian's" dragon head, also carved with interlacing animal bodies but, to quote Oxenstierna:

> It is worked in a quite different manner, in whorls of little, fat, "gripping" animals with snub noses and protruding eyes. They hang on to each other frantically, they claw and paw each other and just about dislocate their clumsy bodies in their grotesque efforts to make room for themselves within the framework of the design. A grip on the throat; six fists crisscross. They tousle the next animal's back hair, snuffle along the edges, bite each other in the rump. And in the end, there is room for them all. Not an interstice of tranquility, nothing but tenseness, motion and writhing life. And all this contained within the confines of a grinning, dragon head with fangs.
> A new style, infused with the Carolingian element, but going its own way.

Greatest of all is the Baroque Master, so named because his two sled shafts and dragon head are done in the grandiose style of the Baroque. (See illustration on opposite page.) His dragon is covered with scales in the form of small oval medallions, each carved with a droll, self-entangled gripping beast with one round staring head but winding limbs and gripping paws everywhere, a lattice-work of these surrounding the centered face. The decorative relief not only spills over the surface, it rears up and makes the surface disappear, as Jan de Vries has said.

The youngest of the three great Oseberg wood sculptors, active about 850, the Baroque Master brought Style III to perfection, with an exotic imagination that plays a piece of rough wood like an organ, pulling out all the stops. A veritable witches' sabbath of raging little animals incessantly in motion is produced with microscopic clarity in the confined space of those oval medallions. Baroque power and magnificence in miniature, done with unsurpassed craftsmanship.

This spectacular "griffin" style soon came to dominate the carvers' and

The gripping beast medallion of the "Baroque master."

goldsmiths' workshops throughout Scandinavia, though the beast emblem itself underwent modifications in the course of time. Its hips became more compact, body and tail thinning and lengthening, threadlike; the rump became a semicircle intersecting throat and neck, until, after the turn of the millennium, the original lion's head began to emerge again. Its variability was part of the liveliness with which it reigned for over two centuries.

Borre Style to Urnes Style

Within these two centuries, Viking art absorbed many influences. After the Viking invasions, massive quantities of booty were brought home to Scandinavia, including much continental art that came to enrich the traditional forms of Norse art. Its sense of unrest, ceaseless activity and change, infinitely elaborated, became its distinctive message.

Art historians distinguish five major styles, apart from local cultures with specialties of their own, beneath the surface of the overall animal ornamentation they all have in common.

First, there is the Borre style, exemplified by a saddle, bridle, and some wooden objects with metal trim, found in 1850 in a grave mound on the Oslo Fjord, that paradise of archaeologists. These objects, about fifty years later in the making than the late Oseberg carvings, combine the ribbon lattice-work with animal shapes into characteristic chain patterns. The gripping beast with its active paws, moving limbs, and mask-like triangular head with button eyes is here, as a reminder of the Carolingian lion's influence in mobilizing the traditional decorative fauna of Viking design. With all its precise, finely worked detail, the Borre style has a certain peasant, almost barbaric flavor, strong, knotty, full of life. Typical of the Borre style are also the carvings and metalwork of the Gokstad find. A perfect prototype is the renowned Swedish Finkarby brooch, a silver disc two inches in diameter, showing four intertwined animal bodies in ribbon form, with spotted thighs and foreheads. The four heads meet in the center, and each passes one eye on to its neighbor; it makes for a complicated but compelling composition.

The Borre style merged into the Jelling style, first represented by a small silver cup found in the north mound at Jelling. The zoological elements in its decoration—heads, limbs, gaping jaws—are reminiscent of pre-Viking art, as are the S-shaped interlaced bodies. Art historians detect an Irish influence, aesthetic booty from the time of the Danish-Norwegian invasions of the Emerald Isle during the first half of the tenth century.

Half a century later, the Mammen style is represented by a fine iron axe-head inlaid with silver, belonging to the Mammen chieftain. Here plant and animal motifs are combined in a new, bold way, in that the traditional spiraling limbs of the beasts end in acanthus leaves. Yet with all its fantastic elements, this heraldic style found on ships' flags, rune stones, and harness and dress clasps, is controlled and elegant. The Jelling Stone, over nine feet high, is the most admired example of the Mammen style: it shows a lion entwined by a serpent (see illustration below). in a life-and-death struggle. Animal and plant forms are stylized into a remarkable ornamental unity. This particular symbiosis of the "royal beast" and the serpent winding into the terminal leafy vines is historically connected with the Danish invasions of England.

An intimate blending of flora and fauna is also typical of the so-called

The great lion of Jelling—the chief example of the Mammen style.

Ringerike style, named for a group of Norwegian rune stones. The foliate element is more emphasized and stylized here; acanthus leaves, small palms, bundled leaves, and pear-shapes flourish here as never before in the European North. This style too is strongly affected by Anglo-Saxon motifs, especially the works of the Winchester manuscript illuminators.

At the end of the Viking era we find the Urnes style, named for the carvings on the gable of a lone wooden church in West Norway. Its flowing lines and rhythms, gazelle-like beasts, and pleasing vines are delightful, and yet all its refinements cannot conceal the incipient decline in Viking art. Like the fin-de-siècle masters of the eighth century, the sculptors, carvers, and goldsmiths of the late eleventh century were intent upon displaying their technical virtuosity, elaborating on existing forms. Compared with the creative impulse and imaginative power of the Oseberg masters, their work is mere imitative routine. With the Urnes style, Viking art was played out as a seminal force.

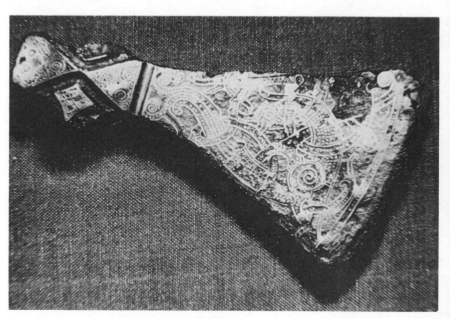

The imitation silver battleaxe of the Mammen chieftain, one of the most beautiful examples of Viking decoration.

Microcosms of Movement

What about this art? What can it tell us about the inner forces of the Viking world? How much light does it cast on the culture?

It was not art as we understand the term today. It did not aim at realistic likenesses nor at exposing evils. It did not concern itself with man, or society, or landscape, with nature as such, reality as such—the Vikings had no such concepts. Their art was no more didactic than that of the Arabs, who were absorbing classical influences at about the same time. Like Islamic art, Nordic art sought to translate dreams and visions into the formal language of decoration. In both, visions were transformed into images that were anything but realistic.

But the work of the Nordic, particularly the Viking masters, has none of the serenity and detachment of Arabic art. Their pulse beats faster, they vibrate with tension. Where an Arabic prayer rug suggests tranquility and harmony, a Viking belt buckle exudes restlessness and passion. Viking art explodes in a fury of lines in constant motion without beginning or end, a microcosm of movement, symbolic of a world whose gods are warriors threatened by titans and monsters, a world they could see only as an enormous battlefield in a never-ending war.

At the same time, their fantastic, intricately knotted lines remain oddly abstract despite their sometimes concrete imagery, oddly well organized; reason is clearly at work here. "Chaos to the indolent gaze, polyphony to the searching eye," they obey strict rules. Where Arab artists created sensuous flowerlike designs, the Nordic masters' mythological beasts were unleashed only to be transformed into ornamental patterns. The opulent splendor of their interlacing animal garlands, so like the ornate, intertwined phrasing of Iceland's bardic poetry, was firmly organized, with strict economy. Otherwise such elaborate imagery could never have been confined to the size of a brooch, a buckle. If the classical principle of life and art, the marriage of contraries, is perfectly illustrated anywhere, it is in Viking art, where the utmost in vitality is wed to the utmost order.

What we do not know as yet, if we ever will, is the possible religious meaning of an art most probably rooted in magic, in mythology, ritual, cult. Holmqvist's suggestion that much of it, perhaps all, was a hieroglyphic language like that of the Egyptians, transmitting information to those who could read it, is conjectural; it must be kept in mind, though it may never be proved.

As an art largely in miniature, mostly decorative and formal, full of unsolved riddles, it has remained on the sidelines of discussion. It is rarely if ever included in the most important works on art, and has remained out of the mainstream of cultural awareness—all the more since the artists remain anonymous, and much of modern culture since the Renaissance, especially the modern idea of the artist, stresses individual personality.

The Fifty Years of Oseberg

A few exceptions within the total legacy of Viking art are widely known, such as the Mammen horse-collar and axe, the two Søllested harnesses, the small silver cup and the large Jelling stone, the gilded bronze weather vane from Heggen in Norway and its Swedish counterpart from Söderala; a number of runestones, several Gotland picture stones. These are almost all the examples of Viking art to have won any degree of fame.

The most famous of all are the works of the Oseberg masters. The sleds, cart, and animal figureheads, and the carvings on the ship itself, all from that excavation in the summer of 1904 which counts as one of the greatest strokes of archaeological luck of this century, have done more than any other surviving work to put Viking art into focus and give cultural historians an appreciation of its high rank. Art historians are convinced that the Oseberg masters were responsible for triggering the great stylistic revolution of the era, seconded by the metalworkers and jewelers.

It was done in the half century between the Academician and the Baroque Master, 800 to 850, the half century during which Scandinavia broke violently into European history. Since 1904, the year of the Oseberg find, we know that this period was also one of the most vital in Norse art.

Part Seven
Finale

Oldest Christian cross in Sweden,
found in a Birka grave, from ca. 900 A.D.

The Hammer and the Cross

Ansgar—Spear of God

The heroic age of the missionaries to the Vikings begins with Ansgar, the Benedictine monk who became the first Archbishop of Hamburg and was called by the Church "the Apostle to the North."

He is thought to have been born in Saxony, about 801, or of Saxon parents in Flanders or Picardy, and sent at the age of five to the monastery of Corbie on the Somme. Fifteen years later he was sent to teach in the brother monastery of Corvey on the Weser. The fame of his erudition and piety spread so rapidly that in 826 Louis the Pious sent him northward with the Danish Pretender Harald, just baptized at Ingelheim, to transform the restless Norsemen into peace-loving Christians.

As his disciple, successor, and biographer Rimbert recorded, Ansgar's first voyage succeeded only partially. He converted many, but the Danes were not yet ready. Their hostility to Harald rubbed off on the Pretender's Franconian missionary, who wisely left the country to await a more favorable time.

Three years later the tenacious missionary embarked on that first voyage to Birka on which he was attacked by Viking pirates and barely escaped with his life. Though he reached Birka alive, and was permitted to stay and preach—the Scandinavians were encouraging Carolingian traders, Christians, to come North without fear, hence the hospitality to their missionaries—the mission did not take hold this time, either. In 832 Ansgar moved with his friends and advisers to the Hammaburg on the Elbe, recently elevated by Pope Gregory IV to the status of an archbishopric. Ansgar converted the fort into an ecclesiastical stronghold, built a church, a school, a hospital, and began to train his students and assistants as missionaries, so creating an organization for the conversion to Christianity of Northern Europe.

Traces of Ansgar's "plant" have been excavated, following the Second World War, on Hamburg's bomb sites, by Reinhard Schindler, who found the remains of pillars for a tripartite hall, and below this the sanctuary of the later Gothic nave of the church, bits of the first baptismal font, and the mission church, as well as remains of monks' cells and workshops.

The Vikings who sailed up the Elbe in their longships in 845 to attack Hammaburg destroyed Ansgar's ecclesiastical colony. Again he barely got away alive, but he continued his missionary work in Bremen, with some success. King Horik the Elder of Denmark permitted him to build a church in Hedeby in 849, and this church became the center of an active Christian community. A second church was built in Ribe, in 854. But though he had gained a solid foothold in Jutland, he did not succeed in converting the Danish kings; although, for the sake of access to the continental trade marts, they allowed their merchants to let themselves be baptized, or at least "have the sign of the cross made over them." Meanwhile they themselves went on offering blood sacrifices to their Aesir and Vanir, gods more suitable to their war-loving feudal ways.

Ansgar died in 865; his Hamburg-Bremen mission did not outlast him for long. His successor Rimbert continued taking the word of God to the heathens, but it was not for another century that organized missionary work succeeded in establishing a stable Christian community. Nevertheless, Ansgar, as "the spear of God" had opened the way; he had been tough, hard to discourage, and diplomatic.

In 934, Henry I, called "the Fowler" and Germany's first Saxon ruler, attacked Hedeby successfully, forcing the Swedish King Knuba, then in possession, to embrace Christianity. A little later he sent Archbishop Unni to Denmark and on to Birka, where Unni died in 936. Henry's son Otto completed his father's work; in 948 at Ingelheim, he founded "in the territory of the Danes" the three bishoprics of Slesvig, Ribe, and Aarhus, appointing German bishops to head them, under the authority of Archbishop Adaldag of Hamburg. In this way he had surrounded the royal Danish residence at Jelling with strongholds of the Church.

Denmark's Stone Baptismal Certificate

Harald Gormsson, called Bluetooth, understood the implied threat well enough to let himself be baptized around 960 by the German priest, Poppo—reported by Adam of Bremen to have demonstrated the power of the Christian God by grasping red hot iron with his bare hands, unscathed.

Otto the Great acknowledged Harald's show of political insight in 965 by granting the three Norse bishoprics tax exemption and judiciary independence.

This form of imperial generosity spelled the beginning of the end of the old pagan cults. Harald arranged to have the old heathen temple at Jelling in south Jutland torn down and replaced by a wooden church, the first Danish stave church according to the archaeologists, which probably housed the mortal remains of Gorm the Elder and Tyra—the same remains that were not found in the north mound in 1861 and in the south mound in 1941.

This second mound was also the work of Harald, but it was empty, a mere demonstration of residual respect for the customs of his clan. Between the two grave mounds was a runestone, the "large Jelling stone" showing on its obverse the renowned acanthus lion, on its reverse the figure of Christ surrounded by tendrils, and on the third face the inscription: "King Harald erected this memorial to Gorm his father and to his mother Tyra—the Harald who conquered all Denmark and Norway and converted the Danes to Christianity.''

It is the most beautlful Norse runestone, Denmark's baptismal certificate in granite.

Leif Ericsson, Missionary

Norway took a few decades longer to turn Christian. King Haakon the Good made a stab at converting the country with the help of Anglo-Saxon priests midway

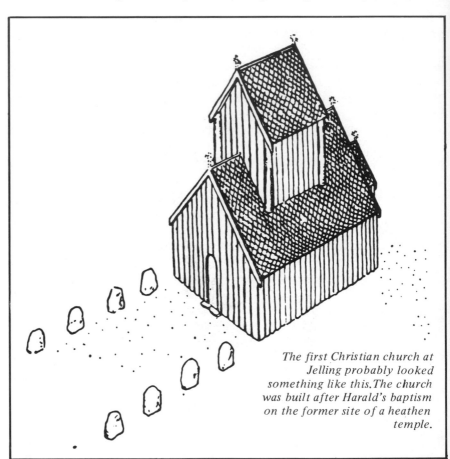

The first Christian church at Jelling probably looked something like this. The church was built after Harald's baptism on the former site of a heathen temple.

through the ninth century, but his independent freeholders drove the foreign monks and preachers out, and Haakon wisely left conversion to his successors. Fifty years later, Olaf Tryggvason and Olaf the Good were powerful, fanatical, and ruthless enough to insist, and succeeded, at least officially.

Iceland, too, did not yield easily. Several missionaries—the Saxon Fredric, in 981, and the German Tankbrand in 998, among them, were forced to leave. But in 1000, following Olaf Tryggvason's baptism, the Icelandic Speaker of the Thing, Torgeir, proclaimed—presumably after taking counsel with his godar— that henceforth the law would have "everyone be a Christian." He was diplomatic enough to leave a few loopholes for hard cases: "With regard to exposing infants and eating horseflesh" the old law continued in force, and those who insisted on making the old pagan sacrifices might do so provided they kept it decently hidden. If they were caught at it, in the presence of witnesses, they would be banished for three years.

Greenland was Christianized the same year—without help from missionaries, in fact. Leif Ericsson, the discoverer of Vinland, returned as a convert from a lengthy stay at the court of Olaf Tryggvason, and persuaded his fellow islanders to follow his example. The sagas report that only his father would not hear of it. Eric the Red hated the priests. His wife, however, underwent baptism. As a result the first church in Greenland, a hut that measured four by four yards, with a gable roof of sod, was built at a respectful distance from Eric's home at Brattahlid—and his obdurately pagan remains may have been given Christian burial there beside those of his Christian wife.

The Swedes clung to the ancestral faith for some time longer still, despite the missionaries of all nations—German, French, Anglo-Saxon, even Greek Orthodox—who tried hard to win them over. Eventually, the missionaries succeeded in forming small Christian communities in the various trade centers, and in persuading the ruling class that conversion was expedient, since trade followed conversion, and trade brought wealth, and the rulers never had enough of the wherewithal to bolster their power. But the Swedish peasants held out for a long time. Soon after the year 1000 they drove out their King Skötkonung because they had heard he meant to destroy the temple at Uppsala. in the second half of the eleventh century they forced their King Inge to leave the country when he refused to take part in the obligatory sacrificial rites. The Cross was not fully established even in the larger settlements until the twelfth century.

But for a long time after that, even, the chroniclers continued to lament the people's frequent relapses into the old barbarism. "If misfortunes, poor harvests, drought, hurricanes or storms" visited the country, the Sveas did not hesitate to

The Christian side of the large Jelling stone, the ins
whole of Denmark and Norv

*informs us that King Harald Bluetooth "conquered the
d the Danes to Christianity."*

revert to "the worship whose ritual they honored." They banded together, in fact, "took vengeance on the priests and tried to drive them out of the country," wrote the Anglo-Saxon monk Aelnoth of Canterbury in the twelfth century.

A Toast to the Mother of God

By and large, however, the Christianization of the far North in Europe was gradual, sensible, and undramatic. Compared with Charlemagne's methods, who went about converting the heathen Saxons by instituting one of history's more spectacular bloodbaths, it went off almost uneventfully. No death sentences, no burning of temples and images, no organized resistance.

The old Teutonic religion, like all polytheistic systems of belief, was tolerant of other faiths. There was always room for new gods in Valhalla. The Vikings sometimes seem to have simply allowed the new Christian god to move in, alongside the Aesir and Vanir, to keep the missionaries and merchants happy. There was always room for another strong protector in the Norse notions of salvation, as well as of expediency.

So the act of conversion may have been regarded as a kind of insurance policy, and the missionaries were broadminded enough to tacitly and tactfully accept it as such. Most baptisms took place after superficial indoctrination, or without any spiritual preparation at all. Persuasion on doctrinal points was usually aimed, not at the people, but their leaders—if the king was baptized, his vassals would not hold off for long, but would normally follow him to the baptismal font in the hope of palpable reward and visible manifestations of salvation.

If rewards did not materialize, or the ritual banquets were omitted from the annual holiday program, then trouble could arise. Usually the old rituals were continued under new names. The guild brothers lifted their cups to Christ, the Mother of God, and St. Michael, instead of to Odin. Besides, the naive Norsemen and their even simpler wives were quite ready to be moved and transported by incense, bells, and candles. The splendor of ecclesiastical robes, liturgical vessels, and the rest of the churchly pomp readily captivated their impressionable souls.

Indifference, therefore, and spontaneous opposition could usually be traced to grave psychological errors made by the missionaries. Or the peasants might detect beneath an overlord's religious zeal a grab for personal or state power. Where clan loyalties were assailed in the name of Christianity, the older, stronger tradition won the unequal battle, as in the story of the Icelander Radbod who withdrew his foot from the baptismal bath when told that his ancestors were condemned to hell even as he went to heaven. The Church learned to circumvent such threats of eternal separation by giving baptism an additional retroactive power.

With tolerance and patience, the missionaries allowed the converted time to forget the old gods. Heathen temples were transformed into Christian churches, with many of the old rituals preserved under a new dispensation; backsliders were not threatened with instant damnation but wooed back. The Icelandic *Landnamabok* tells of a man named Helgi who was of "mixed faith." Though baptized, if the winds were favorable at sea, he would invoke his old friend and helper Thor.

A Mixed Faith

Such Helgis must have been common in any district long after nominal conversion. The period of transition is clearly discernible in lists of archaeological finds. The masters of the heathen runes spelled out Christian formulae with them. Dragon heads appear side by side with Christian crosses, stylized to fit in, on Swedish picture stones. The stone sarcophagi of the early bishops were decorated with Norse designs. Heathen gifts were Christianized by the addition of cross pendants. One Jutland craftsman succeeded in making a mold which could be used to make either the Hammer of Thor or the Cross of Jesus—perhaps an ultimate in symbolic assimilation.

By this time the victory of Christianity was never in doubt. The dynasties of Aesir and Vanir were done for—vanquished not by the resurgence of the Titans, not by Nature's rebellion against the gods as feared, but by a new force none of the Norse visionaries and poets had foreseen: the pale Galilean, backed by a vast, powerful, highly sophisticated organization, the militant Church. Conquered by men of the Book, by intellectuals, whose runes were infinitely more potent than poor Odin's comparatively primitive little wooden sticks and rods with their country magic. The old Norse mythology was giving ground, its gods felt doomed, as reflected in the apocalyptic mood of the *Edda*. Christianity was a far more mature and ethically viable religion, beside whose spiritual power the poetic but oddly diffuse Teutonic mythology looks like a wooden rural temple next to the Roman Pantheon. The Church worked in close collaboration with the secular powers. That Ansgar the missionary was sent to the Norsemen by the head of the Holy Roman Empire is a telling fact, not a matter of chance. The Church played a dominant part throughout the continental network of trade centers. Once Norse leaders had discovered that trade, and orderly business relations, paid off far more

Cross and Thor hammer—Christian and heathen symbols. In the center th

land trader with which both cross and Thor hammer could be made.

quickly and far more than piracy and war, the ultimate accommodation with the Church was a foregone conclusion. At first, a few of these leaders were bribed to accept baptism; after a while, bribery was no longer necessary.

In simple, day-to-day terms, the Vikings came to bring home from their forays not only countless cargoes of goods and people, but a new, enlarged world view. Just as the Romans conquered Greece only to be conquered inwardly by Greek ideas, learning, and art, the Vikings' subjugation of many European lands ended finally with their being subjugated by the European culture, of which the chief carrier had become the Christian religion.

The Old and the New Europe

It worked both ways, of course. Christian Europe changed the North, economically, ethically, politically. But the Norse invasions had certainly left traces all over old Europe, injected a powerful stimulant and helped to transform it into something new, as well.

The Svea and Varangians laid the foundations for a new Russia, with their trade routes bringing together formerly discrete regions, bridging language differences, among others, among formerly hostile tribes. The one-time Norse scourges of Europe's Atlantic coasts who came to settle Normandy eventually brought together Scandinavians and Anglo-Saxons and founded England, the second naval world empire. The Norman states in the Mediterranean and the Christianity they practiced—"the most persistent, most active, and most clearheaded kind of Christianity . . . ever . . . in pre-Puritan times" became the most powerful bulwarks in the battle against Islam and the spread of Arab power. In these southern Norman dukedoms the modern state was born, mingling Arab with Byzantine and classical Roman traditions of government that would eventually emancipate the secular power from the tutelage of the Church.

The Vikings also laid the foundations for modern economics by the stimulus and the organization they gave to far-flung networks of trade, beginning as intrepid explorers, ruthless takers of riches and power, and ending as creators of new worlds, new wealth, and statecraft. By the end of the Viking era trade had become highly organized. Merchants were no longer necessarily the leaders of their own expeditions, but sent employees far and wide over land and sea. They had business associates and friends everywhere, they had their protective associations and banking facilities. They could even write out bills, and give and receive credit.

Their conquests, however, mostly the result of sporadic exercises in acquisition by force, tended to be absorbed by the conquered territory and culture in time.

Duke Rollo's Normandy became Romance territory a hundred years later. William the Conqueror's knights spoke and thought in French. Only a few place names, family names, and features of Norse physiognomy serve as reminders that the landscape between Rouen and Avranches was once held by Danes and Norwegians.

In England, the Norse inheritance has become a matter of academic interest to archaeologists and philologists, to whom the old Danelaw areas in particular are a valuable hunting ground. The Atlantic islands have even more to offer the philologists. Of the 125 village and farm names on the Hebrides, 99 are of Norwegian derivation. On the Shetlands and Orkneys, where the Norse idiom survived into the seventeenth century, 10,000 words were catalogued as Viking in origin in 1900. Ireland still has many stone towers that were originally built as refuges from Viking attacks, and many objects found here and in Great Britain, from arrowhead to brooch, sword to gravestone, are Norse imports. Norse stone crosses on the Isle of Man have contributed to the history of art. Here, too, the people still meet at the Viking Thing mound, a square twenty-seven by twenty-seven yards and nine feet nine inches high, to give formal approval to the laws from London, as a matter of custom rather than politics.

The Norwegian-Icelandic colony on Greenland survived the rediscovery of America by Columbus, flourishing intermittently. In times of prosperity during the twelfth and thirteenth centuries, it is known to have had a bishop's palace in Gardar, near the Eastern Settlement, sixteen churches, and two monasteries. The chances are that it sent out ships every summer until the late fourteenth century to Newfoundland, to bring back timber and furs.

But the population seems to have degenerated. The dead of Herjolfsness, dug up by Paul Nørlund in the dig of 1934-41, preserved for over five hundred years as though in a freezer, were dressed in the fashion of their times, but they showed signs of interbreeding and malnutrition. Rickets, dwarfishness, rheumatic disease, tuberculosis, and early death seem to have been their fate in late Viking times. When the Icelander Jon landed on Greenland in 1540 he found huts, barns, and drying sheds for fish, but no people, except for one unburied corpse clothed in sealskin and fur cap, a curved dagger by its side.

The Republic of Iceland alone of all the Viking states has survived and preserved the traditions of the *Landnamabok* to this day. Their parliament is still called the Althing, and meets every summer on the lava field of Thingvellir, to celebrate Iceland's independence, regained in 1944. Icelandic is the only one of the Teutonic languages to have preserved its medieval structure—making it, together with the *Edda*, the promised land of Norse philology.

And what about Russia? And the Norse settlements in the Baltic lands? And those in Arabic-Byzantine country?

The Viking trade monopoly there was broken by the year 1000. The Arab silver mines were exhausted. The mines in the Harz country, opened up by the Saxon emperors, rerouted the exchange of goods, to the advantage of the growing continental trade routes. Bulk cargo was carried by Frisian cogs, and the Scandinavian merchant seafarers were edged out by the growing Hanseatic League.

In the east of Europe, hardly a trace remains of the Viking era. Between Volga and Vistula, reminders of the Norse centuries of dominance are even rarer than in Western Europe, and even less popular. Today's Slavophile Russians have expurgated the ancient Rus from their memory.

The Hunters Become the Hunted

The end of the Viking era is not marked by any dramatic counterpoint to its beginning, the gory raid on Lindisfarne. The heroic age peters out in a matter of decades during which the conversion to Christianity is consolidated. In Denmark, this was around 1000, in Norway, fifty years later, in Sweden, a hundred years later still. In 1135 Slav pirates attacked the town of Kungahälla on the west coast of Sweden, plundered and ravaged it, and then sold 7,000 Norsemen on the slave markets of Mecklenburg. Eight years later the Danish Bishop Absalon began to build a fort on the Oresund, at the site of present-day Copenhagen, as a defense measure against the increasingly frequent attacks of the Wends. In 1187 the Swedish mart of Sigtuna was attacked and burnt to the ground by Est pirates.

The hunters had become the hunted.

Appendix

Keys to the Viking World:
Sources

Chronicles
Rune Stones
Illustrated Fabrics
Documents from the Earth

Keys to the Viking World

The first man to discover the extreme North of Europe and report on it was Pytheas, a Greek mathematician and geographer of the fourth century B.C. Alexander the Great was king when Pytheas traveled by way of Spain and Britain to Ultima Thule (probably Iceland), to central Norway, then to the German sea coast and home to Massilia (Marseilles). His book *About the Ocean*, though known to us only indirectly from the use made of it by later writers, served as a source to the earliest known world geography, in Latin, three hundred years later, by Pomponius Mela of Spain, who refers frequently to Codannovia, later called Scandinavia by Pliny the Elder. The name means Dangerous Island.

About a hundred years later, Tacitus has considerably more to say on "the Suiones, distinguished not only for arms and men but for their powerful fleets" in the forty-fourth chapter of his *Germania*. A geography of Northern Europe, by Ptolemy of Alexandria, about the middle of the second century A.D., describes four Scandia islands east of Jutland, the three Danish islands, and also gives the names of some of the nations inhabiting Scandia, such as the Laps and Goths. The Goth Jordanes, in his *Getica*, named about thirty Norse clans. He also wrote of the endless dark winter nights, the midnight sun, the splendid horses and precious furs of the Swedes, their tall stature, their valor, and their zest for war and adventure. The most impressive account of the customs of Northern Europe is provided by the Byzantine Procopius, in the reign of Justinian. Writing of Thule, in the sixth century, Procopius gives a great early description of the forty days of sunlight and the thirty-five days of winter darkness, the end of which is celebrated as the most important festival of the year, in the land of the midnight sun. Even more impressive is the following vignette of primitive tribal Norse life in those latitudes:

> One tribe on that island lives on the level of the wild beasts, the Scrithifinoi [Stridefinns?]. They wear no clothes or shoes, drink no wine, do not grow their food on cultivated fields. Men and women alike live by hunting, eating the meat of the beasts they have killed, and wearing their skins. All the other inhabitants live like ordinary people. They do worship many gods and spirits in the sky, the air, on the earth and in the sea . . . in springs and rivers. They sacrifice regularly to their gods and to the dead. They regard as the best sacrifice the first man captured in battle, whom they offer up to the king of their gods . . . they hang him on a post, throw his body on a bed of thorns, or kill him by similar horrible means . . .

Procopius's image of the Norse world must be that of the best-informed minds of his period and for centuries thereafter, until the Franconian chroniclers came up with a great deal more eyewitness testimony.

The first of these monastic reporters is Einhard, biographer of Charlemagne. He had clear ideas of Scandinavian geography, including the Baltic Sea, even though he did not know where "the great German bay" ended. The Franconian chronicles and annals provide our basic, indispensable accounts of the Viking era, beginning with the Danish invasions of 828-29 and ending with the catastrophic years between 874-900. It is a phase that could be labeled "Lamentations and Apocalyptic Terrors."

The *Anglo-Saxon Chronicle* registers the important events of the Viking era in England. It is a sequence of mutually supplementing annals, probably written toward the end of the ninth century and recording events for more than a century past under the recurring headline "In this year . . ."

From this point on documentation of the Vikings increases in the form of letters, genealogies, protocols of synods, church council records, and royal capitularies. All the Medieval histories and records are dominated by the somber, moralistic, black-and-white point of view of Churchmen who tended to regard the Norse pagans as the incarnation of evil.

The first really knowledgeable Christian account of the life, thoughts, and customs of the Norse peoples, not dictated so largely by anger, fear, and superstitions, may be found in Rimbert's biography of Ansgar, c. 880. And by 1040 there was a Christian chronicler, Dean Dudo of St. Quentin, who wrote panegyrics of Viking exploits, especially those of the Dukes of Normandy. Toward the end of the eleventh century the Vikings found their Tacitus in Adam of Bremen, head of the Cathedral School of Hamburg-Bremen, under Archbishop Adalbert. Adalbert must be mentioned here for his enormous achievements in Christianizing the Norse lands even beyond Iceland and Greenland. In order to pursue his goal of establishing a Norse patriarchy to unite all churches in the North, he declined the Papal crown in 1046. Adam's *History of the Archbishops of Hamburg-Bremen* was written to bolster this grandiose plan. Adam absorbed uncritically whatever he found in all the chronicles, annals, and the rest, and his history is accordingly full of myths, fantasies, and tall tales—but also much information gathered from other monasteries and "live" interviews with mariners, kings, bishops, merchants, princes, ambassadors, and missionaries. It is a fundamental source book for Viking scholarship to this day.

Dictated by the thirst for knowledge rather than by having any axe to grind, the writings of King Alfred the Great of England, and the Byzantine Emperor Constantine Porphyrogenitus on ethnographic, cultural, and economic aspects of the Viking world are especially popular with historians. Constantine, in whom the Macedonian Renaissance of the Eastern Empire reached its culmination, contributes an invaluable chapter on the Rus peoples in his realm, based, like King Alfred's account of Ottar and Wulfstan, on oral interviews—in his case with actual Varangian itinerant traders. Most of the information about the Rus and Varangians is supplied by Arab travelers, diplomats, and geographers, with their keen, objective eye for a wealth of cultural material quite beyond the range of the

Nestor Chronicle (1056-1156) with its emphasis on the Christianization of Kiev. The Arabs, whose trade connections in the eighth century extended as far as India and China, had the necessary cosmopolitan and scholarly objectivity for such a task; besides, they wrote professionally, for sale and largely for entertainment, but also to make available genuinely helpful information.

Of the Arabs who deserve special mention here, the diplomat Ibn Fadlan was fascinated by the customs and habits of the Rus-Varangians—he ranks as their true discoverer—their contempt for all physical hygiene, their trading ceremonies, sacrificial rites, indifference to human life, burial customs, everything that would cause a pious Muslim in the 920's to wonder. A few decades later, the astronomer and geographer Ibn Rustah continued the documentary record on Vikings in early Russia by putting together a reliable compilation from many originals. We have quoted also the Jewish slave dealer Ibrahim ben Jacqub's impressions, in a report for the Caliph of Cordoba, of 973; those of the merchant Al-Tartushi who traveled to Soest, Paderborn, and as far as Hedeby. Most of these and some others were compiled by the Arab scholar El Bekri in a geographical handbook, with important dates on the appearance of Vikings in the Mediterranean, at the end of the eleventh century.

From northern Europe, somewhat later, comes the *History of the Danes*, a splendidly martial parade of heroes and great deeds in battle, by Saxo Grammaticus, a lay preacher from Zealand who died in 1220; it is Denmark's contribution to Viking historiography. From Sweden we have a few meager chronicles in verse; from Norway, nothing in written form. Old Norse historical works originated only on Iceland. Patriarch of this Old Norse literature was Saemund the Learned, a priest who had studied in Paris before gathering a flock of adepts around himself in 1100, on his father's property in Oddi. There are no Norwegian or Icelandic heroes whose deeds have not been celebrated by Saemund's disciples.

The Homer of old Icelandic literature was Snorri Sturlusson. He was not only one of the richest men and a political leader on the island (twice president, he was murdered by his opponents) but also a great spiritual and cultural light in the first half of the thirteenth century. The first university on Iceland, at Reykjaholt, was founded by him; here all the old sagas, bardic poems, prose epics, hitherto preserved only by oral tradition, were recorded in a voluminous collection. (Saga, related to German *sagen*, is simply what was *said* by the Sagamann, the Sayer of the traditional stories, in verse or prose.) The heroes of this literature were chiefly the northern Norwegian peasants, who had been the first to venture across the Atlantic to settle the forbidding island with their families, servants, and beasts. The sagas' style reflects the harshness of pioneer times; it is tart, monosyllabic, manly, understated, objective. These are tales of action; the author remains anonymous, invisible. The three important cycles are *The Iceland Book* by Ari Thorgilson, who wrote the first history of his country in Icelandic in 1130; *The Landnamabok*, c. 1200, the story of how Iceland was settled, containing over four hundred names of the first generation of immigrants; and *The Saga of Icelanders*, prose tales of the thirteenth century, dealing chiefly with various heroes and families. The two Greenland manuscripts belong to the same category: *The Greenlanders' Saga*, about the voyage of Eric the Red, and *The Saga of Eric the Red*, which deals chiefly with Karlsefni's Vinland expedition.

But the Icelandic saga writers dealt also with Norwegian history. Snorri Sturluson's *Heimskringla* is their leading prose epic; in sixteen parts, it combines legend and valuable historical information to tell the story of Norway until 1177 in much colorful detail. Our knowledge of the splendid great maze of Norse bardic poetry, mostly Norwegian and Icelandic, is based mainly on two large collections, the *Prose Edda* of Snorri Sturluson, which is both a treatise on the art of poetry and a compendium of Norse mythology, and the *Poetic* or *Elder Edda*, which for a long time was ascribed to Saemund the Learned. The older work is the bible of the Teutonic religious creed. Its thirty myths in verse, collected anonymously in the second half of the thirteenth century although written earlier, set forth the vision of the Viking universe as a gigantic cosmic trinity: Asgard, the home of the gods, Midgard, the battlefield of men, and Hel, the realm of the dead. By the time these myths were written down, the Scandinavian countries had been Christianized for two centuries; they accordingly have a certain mellow glow of transfiguration by memory, a certain sadness, and a beauty that has lived to inspire many great artists. Examples cited in our text include the *Voluspa* epic stories of the gods, and the *Rigsthula*, the story of the god Heimdall's amorous adventures on earth. *Brynhild's Helfahrt*, a lyrical ballad about the death of a heroine, is unique in having a female protagonist.

A quite different kind of historical documentation is given by the rune stones. The first rune alphabet, thought by scholars to be based on the Latin or Etruscan and brought North from the Rhineland or the Baltic shores, had twenty-four characters whose angular shape suggestthey were originally carved in wood. By the time of the Viking era, there were only sixteen characters in use as a secret code of the initiated few, for incantatory, ritual purposes, as protective magic, often concealed. Their historical value lies in their having been used on memorial stones, giving names and dates. The two hundred Danish rune stones, spread fairly evenly throughout the country, date from 950 to 1050; Norway's rune stones are concentrated south of Stavanger in Järem. Sweden is the Eden of ru, with its 3,000 rune stones, 1,000 of them in Uppland, whose highly ornamented memorial stones play a great role in the Norse history of art. Their inscriptions are a rich source of all kinds of information. And the Vikings of course left memorial stones wherever they went, outside of their home lands.

A special group of memorial stones, the Gotland picture stones, found only on that island in the Baltic, bear their own kind of witness to the Viking age from the fifth to the eleventh centuries, as ornamented illustrations of Norse life and its appurtenances—ships above all. Their basic form is that of an upright rectangle from one to three yards in height, carved in low relief, often painted, or even gilded, like Russian icons. They picture everything from battle scenes to genre scenes of daily life, myths, burials, animals, tools, jewelry, and tales from the sagas.

Equally informative and beautiful in one are the Bayeux tapestry, the Oseberg tapestry, and their like. This brings us to the invaluable and still ongoing contributions made to Viking history by the archaeologists in modern times, in some ways surpassing the historical and the literary sources; the greater part of this book bears witness to their efficacy in unlocking the Viking world, and filling in the blanks in our image of it in such detail that the most searching questions need not go unanswered for long.

Chronology

301

880-81	Vikings defeat the Duke of Saxony, rage along the Rhine and in Lorraine, destroy the palatinate of Aachen (Aix-la-Chapelle), attack Cologne, Mainz, Bonn, Worms, and Metz
881-88	Charles the Fat, King of a united France, enriches the Vikings at Elsloo with tribute and lands in Frisia
885	Siege of Paris
886	Alfred of England and Guthrum of the Danelaw in England agree on a division and border between them
890	Alfred the Great records his talks with Wulfstan and Ottar of Halogaland about the Far North
892	End of the "great army" by famine and disease; remnants retreat to England
	Alfred the Great has to fight Vikings again
896	Alfred's "royal navy" battles Viking ships near the Isle of Wight
c. 900	Bards at the Court of Norway
	Beginning of Swedish rule in southern Denmark and Hedeby
901	The Irish reconquer Dublin
911	Viking Rollo becomes Robert I, Duke of Normandy and accepts baptism a year later
	Trade treaty Kiev-Constantinople
912-50	Emperor of the East, Constantine VII, Porphyrogenitus
916 ff.	The Norway Ivar clan in Ireland
c. 920	Ibn Fadlan in Bulgar
920 ff.	The English reconquer the Danelaw territories
930	Norwegian immigration to Iceland comes to a halt
	The Althing established
934	Hedeby conquered by King Henry I
	King Knuba accepts baptism
936	End of Swedish power in Hedeby
	Jelling becomes a royal residence in Jutland
c. 940	Gorm the Old and Queen Tyra in Jelling
940-45	Eric Bloodaxe, King of Norway
c. 945-60	Haakon the Good, King of Norway
c. 950	Egil Skallagrimsson, Iceland's great bard
	Death of Gorm the Old
	The Arab merchant Al-Tartushi from Cordoba in Hedeby
c. 960	Harald Bluetooth is baptized and "makes the Danes Christians"
c. 980	Renewed Viking attacks on England
	Kiev becomes the capital of the Rus
980-1015	Vladimir I, Duke of Kiev
982	Eric the Red outlawed in Iceland
985-86	Eric begins the settlement of Greenland
986	Bjarni Herjulfsson's voyage of discovery; first sighting of the Western Hemisphere?
986-1014	Sven Forkbeard, King of Denmark

987	Vladimir I of Kiev baptized
994	Olaf Lapking of Sweden baptized
	Olaf Tryggvason and Sven Forbeard sail on London with a hundred longships
	Olaf Tryggvason becomes a Christain
995-1000	Olaf Tryggvason, King of Norway
c. 1000	Viking military camps Trelleborg, Fyrkat, and Nonnebakken are built
	Leif Ericsson goes to Vinland
1000	Death of Olaf Tryggvason
	Danes occupy Norway
	Christianity brought to Iceland and Greenland
1000-1016	Eric Jarl and Sven Jarl, Kings of Norway
1002	Danes massacred in England
1003-4	Sven Forkbeard the Dane wages war on England in revenge
1013	Sven Forkbeard, King of England
1014	End of Viking power in Ireland
1014-18	Harald King of Denmark
1016-30	St. Olaf King of Norway
	Christianization of Norway and centralization of power
1016-35	Canute the Great, King of Denmark
	Greater Danish Empire on the Baltic
1020	Normans in Southern Italy
1035-47	Magnus the Good of Norway becomes also King of Denmark in 1042
1035-87	William I, Duke of Normandy and in 1066, King of England
1043	First mention of Copenhagen
	Normans conquer Arabs in Italy
1043-66	Edward the Confessor King of England
1047-66	Harald Haardraade (the Ruthless) King of Norway
1048	Oslo founded by King Harald
1060	Robert Guiscard, Duke of Apulia
1061-91	Normans conquer Sicily
1066	King Harold of England conquers the Norwegian Harald Haardraade at Stamford Bridge
	A Norman army lands in England; Battle of Hastings King Harold slain
	Hedeby sacked by the Wends
1066-93	Olaf the Peaceful of Norway
1072	Normans conquer Palermo
c. 1075	Adam of Bremen's *History of the Archbishops of Hamburg-Bremen*
1085	Last effort to win England back for Denmark
c. 1100	The Nestor Chronicle is written in the cave monastery of Kiev.
	Under Saemund the Wise (1056-1133), history begins to be written on Iceland
1116	Second edition of the Nestor Chronicle
1135	Slavs attack Kungahälla
c. 1200	The *Landnamabok* of Iceland and Saxo Grammaticus's *History of the Danes*

Old Uppsala

ke Mälar

Stockholm

Visby

Gotland

Öland

Baltic Sea

A Viking
Travelogue
(or, Visiting the
Vikings)

Copenhagen   The Danish Collections at the National Museum, Prehistoric Division, include weapons, jewelry, models of the Ladby grave, the Trelleborg and Jelling finds, rune stones, and bog finds.

Stockholm   The Historical Museum has rune stones, picture stones, weapons, jewelry, Birka finds, coins, silver art objects, and much else. One-day excursion to Uppsala, which has a museum of Norse antiquities, and cultural-historical collections at the University. Five miles north of Uppsala there is Old Uppsala with its royal burial mounds, Romanesque church where the pagan shrine once was—and a mead bar at the Hotel Odinsborg! Sigtuna with its prehistoric museum and other places of interest are within easy access. Another excursion, by ship, to the ancient island Bjorkö (Birka) in Lake Mälar, with its hill-fortress with Ansgar Cross and Viking graves, can also be done in one day. Gotland can be reached by air in forty-five minutes from Stockholm; by ship in five hours. A museum of antiquities in Visby. Many excursion possibilities in the area.

Oslo   Historical Museum with the famous University collection of antiquities and Viking Hall. Viking Ships Museum on the Bygdoy Peninsula with the restored Oseberg, Gokstad, and Tune ships. The Oseberg Collection: carvings, sleds and carts, textiles, kitchen equipment, farming utensils, ships' gear. Gokstad and Borre finds. Excursions to Borre National Park with great grave mounds and two huge stone collections. Most impressive grave site in Norway on the west side of the Oslo Fjord; probably the burial site of the Yngling Kings.

(continued on next page)

100   150 km

305

Aalborg Excursion to Lindholm Høje, the largest Viking grave site, with about seven hundred burials, largely ship burials. A field with traces of furrows ploughed 900 years ago. Excursion to Hobro, near which is one of the great military encampments from the time of Canute the Great, the Fyrkat-Ringwall.

Aarhus Viking Museum on original Viking site. The nearby famous Prehistory Museum contains bog finds.

Schleswig Museum for Pre- and Early History in Castle Gottorf. Significant collections and the Nydam Boat. In Hedeby: fieldstone church Haddeby (c. 1200) and castle. Several important grave sites. Nearby, Kograben, the oldest part of the Danework, built in 808, and ten miles of Danework fortifications between the Schlei and Treene rivers.

Ny Hedeby (Returning from Schleswig, back over the Danish border about 20 kms. north of Flensburg) Pioneer camp modeled on Hedeby. Numerous grave sites.

Ladby Ship (By way of Kolding, Fredericia, and Odense) A grave mound become a museum with the remains of a 72-foot Viking ship, on the Kerteminde Fjord.

Trelleborg (Off the road between Korsör and Slagelse) Reconstruction of a late tenth-century house and barracks for seamen's encampment.

Roskilde Five Viking ships brought up by Danish archaeologists from the bottom of the Roskilde Fjord. Maps, drawings, photos, finds. A twenty-minute colorfilm documentary of the "dig." Restoration of the Skuldelev ship in progress can be seen by visitors in the exhibition hall, which also serves as a workshop.

From Roskilde, the highway back to Copenhagen.

The map indicates a possible complete itinerary, beginning and ending in Copenhagen, but of course the round trip can be made from any starting point at the traveler's convenience. Jelling, not shown here, with its two great grave mounds among other antiquities, can be reached from Aarhus via Vejle by Highway 18.

Selected Bibliography

Adam of Bremen. *Gesta Hammaburgensis Ecclesiae Pontificum* (History of the Archbishops of Hamburg-Bremen). Edited by B. Schmeidler. Translated by Francis Tschan. New York: Columbia University Press, 1959.

Almgren, Bertil (ed.). *The Viking.* London: C. A. Watts, 1966.

Arbman, Holger. *The Vikings.* Tr. by Alan Binns. New York: Praeger, 1961.

Blair, Peter Hunter. *An Introduction to Anglo-Saxon England.* London: Cambridge University Press, 1954.

Brogger, A. W., and Shetelig, H. *The Viking Ships.* New York: Twayne, n.d.

Brøndsted, Johannes. *The Vikings.* Rev. ed. Tr. by Kalle Skov. Baltimore and Harmondsworth: Penguin, 1965.

Cohen, S. L. *Viking Fortresses of the Trelleborg Type.* New York: Humanities Press, 1966.

Davidson, H. R. Ellis. *Pagan Scandinavia.* London: Thames and Hudson, 1967.

De Vries, Jan. *Study of Religion: A Historical Approach.* New York: Harcourt, Brace & Yovanovich, 1967.

Foote, P. G., and Wilson, D. M. *The Viking Achievement: A Comprehensive Survey of the Society and Culture of Medieval Scandinavia.* New York: Praeger, 1970.

Hagen, Anders. *Norway* (Ancient Peoples and Places Series). New York: Praeger, 1967.

———. *Rock Carvings in Norway* (Norwegian Guides Series). New York: International Publications Service, 1965.

Ingstad, Helge. *Land under the Pole Star.* Tr. Naomi Walford. New York: St. Martin's, 1966.

———. *Westward to Vinland.* Tr. Erik J. Friis. New York: St. Martin's, 1969.

Jones, Gwyn. *A History of the Vikings.* New York and Toronto: Oxford University Press, 1968.

———. *The Norse Atlantic Saga.* London: Oxford University Press, 1964.

——— (ed.). *Eirik the Red and Other Icelandic Sagas.* London: Oxford University Press, n.d.

Kendrick, T. D. *A History of the Vikings.* New York: Barnes & Noble, 1968 (reprint of 1930 edition).

Kivikoski, Ella. *Finland* (Ancient Peoples and Places Series). New York: Praeger, 1967.

Klindt-Jensen, Ole. *Denmark* (Ancient Peoples and Places Series). New York: Praeger, 1957.

Körner, S. *The Battle of Hastings: England and Europe, 1035-1066.* Lund, Sweden: Gleerup, 1964.

Lewis, A. R. *The Northern Seas, Shipping and Commerce in Northern Europe, A.D. 300-1100.* Princeton, N. J.: Princeton University Press, 1958.

Loyn, H. R. *Anglo-Saxon England and the Norman Conquest.* New York: St. Martin's, 1962.

Magnusson, Magnus, and Palsson, Hermann. *The Vinland Sagas: The Norse Discovery of America.* Baltimore and Harmondsworth: Penguin, 1965.

Norlund, P. *Viking Settlers in Greenland and Their Descendants During Five Hundred Years.* Millwood, N. Y.: Kraus Reprint (reprint of 1936 edition.)

Oxenstierna, Count Eric. *The Norsemen.* Tr. and ed. by Catherine Hutter. Greenwich, Conn.: New York Graphic Society, 1965.

Sawyer, P. H. *The Age of the Vikings.* 2nd ed. New York: St. Martin's, 1971.

Shetelig, Haakon (ed.). *An Introduction to the Viking History of Western Europe. Viking Antiquities in Great Britain and Ireland.* 4 vols. Oslo, 1950-54.

Simpson, Jacqueline. *Everyday Life in the Viking Age.* New York: Putnam, 1968.

————. *Northmen Talk: A Choice of Tales from Iceland.* Madison, Wis.: University of Wisconsin Press, 1965.

Stenberger, Marten. *Sweden* (Ancient Peoples and Places Series). New York: Praeger, 1962.

Stenton, Frank M. *Anglo-Saxon England.* 3rd ed. London: Oxford University Press, 1971.

————. *Free Peasantry of the Northern Danelaw.* London: Oxford University Press, 1969.

Sturluson, Snorri. *Heimskringla: History of the Kings of Norway.* Ed. Lee M. Hollander. Austin, Tex.: University of Texas Press, 1964.

————. *Heimskringla, Part I: The Olaf Sagas.* 2 vols. *Part II: Sagas of the Norse Kings.* New York: Dutton, 1961, 1964.

————. *King Harald's Saga: Harald Hardradi of Norway.* Tr. Magnus Magnusson and Hermann Palsson. San Francisco: Gannon, n.d.

————. *The Prose Edda of Snorri Sturluson: Tales from Norse Mythology.* Tr. Jean I. Young. Berkeley: University of California Press, 1964.

Thomsen, Vilhelm. *The Relations Between Ancient Russia and Scandinavia and the Origin of the Russian State.* Rev. ed. New York: Burt Franklin, 1964 (reprint of 1876 edition).

Turville-Petre, Edward Oswald Gabriel. *Myth and Religion of the North.* London: Weidenfeld & Nicolson, 1964.

Vernadsky, G. *Kievan Russia (A History of Russia,* vol. 2). 2nd ed. New Haven, Conn.: Yale University Press, 1973.

————. *The Origins of Russia.* Oxford: Clarendon Press, 1959.

Wilson, David M., and Klindt-Jensen, Ole. *Viking Art.* Ithaca, N.Y.: Cornell University Press, 1966.

Index

References to maps and illustrations are printed in boldface type.

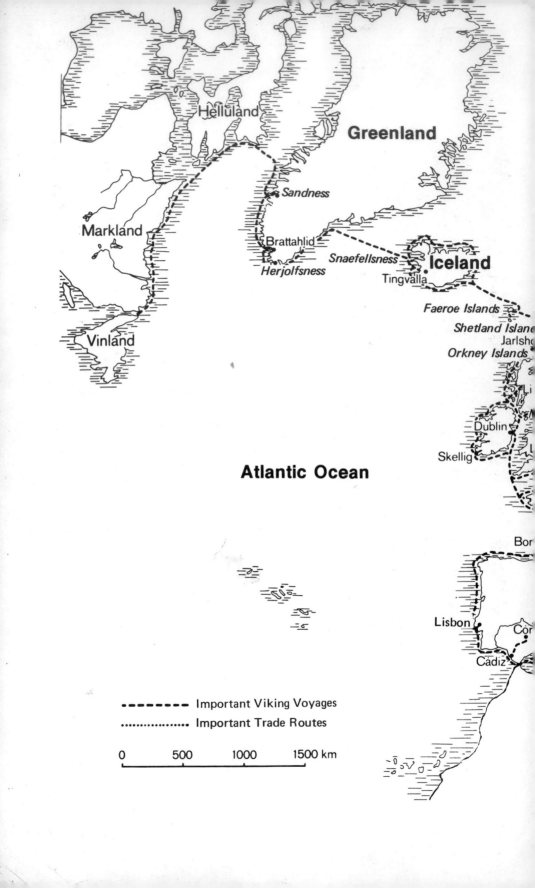

Helluland

Greenland

Sandness

Markland

Brattahlid

Snaefellsness •**Iceland**

Herjolfsness

Tingvalla

Faeroe Islands

Shetland Island

Jarlsho

Orkney Islands

Vinland

Li

Dublin

Skellig

Atlantic Ocean

Bor

Lisbon

Cor

Cadiz

- - - - - - - Important Viking Voyages

. . . . Important Trade Routes

0   500   1000   1500 km